Sport, Education and Social Policy

This important study brings together world-leading researchers to reflect upon the state of the social scientific study of sport. Addressing three core themes in sport studies – equality, education and policy – the book looks back over the development of sport research in recent decades and offers new insights into future lines of enquiry.

Presenting a unique collection of authoritative perspectives from some of the best-known scholars in the social scientific study of sport, the book engages with key contemporary issues such as gender stereotypes in physical education, ethnicity, inclusion and critical race theory, physical literacy, physical activity and health and international sport governance. Its chapters address major topics such as the globalisation of physical activity initiatives and the involvement of the EU in developing sport policies, as well as shedding light on new areas of research such as the growing participation of Muslim women in sport.

Sport, Education and Social Policy is fascinating reading for any researcher or advanced student working in sport studies, physical education or kinesiology.

Gudrun Doll-Tepper is a professor at the Freie Universität Berlin, Germany.

Katrin Koenen is Director Scientific Affairs at the International Council of Sport Science and Physical Education (ICSSPE).

Richard Bailey is a writer, researcher and former university professor in the UK.

ICSSPE Perspectives
The Multidisciplinary Series of Physical Education and
Sport Science

By publishing Perspectives, ICSSPE aims to facilitate the application of sport science results to practical areas of sport by integrating the various sport science branches. In each volume of Perspectives, expert contributions from different disciplines address a specific physical education or sport science theme, which has been identified by a group of leading international experts.

Also available in this series:
Published by ICSSPE – www.icsspe.org
Published by Routledge – www.routledge.com/sport

Sport, Education and Social Policy

The State of the Social Sciences
of Sport

Edited by Gudrun Doll-Tepper,
Katrin Koenen and
Richard Bailey

 Routledge
Taylor & Francis Group

LONDON AND NEW YORK

First published 2017
by Routledge
2 Park Square, Milton Park, Abingdon, Oxon OX14 4RN

and by Routledge
711 Third Avenue, New York, NY 10017

Routledge is an imprint of the Taylor & Francis Group, an informa business

British Library Cataloguing-in-Publication Data
A catalogue record for this book is available from the British
Library

Library of Congress Cataloging in Publication Data
A catalog record for this book has been requested

ISBN: 978-1-138-22343-1 (hbk)
ISBN: 978-1-315-40486-8 (ebk)

Typeset in Sabon
by Wearset Ltd, Boldon, Tyne and Wear

To Professor Dr Margaret Talbot OBE

Contents

Illustrations

Figures

Tables

Contributors

Chantal Amade-Escot is Professor of Education and was co-director of a multidisciplinary educational research centre at Toulouse University, France. Her primary research subject concerns 'didactics' as a research programme for the studying of the situated process of teaching and learning. Her interests focus on two main areas: teacher's practical epistemology, and gender issues. She has authored over 50 refereed papers on didactics, physical education, sport pedagogy and teacher education. She was a Board member of the International Association for Physical Education in Higher Education (AIESEP) from 1998 to 2002. As a French delegate, she participated in the European Women and Sport network from 1999 to 2006. She was involved in establishing the Association of Research on Comparative Didactics (ARCD) that she co-chaired from 2003 to 2007. She currently acts as a scientific authority for educational research at the French national agency HCERES.

Richard Bailey is a writer, researcher and former university professor in the UK. His work has focused on the relationship between physical activity, human development and education. He is the author of 20 books, more than 100 articles and chapters, and he currently writes a popular blog ('Talking Education and Sport') and a column for *Psychology Today* magazine on sport and learning ('Smart Moves').

Tansin Benn is currently visiting Professor at the University of Plymouth, UK. Having led IAPESGW, as its President, to a successful 17th World Congress in Cuba, April 2013, she continues to support the Association as chair of the committee of consultants on IAPESGW's Executive Board. She also served on the executive board of ICSSPE from 2009 to 2013. Her main research interests are in the field of gender, ethnicity and religion in the UK and internationally, and she has authored many scholarly articles and books, including being lead editor of *Muslim Women and Sport* (2011, Routledge). She won a Leverhulme Research Fellowship award in 2008 to work with women in Oman. She was awarded the Outstanding Contribution Award of the Muslim Women's

Sport Foundation (UK) in 2012, the Philip Noel-Baker Research Award (ICSSPE) in 2012 and the Women's Sport Foundation International Research Award (USA) in 2013.

Jonas Burgheim has contributed as founder of Sport Cares and Polity Cares, a consultancy project. He has international professional experience in both sport policy and research (funding) policy fields with a background in European integration, human rights law, international relations and structural analysis.

Ed Cope is a Lecturer in Sports Coaching and Performance at the University of Hull, UK. His main areas of expertise are the pedagogical practices employed by sports coaches and the consideration of young people in the coaching process. He completed his PhD at the University of Bedfordshire examining the pedagogical practices employed by coaches and how these were formed. Since completing his PhD he has continued his work examining coaches' practices and underpinning rationales, which has led to research publications in journals such as the *Sports Coaching Review*, *Reflective Practice* and *Qualitative Research in Sport, Exercise and Health*, as well as several book chapters on similar topics. He is currently involved in writing a special issue for *Soccer and Society*, focusing on the potentially holistic benefits of participation in football. He regularly reviews papers for other journals such as *Sport, Education and Society*, *Physical Education* and *Sport Pedagogy*, and is currently involved in a funded research project with the International Olympic Committee exploring young peoples' perceptions, interests and outcomes of participating in sport and physical activity.

Gudrun Doll-Tepper is a Professor at the Freie Universität Berlin, Germany. She has authored and co-authored over 350 publications in sport science, sport pedagogy, and adapted physical activity and sport for persons with a disability. She is former President of the International Council of Sport Science and Physical Education (ICSSPE) and of the International Federation of Adapted Physical Activity (IFAPA), and is an Invited Fellow of the European College of Sport Science (ECSS). Since 2006 she has been Vice-President of the German Olympic Sports Confederation and since 2007 Chairperson of the German Olympic Academy Willi Daume.

Kari Fasting is a Professor Emerita at the Department of Social and Cultural Studies at the Norwegian School of Sport Sciences in Oslo, Norway. She became the first elected chair of this institution and served as the Rector from 1989 to 1994, and is past President and honorary member of the International Sociology of Sport Association. She was a founding member of WomenSport International (WSI), and has served as the President of this organisation. Kari Fasting has over 300 publications, and is often invited as a keynote speaker to international conferences. During the last 30 years her research has been concerned with various aspects related to 'equality and diversity' in sport, with a focus on sport and exercise in the lives of women. Her most recent research area is sexual harassment and abuse in sport. In this area she is also working as an expert consultant for IOC, UNICEF and EC.

Anneliese Goslin is currently serving as Vice President of the International Association of Physical Education for Girls and Women, is an executive Board member of the International Council for Sport and Physical Education (ICSSPE) and has held leadership positions in Trim and Fitness Sport for All (TAFISA), Recreation South Africa (RECSA). She is the appointed chair of the South African Ministerial Advisory Committee on Recreation (MACRe). She was presented with an IOC Award for the Advancement of Sport for All in Africa, the South African State President Sport Award and an NAGWS award for research on sport and physical activity for girls and women. She is a full Professor in the Department of Sport and Leisure Studies at the University of Pretoria, South Africa, is a recognised scholar in the field of sport leadership and sport management and has published over 60 scholarly research articles.

Kevin Hylton is Professor at the Diversity, Equity and Inclusion Research Centre at Leeds Beckett University, UK, and is the first black person to hold this title. Kevin was heavily involved in community sport development in the 1980s and early 1990s and worked with marginalised groups and representative equality bodies in different settings. His early research focused on race equality in local government and he has continued research into the nature and extent of racism in sport, leisure and education. He has published extensively in peer reviewed journals and high-profile book projects. He has recently concluded three research projects related to 'race', ethnicity, coaching and participation for Sports Coach UK (2014), the English Cricket Board (2014) and the Yorkshire Cricket Partnership (2015). He is a patron of the Black British Academic, Walk Off and Board member of the Institute of Black Culture, Media and Sport, and Editorial Board Member for the *International Review for the Sociology of Sport* and *Journal of Global Sport Management*.

Haifaa Jawad is Senior Lecturer and Director of the Centre for Islamic and Middle Eastern Studies, University of Birmingham, UK. Her recent work includes the book, co-authored with Maria Holt, *Women, Islam and Resistance in the Arab World* (2013, Lynne Rienner). Her research interests lie within Islamic studies and Middle Eastern politics and history; her research and publications cover areas such as the socio-political study of Islam, modern and contemporary Islamic thought, women in Islam, feminism and Islam. She is co-editer of the book *Muslim Women and Sport* (2011, Routledge).

Darlene A. Kluka is Dean of the School of Human Performance and Leisure Sciences, Barry University, USA. As an advocate for girls and women in sport since 1972, she has served as President of the National Association for Girls and Women in Sport (NAGWS/AAHPERD/ SHAPE) in the USA and as President of the International Association of Physical Education and Sport for Girls and Women (IAPESGW). She has been a member of the Women's Sports Foundation (WSF) International Committee, and has held leadership positions in USA Volleyball (USAV), United States Olympic Committee (USOC), American Volleyball Coaches Association (AVCA) and the International Council of Sport Science and Physical Education (ICSSPE). She has been inducted into AVCA Hall of Fame, the SHAPE Hall of Fame, the Illinois State University College of Applied Sciences and Technology (CAST) Hall of Fame, has received the NAGWS Honor Award, WSF President's Award and was awarded an Honorary Life membership in IAPESGW. She is also an established scholar in sport with over 80 refereed articles.

Katrin Koenen is Director Scientific Affairs at the International Council of Sport Science and Physical Education (ICSSPE), where she is responsible for scientific publications. She is also the organiser of scientific events and developer of publication and event concepts. Her core areas in sport science are Physical Education, Adapted Physical Activity/sport for persons with a disability, Inclusion and Sport for development. She regularly publishes articles for journals and has written book chapters.

Joseph Maguire is Professor in the School of Sport and Exercise Sciences at Loughborough University. He completed his PhD in Sociology at the University of Leicester, UK. He is a two-term former President of the International Sociology of Sport Association. He is currently an executive board member of the International Council for Sports Science and Physical Education and Visiting Professor at the University of Copenhagen and University of Johannesburg. His research on globalisation examines inter-civilisational relations, the Olympics and mega-events, migration, media and national identity and sport and development.

Victor Matsudo is a full Professor of Medicine at Gama Filho University, Brazil and invited Professor at Santa Casa Medical School, Department of Preventive Medicine; he is a medical doctor, specialised in orthopedic and traumatology, and in sports medicine. He is a Scientific Director and Past-President of the Physical Fitness Research Center of São Caetano do Sul, and a Past Vice-President and Regional Director of the International Council of Sports Sciences and Physical Education. He is also Chairman of the Agita São Paulo Program, organised by the

State Secretariat of Health, São Paulo State. He is a Founder Member and Chairman of the Physical Activity Network of the Americas; and a member, a founder and a chair of several other organizations and committees. He has been a member of several Editorial Boards and has published many relevant publications in the area of medicine and sport science. He has been awarded several international prizes, such as the International Prize of Sports Medicine, 'Philip Noël Baker' Award of ICSSPE, International Principe Faisal Award of FIEP, World Health Association Award, International Prize of Physical Activity and Health and American College Citation Award.

Patricia Maude, MBE Emeritus Fellow, taught physical education in Primary, Middle and Secondary schools and has worked in the School Advisory Service and then in Initial Teacher Education at Homerton College, University of Cambridge, UK. Along with her role as Senior Coach of Homerton Gymnastics Club for over 30 years, she has gained significant experience in children's movement development, physical literacy and in helping children, trainee teachers and other professionals to learn. She is the author of Movement Observation packages and other interactive tools and books, including 'Observing Children Moving – Investigating Physical Literacy' (2001) and is co-author, with A. Pickard, of *Teaching Physical Education Creatively* (2014). In addition to conferences and courses for teachers in the UK, she has taught and presented in Europe, Canada, USA, South Africa and UAE. In 2000 she was awarded an MBE for Services to Physical Education.

Michael McNamee is Professor of Applied Ethics in the College of Engineering at Swansea University, UK. His teaching and research interests are in the philosophy and ethics of engineering, medicine, research and sports. He has held Visiting Professorships at Hunan Normal University, China; Linfield College, USA; Norwegian University of Sport and Exercise Sciences; University of Canterbury, New Zealand; Universities of Gent and Université Catholique du Louvain, Belgium; and University of Peloponnese, Greece. He is a former President of the International Association for the Philosophy of Sport and was the founding Chair of the British Philosophy of Sport Association. He serves or has served on the executive committees of many national and international associations, including the European College of Sport Science, the International Council for Sport Science and Physical Education and the Philosophy of Education Society of Great Britain. The founding editor of the journal *Sport, Ethics and Philosophy*, he has written or edited 16 books in applied philosophy and ethics, and is a founding co-editor of the landmark book series, *Ethics and Sport* (1998–, Routledge). His most recent books are *Sports, Virtues and Vices* (2008, Routledge), *Sport, Medicine, Ethics* (2014, Routledge) and *Handbook* *of the Philosophy of Sport* (2015, Routledge) co-edited with William Morgan. His current project is a co-authored book, *Bioethics, Genetics and Sport*, with Sylvia Camporesi.

Dan Parnell is a Senior Lecturer in Business Management at Manchester Metropolitan University, UK. Dan is primarily interested in the social role of sport (specifically football). Dan completed his PhD at the Research Institute of Sport and Exercise Sciences at Liverpool John Moores University. Dan manages the evaluation of organisations and interventions using mixed and multi-method approaches both quantitative and qualitative. He currently conducts research with a number of football clubs in England and key strategic stakeholders in football, including the Football League Trust, the English Premier League and the Football Foundation (the UK's largest sports charity). This work concerns research with participants across the lifespan (including 'hard-to-reach' groups), and extends to coaches, managers, chief executives, funders, policymakers and other stakeholders. He has led a number of club-based interventions based on his work within the Everton Active Family Centre and has completed the national evaluation of the Extra Time programme. In addition, he is interested in the impact of austerity-driven policy measures on the provision of sport and leisure, sport management and public health; and in utilising various communication methods to share and raise the awareness of the findings of his research to the public (individuals, families, communities, organisations, commissioners and policymakers).

Karen Petry is Deputy Head of the Institute of European Sport Development and Leisure Studies at the German Sport University. She is responsible for teaching and research in the areas of European sport policy, sport and development, social work and sport.

Gertrud Pfister is a Professor at the Institute of Exercise and Sport Science at the University of Copenhagen, Denmark. She has had a long academic career starting with a PhD in history, followed by another PhD in sociology. From 1980 to 2000 she was employed as Professor at the Freie Universität Berlin and was appointed Professor at the University of Copenhagen in 2001. She received two honorary doctorates. She has conducted several large national and international research projects, and has published more than 200 articles and 20 books. A specific focus of her work is research about, and support of, Muslim girls and women, including co-editing *Muslim Women and Sport* (2011, Routledge). She plays a leading role in various sport-related scientific communities. From 1983 to 2001 she was President of the International Society for the History of Sport, from 2004 to 2008 she was the head of the International Sport Sociology Association. Currently, she is a member of the executive board in Women Sport International. All her life, she has been active in sport, in particular in skiing, tennis and long-distance running.

Matthew J. Reeves is a Senior Lecturer in Sport Pedagogy and the Programme Leader for the MSc Sport Coaching at Liverpool John Moores University (LJMU), UK, and is also a doctoral student in the School of Sport and Exercise Sciences at LJMU. Matthew is primarily interested in the identification and development of talent in youth sport. His work is currently examining concepts of talent across various sports in Europe and the United States. He is an experienced researcher, working on a variety of national and international projects and evaluations for organisations such as the Premier League, Sport England, Youth Sport Trust, UNESCO and UEFA, and also regularly reviews papers for *Sport, Education, and Society* and *International Journal of Sport Science and Coaching*. He is currently involved in a funded project with Sports Coach UK exploring the use of technology in sport coaching.

Ben Weinberg is an independent scholar and writer, whose areas of interest include political, historical and cultural aspects of sport and physical activity. He has gained expertise and experience in advising governments and international non-governmental organisations on sport policy and sport-for-development.

Margaret Whitehead is visiting Professor at the University of Bedfordshire, UK, and Adjunct Professor at the University of Canberra, Australia. She is President of the International Physical Literacy Association. She has had a career in teacher training, specialising in pedagogy. Since retiring she has developed the concept of physical literacy, a concept which is now changing practices in engagement in physical activity for people of all ages across the world. In 2013 she was honoured by the International Association of Physical Education and Sport for Women and Girls with the Audrey Bambra Legacy Award for a life's work that continues to influence the lives of girls and women in physical education at local, national and international level. She has published widely on physical literacy and has presented in Europe, North America, Australia and New Zealand.

Margaret Talbot

A light that continues forever

Victor Matsudo

When I started to try writing these words, Margaret was still alive. Her death was such a terrible impact that I lacked the energy to go ahead. Without the understanding of the editors I would probably have given up the task. However, my friends tell me that I am persistent, and that is why I am sharing with you some of my feelings.

My first steps in ICSSPE were as a Corresponding Member of a Scientific Committee organized by Marcel Hebbelinck, back at the start of the 1980s. After that, I received an ICSSPE Fellowship to attend the Pre-Olympic Conference at Eugene-Oregon. I was also, at this time, involved with the Kinanthropometry Group, as founder of its Society. From my first contact with her, I could see what a special person Margaret was. Later, I was elected to the Executive Board of ICSSPE. In 1986, I attended my first meeting of the Executive Board in Quebec, and that was the first time I met Margaret Talbot.

I was just starting my international career; meanwhile she was already a well-known professional in the fields of physical education and, particularly, women and sport. Everybody in international sport knows of Margaret's competence and dedication, but in my opinion her commitment to the defence of women's rights in the physical education, sports, and sport science areas was her greatest service to society. When discussing these issues, she became transformed. Her fine black eyes became shining and bright. She became a brave warrior, fighting for her dreams.

Another passion of hers was 'quality physical education', and in more recent years her involvement spread to 'physical activity and health'. In many different settings she tried to disseminate and promote the concept of quality physical education. I can personally testify to her tenacious attitude on many occasions: in Berlin, Havana, Tel-Aviv, Dresden, Helsinki, São Paulo, Oslo, Thessaloniki, Seoul, and in Guangzhou, where she was elect President of ICSSPE.

I did not know her well enough to learn from where Margaret took her beliefs and attitudes in defence of physical education, and particularly feminism. But it was fantastic to see her contributions published in different regions, not only in Europe, as can be seen in papers published even in the Muslim world, in African countries, and the Middle East.

Her leadership was natural, based upon an intelligent and elegant means of action. I had the experience of working with her on many issues, but on one occasion she learned how difficult it was for sports groups to find a common agenda with the World Health Organisation (WHO). Despite her (and my) efforts to convince WHO authorities of the great avenues of opportunities which could be opened if sport and health worked together, the conclusion on that occasion was, to say the least, unsatisfactory. What was interesting, however, was that the decision did not take away Margaret's humour and motivation. She looked at me and said: 'They are not ready to understand this programme, but next year we will come again.'

Another of Margaret's characteristics was her attention to the development of young professionals and students, particularly from the developing world. I had many opportunities to see her, late in the evening, in a corner of a conference, or even at a restaurant table, talking to those she considered to be 'the fresh intellectual blood' and 'the opportunity for a better future'. She was always open to discuss someone's dreams.

She was also open to talk to colleagues in other disciplines. It is extraordinary to realize that Margaret was also recognized and respected by international experts in areas as diverse as management, sport coaching, sport development, policy, research, health, sponsorship, sport industry, culture change, fundraising, and of course physical education, among others!

Another of Margaret's qualities was her capacity to establish a positive relationship with any person, and many friends. I cannot detail all these relations, but I had a close observation of her relationship with Sandra Matsudo. I remember well when Margaret first came to assist a lecture delivered by Sandra – and she attended many others. Although Sandra's and Margaret's styles were quite different, they defended with the same emphasis women's participation in sports, exercise, physical activity, and in society as a whole. Margaret accompanied Sandra to many conferences around the world, and I well remember two that really touched Sandra's career: the World Congresses of Women and Sports in Canada and in Japan. Margaret and Sandra became friends, and even during Margaret's last years and months they kept up the conversation. I was emotionally touched when I saw, once in a while, emails from Margaret informing Sandra about the status of her health.

Something very personal that I had in common with Margaret was the attraction to ocean islands. Ilhabela is the largest island on the Brazilian coast, with 1,400-metre high mountains, covered with beautiful Brazilian green forest. It has over 70 waterfalls, and dozens of wonderful beaches, where the coconut trees are a special feature of the environment. That is the site of our 40-year research project with the island children and adolescents. As a consequence of this I received with great pleasure the title of honorary citizen of Ilhabela. Meanwhile, Margaret just loved to spend time in the Greek islands. Many times she escaped from 'grey' England to the 'shining' Greece. There she could contemplate the Mediterranean Ocean waves that probably gave her enough energy to face her everyday challenges.

Even in this situation, she kept her professional commitment and managed to cope with her burdensome workload. As her illness developed she spent more and more time in the fantastic Greek islands. I am left wondering if she is now teaching English, or classes on how to live with dignity, to the Greek Gods!

Introduction

In gathering the contributions to *Sport, Education and Social Policy: The State of the Social Sciences of Sport*, we had two main objectives. The first was to survey some of the dominant themes that have occupied researchers of the social scientific aspects of sport. By inviting some of the most influential theorists from around the world to talk about the development and current context of their areas of expertise, we wanted to produce a unique document that looked simultaneously back, to the changing and evolving research programmes that continue to influence academic discourse, and forwards, emerging lines of enquiry and under-explored topics. In doing so, we hoped to communicate some sense of the excitement generated by the social sciences of sport, and to inspire new and emerging scholars to take up the challenges presented.

Our second objective was to honour and celebrate the contribution of one particular scholar, Professor Margaret Talbot, who died during the production of this collection. As a researcher, Margaret made a unique and extraordinary contribution to a number of fields: physical education, gender studies, international policy development in sport, and others. As an administrator and policy-driver, herself, Margaret's legacy is possibly even greater. She was a life-long advocate and activist for equity in sport and physical education, and fought continually to defend the statutory entitlement to quality physical education around the world. Among her countless roles, Margaret Talbot was elected as President of the International Council of Sport Science and Physical Education (ICSSPE) in 2009, and prior to this, she was Vice President. Margaret Talbot had been President of the International Association of Physical Education and Sport for Girls and Women, Chief Executive of the Central Council of Physical Recreation and Chief Executive Association for Physical Education, both based in the United Kingdom. She was also Chair of the Education Committee of the International Paralympic Committee.

So, *Sport, Education and Social Policy* should also stand as a 'Festschrift' for Margaret. Appropriately a German word, as Margaret's last formal position was as head of the Berlin-based ICSSPE, *Festschrift* literally means 'celebratory volume' and it is now a widely used term to describe a book honouring an exceptional scholar. The career of every contributor to this book has been touched in some way by Margaret's work, mission and personality. It is a testament to her legacy that we were able to draw together so many world-class scholars in one volume.

The title of this book was also inspired by Margaret Talbot. Three overarching themes were identified that address some of the central concerns of researchers and practitioners. These represent both some of the perennial themes in the social sciences of sport, and the three dominant topics of Margaret's own work: equality (focusing particularly on gender and ethnicity), education (which considers physical education, in particular) and policy (especially, of course, sport policy). We have chosen not to divide the book into discrete sections as, predictably, the most interesting and intractable problems cut across simple boundaries. Nevertheless, these three themes offer, together, some unifying sense of interest and priorities.

A number of chapters address issues of equality and gender. Kari Fasting's chapter focuses on the need to break stereotypes as a means towards equality in sport. She discusses the relationship between gender, gender stereotyping and equality in sport. Tansin Benn, Gertrud Pfister and Haifaa Jawad examine the largely under-researched, but clearly highly topical area of the inclusion of Muslim girls and women in sport and physical education. This contribution can be situated in the fields of gender and culture as they permeate sport, education and health. Gender and equality are also the foci of Darlene Kluka and Anneliese Goslin's chapter. Kluka and Goslin integrate a range of concepts, including women's empowerment, gender mainstreaming, gender equality and gender equity, to articulate a new framework for understanding and influencing policy development to promote women's quality of life through sport. Chantal Amade-Escot addresses the issues of gender in physical education by introducing French *didactique* research, an approach that has generally been overlooked by English-language scholars. Amade-Escot's analysis offers fascinating insight into three interwoven topics at the heart of the co-construction of unequal learning: the teacher's appraisal of student ability in the subject, the knowledge facets privileged by the teacher when teaching and the non-verbal dimension of classroom interactions.

Two chapters consider issues of inclusion, although with very different perspectives. Gudrun Doll-Tepper surveys the evolving conceptions of integration and inclusion in education, physical education and sport. She focuses, in particular, on adapted physical activity for people with disabilities, but her analysis also touches on inclusion in a broader sense, for all individuals who are lacking equal access and participation, e.g. because of gender, socio-economic, religious and cultural backgrounds, sexual orientation and ethnicity. Kevin Hylton takes up the topic of ethnicity in his chapter. He offers a personal account of Critical Race Theory (CRT) in relation to past and present issues in sport, leisure and society. Drawing on an extensive body of work he reflects upon his application of CRT and the necessary challenges that prevail if we are to ensure racial justice or even racial transformations become goals in the way we do business.

Joseph Maguire's chapter can be read as a theoretical centre-point for many of the other chapters. Maguire makes a compelling case for the urgent need for a social scientific perspective on sport and physical activity. A social scientific perspective is needed, he argues, not just as a complement to the natural sciences that continue to dominate in sport science, but as necessary dimension of an understanding of phenomena that are evident in global sport and physical cultures today.

Jonas Burgheim, Karen Petry and Ben Weinberg turn specifically to sport policy. They explore how the European Union and the United Nations have contributed to advocating holistic policies and thereby to 'walking the talk'. Their analysis points to the potential for instigating comprehensive sport policy approaches which relate to and are based on a sport governance system including all relevant stakeholders. Richard Bailey, Ed Cope, Dan Parnell and Matthew J. Reeves' presentation of the highly influential 'Human Capital Model' (HCM) can be read as an empirical complement to the policy analysis of Burgheim, Petry and Weinberg. The HCM is, in part, an over-arching framework for understanding the relationships between sport and physical activity and different aspects of human development. It proposes that the different outcomes associated with physical activity can be framed as differential 'capitals' that represent investments in domain-specific assets. These investments, especially when made in childhood, can yield significant rewards, both at that time and for years to come.

Discussions of the nature and pedagogy of 'physical literacy' have transformed physical education and sports coaching in recent years, although the concept has a much longer history. Margaret Whitehead and Patricia Maude are the scholars most responsible for its wide-scale acceptance, and their chapter charts the creation and development of the concept of physical literacy. Whitehead and Maude provide a first-hand account of the context in which the concept was formulated, significant milestones in the dissemination of the concept of physical literacy, the current challenges being addressed by its advocates. The final chapter, written by the philosopher Michael McNamee, reproduces a 'classic' paper that can be read as addressing similar themes to the chapters by Bailey and colleagues, and Whitehead and Maude, but taking a different perspective. McNamee offers some conceptual 'housekeeping' for those wishing to discuss the values and value of sport and other leisure activities. In doing so, he provides a framework in which different accounts of the value of leisure practices may be contested.

Whether taken individually, or as a whole, these different contributions provide a unique introduction to many of the most pressing topics that currently occupy social scientists of sport, and they are likely to occupy them for some time to come. Our intuition is that the greatest benefit will come from reading the book as a whole, as it is only then that the synergies and tensions between them will become properly apparent. But either way, we hope that this collection inspires, provokes and challenges fellow and future scholars.

We also hope that this collection – this Festschrift – acts as a suitable testament to the lasting influence of Margaret Talbot. We, the editors, as well as all of the contributors to this volume have benefitted from her vision. Perhaps, in some small way, readers of this book will have some sense of her work, too.

We asked one of Margaret's colleagues and friends, Professor Victor Matsudo from Brazil, to write a personal account of his experiences with this extraordinary woman; this can be found immediately preceding this Introduction. Other statements can be found at the ICSSPE website (www. icsspe.org), and also at the website of the International Association of Physical Education and Sport for Girls and Women (www.iapesgw.org.uk).

Gudrun Doll-Tepper
Katrin Koenen
Richard Bailey

Chapter 1

Breaking the gender stereotypes in sports

Kari Fasting

Introduction

In 1910, one could read the following in *Illustrierte Zeitung* about a young woman, called the Jumping Baroness:

> An excellent female ski jumper is Baroness Lamberg from Kitzbühel. At ski competitions this lady, who is an avid, enthusiastic skier, was able to perform two jumps without falling.... It is understandable that ski jumping is performed very rarely by women, and taking a close look, not really a recommendable sport. One prefers to see women with nicely mellifluous movements which show elegance and grace, like in ice skating or lawn tennis. One does not like to see athletic exercises performed by a woman.... And it is not enjoyable or aesthetic to see how a representative of the fair sex falls when jumping from a hill, flips over and with mussed-up hair glides down towards the valley in a snow cloud.
>
> (Hofmann, 2011, p. 6)

This quote shows that female ski jumping is not new, but it also reminds us that it took about 100 years before female ski jumpers were allowed to jump in the Olympic Games. The quote is a good example of the gender stereotyping of women, because women at that time were expected to be elegant and graceful if they were to be 'feminine'.

As the title indicates, this chapter discusses the relationships between genders, gender stereotyping and gender equality in sport. To illustrate these, examples from sport history, such as the relationships between sport participation and masculinity and the views of medical doctors on women's sport participation in the past will be presented. Thereafter the focus will be on some examples of the change in the perception of gender stereotyping in sport, illustrated by ice skating and cheerleading; and further how gender stereotyping and inequality still exist in sport today by using women in elite-level coaching and men's rhythmic gymnastics as examples.

The chapter will end with discussing strategies used for breaking the gender stereotypes with a focus on gender mainstreaming. But first it is necessary to clarify some concepts.

Gender and gender stereotyping

To understand the development of both women's and men's sport it is important to have in mind that the concept of gender concerns the psychological, social and cultural differences between males and females. Gender refers to cultural meanings and connections associated with one's biological sex. It refers to what is appropriate behaviour for women and men and thereby to what is masculine and what is feminine. It differs within and between cultures. Even if men and women are doing the same activity, it can have a different meaning and a different message. The social construction of gender in individuals reproduces the gendered societal structures; as individuals act out gender norms and expectations in face-to-face interaction, they are constructing gendered systems of dominance and power (Connell, 2009; Lorber, 1994).

An illustration of this would be when a female athlete's behaviour expresses frailty or weakness compared with the strength of male athletes. For example, in figure skating we seldom see a female athlete lift her partner. This means that there is an unequal power relationship with male domination and female subordination in many spheres of life, including sport. Since gender is not something we are, or have, but rather something we produce and do, gender and thereby power relations between women and men can change.

Gender is not a simple and one-dimensional construct. At the level of the individual, gender is formed from the sex category, i.e. categorisation of gender according to physical attributes, and from various aspects of gender ranging from gender identity via gendered sexual orientation to gender display. Being a man or a woman is not a fixed state. People construct themselves as masculine or feminine.

Psychological research suggests that the great majority of us combine masculine and feminine characteristics, in varying blends, rather than being all one or all the other. We also do not talk or write about these concepts in the singular anymore, but in the plural, i.e. masculinities and femininities (Connell, 2009; West and Zimmerman, 2009). But doing gender involves behaviours that 'sustain, reproduce and render legitimate the institutional arrangements that are based on sex categories' (West and Zimmerman, 1987, p. 146). As a result, both men and women draw on culturally gendered stereotypes to ensure that their behaviour in the context is gender-appropriate.

What is regarded as gender-appropriate behaviour varies across time, ethnic groups and social situations, but following Deutsch (2007, p. 107) 'the opportunity to behave as "manly" men or "womanly" women is ubiquitous'. Since doing gender is a social construction, there is a possibility to undo gender, and breaking the gender stereotypes can be looked upon as a way of undoing gender.

According to Lorber undoing gender refers to the end of gendered practices that maintain gender inequality (Lorber, 2005). Undoing gender evokes resistance (Deutsch, 2007), and becomes obvious when people experiment with gender characteristics such as the phenomenon of transgendering. 'Transgender' is an umbrella term and involves a range of behaviours, expressions and identifications that challenge the pervasive bipolar gender regime in a given culture (Carroll *et al.*, 2002; McKenna and Kessler, 2006). The term includes a number of possibilities, such as gender bending – when elements of masculinity are mixed with elements of femininity (Carroll *et al.*, 2002; Pfister, 2010).

Hegemonic gendered meanings can therefore both be challenged and changed through actions and social interactions. As a result gender differences can be reduced and gender can be viewed as 'undone' (Claringbould and Knoppers, 2008). West and Zimmerman (2009) disagree and argue that abandonment of attribution/accountability to a sex category is impossible. According to them gender can never be undone, only redone. But both undoing and redoing genders upset the gender binary and develop a greater awareness of gender inequality. This is supported by Lorber (2005) who emphasises that gender troublemakers are needed to challenge the way that gender is still built into the Western world's overall social system.

Research reveals that in any culture or institution there is a particular pattern of masculinity which holds the dominant position. Connell (1987) has called this hegemonic masculinity, which means that in any given setting, the pattern of masculinity that is most honoured is that which is most associated with authority and power. Connell argues that all other forms of masculinities and all femininities are formed in positions of subordination to hegemonic masculinity. Emphasised femininity is an important complement to hegemonic masculinity. It is oriented to accommodating the interests and desires of men and is characterised by heterosexual attractiveness, compliance, nurturance and empathy. It is what many people in Western society will associate with femininity. This was illustrated in the quote on a woman ski jumping in 1910 that opened this chapter.

Even though this type of femininity is still alive, Connell and Messerschmidt (2005, p. 848) wrote some years ago that:

> The concept of emphasized femininity is focused on compliance to patriarchy, and this is still highly relevant in contemporary mass culture. Yet gender hierarchies are also affected by new configurations of women's identity and practice, especially among younger women – which are increasingly acknowledged by younger men.

What then about gender stereotypes? As just mentioned both women and men draw on cultural gender stereotypes to ensure that their behaviour is gender-appropriate. Pilcher and Whelehan (2004, p. 167) define it as 'a standardized and often pejorative idea or image held about an individual on the basis of their gender'. As examples of such shared elements of the content of gender stereotypes they mention that women are emotional and unpredictable, and are bad drivers, and that men are rational and instrumental, bad at housework and like sport. Gender stereotypes are simplistic generalisations about the gender attributes, differences and roles of individuals and/or groups.

When people automatically apply gender assumptions to others regardless of evidence to the contrary, they are perpetuating gender stereotyping. Just as masculinities and femininities vary and change historically and culturally, this also happens with gender stereotypes. According to Paoletti (2012), for example, the fact that the colour pink is for a girl is a recent idea. A 1918 editorial from Earnshaw's Infants' Department stated that pink was 'a more decided and stronger colour ... more suitable for the boy; while blue, which is more delicate and dainty, is prettier for the girl' (Paoletti, 2012, p. 6). Now, what does all this have to do with sport? How do gender stereotypes and people's conceptions of femininities and masculinities affect our thinking about sport, and about equality in sport? It is easy to see in relation to competitive sport because attributes like the display of muscles, active physicality, aggression and the desire for competition have been associated traditionally with both hegemonic masculinity and sport. One used to say that by participating in sport men reinforced their masculine identities. This was not true for women. Many sportswomen had to negotiate their complex and often contradictory gendered and sexualised identities. By doing this these pioneering sportswomen were bending gender, often with much external resistance. The debate has however shifted from the early emphasis on women's individual 'conflicts' with their femininity to structural accounts of how femininity is constructed, reconstructed and resisted through sport. Central to this work is the concept of power – the power to define a sportswoman as both gendered and sexualised and the power of women to resist and thus become empowered and self-defining. According to Jay Coakley (2009, pp. 259–260) the sport worlds are usually organised to be the following:

1   male-dominated so that the characteristics of men are used as standards for judging qualifications;
2   male identified so that the orientations and actions of men are used as standards for defining what is right and normal;
3   male centred so that men and men's lives are the expected focus of attention in sport programs, stories, legends and media coverage.

Normative boundaries associated with masculinity seem to be more restrictive and more closely regulated than the normative boundaries associated with femininities. This is explained by the fact that masculine characteristics are believed to be consistent with positions of power and influence; therefore, men have more to lose collectively if they do not conform to gender expectations. That is why men strictly police their gender boundaries and sanction those who push or move outside them. This means that men have less social permission to express the feelings, thoughts and actions associated with masculinity. This is, according to Coakley (2009), why male ballet dancers (who also are bending gender) are less likely to be socially accepted in society than are female rugby players. Maybe this also has something to do with why there are so few open male homosexuals in sport, and why men cannot participate in rhythmic sportive gymnastics and synchronised swimming, at least not in the Olympics.

Messner (2002) writes that the reason that sports become important in connection with gender is that gender categories are embodied dimensions of people's lives – that means that they are built into the way people move and experience the world with and through their bodies. Accordingly sports have been important sites and activities for preserving gender ideology in most cultures. But one can also question whether sport can contribute to a change in the gender ideology in society at large, when male and female athletes are challenging traditional gender ideology by pushing and bending gender boundaries. Gender stereotyping in sport has been and still is reinforcing gender inequality. This is stated in a new publication from the European Commission (2014, p. 22):

> Gender stereotypes in and about sport are still deeply rooted in European societies where sports are predominantly divided into male and female domains, and where mixed gender participation has not been accepted for a long time. Traditions (often perpetuated by family members, coaches and teachers), sport governing structures, and the media confirm these stereotypes rather than challenge them.

History – the view of medical doctors

Looking at how gender and sport have changed through history may give us a better understanding of how gender and sport are socially constructed and how the gender stereotypes have been changed and are changing. The male medical profession's power, and thereby medical discourses, have had a large influence on both women's and men's participation in sport, and therefore also on the view of gender. From the perspective of sports medicine women were the 'weaker sex', provided with a body whose female functions constituted its weaknesses.

Pfister (2005) shows in an interesting article how the view on gender and long-distance running has changed. According to her, doctors in the past warned men against excessive exertion, especially in endurance sports, and believed hearts, kidneys and lungs to be at risk, a view that changed dramatically some years later. The medical view of long-distance running is also a good example of the evolution of the construction of gender differences. It changed from being considered dangerous for men to the more recent conception of it being very healthy at the same time that it was a demonstration of superhuman performances and a manifestation of heroic masculinity.

The medical interest in the case of women focused on the uterus and the effects of sport on bearing children. As a rule women were barred from competition except for a few sports. They were also restricted by their clothing. Additionally women were confronted with a 'double bind situation' when their bodies or performances reached male standards, they were accused of bisexuality and virility. When women proved themselves able to participate in some of these 'unfeminine sports', they were not 'real' women and as such also contributed to the construction of the binary gender ideology. Views of the female body and women's sport led to women's long-distance running being judged wholly unsuitable. This was based on three arguments: first, the female pelvis and knock-knees, which allegedly made running for women not only difficult but also unaesthetic; second, the deficiencies of the cardiovascular system, which seemingly did not allow for high performance in endurance disciplines; and, finally, the limited amount of energy available to women, which ought to be saved for childbirth and bringing up children (Pfister, 2005).

The earlier medical discourses about women's sports have changed dramatically. What is surprising is that every time women have tried to get access to a new sport, often with much support from their male coaches, it has been met with resistance – with women's biology and gender being used as a reason for delaying or refusing access. This happens even today, and demonstrates the strength of gender stereotyping in connection with sport. When the female ski jumpers started their fight to get into the World Cup and the Olympics not that many years ago, Gian-Franco Kasper, head of the International Ski Federation (FIS) said:

> Ski jumping is just too dangerous for women. Don't forget, the landing it's like jumping down from, let's say, about two meters to the ground about a thousand times a year, which seems not be appropriate for ladies from a medical point of view.
>
> (Laurendeau and Adams, 2010, p. 440)

A few years earlier, he told reporters that a woman's uterus might burst during landing. His non-verifiable viewpoint illustrates how biology is still at play and how difficult it is to change the myth or the stereotype about women as the weaker sex.

Recent changes in the perception of feminine and masculine sports

As mentioned earlier, gender stereotypes tell us what are acceptable behaviours for women and men, and have consequences for which sports are looked upon as acceptable for women and for men. As indicated above, since masculinities, femininities and stereotypes are social constructions they also sometimes are undone or redone. For example, who would dare to say today that women should not participate in the marathon?

Below are two examples of what consequences gender stereotyping in sport has had and still have for women and men. The development of figure skating and cheerleading further illustrate how a sport activity is gendered and how this can change over time.

In the second half of the nineteenth century, Jackson Haines revolutionised figure skating, by adopting elements of dance and artistic exercises (Pfister, 2000). When women started to compete in figure skating at the beginning of the twentieth century the long skirt and the rules of morality and proper feminine behaviour made many figures and jumps impossible, which increased the gender difference in figure skating. In the 1920s women's figure skating increased in difficulty, at the same time that the skaters used more and more elements of dance and glitter and glamour. This feminisation of figure skating forced the male skaters to distance themselves and to increase their representations of masculinity. Male figure skaters reproduced gender difference by jumps and an increasingly athletic style. At the end of the 1970s, however, a 'demasculinisation' of the sport began to emerge. A refusal of traditional male signals and symbols, like the rigid postures of the arms and the upper body were diminished. The male skaters today are bending the former male-skating role, by combining soft gracious movements, which had been defined as female, with the traditional male movements of high technical difficulty.

Cheerleading is also interesting because it was originally an all-male activity. Characterised by gymnastic stunts and crowd leadership for football games, cheerleading was considered equivalent in prestige to an American flagship of masculinity, American football, according to Lisa Wade (2012). She also points to the fact that cheerleading helped launch the political careers of three US Presidents: Dwight D. Eisenhower, Franklin Roosevelt and Ronald Reagan, who had all been cheerleaders.

According to Coakley (2009) the first women who became cheerleaders were defined as rebels or deviants, invaders of male space. Up through the 1940s they received warnings from educators that cheerleading was too masculine for women, bad for their health and their overall development as women. Ultimately the effort to preserve cheer as a man-only activity was unsuccessful. But the presence of women changed how people thought about cheering. Because women were stereotyped as cute instead of 'valiant', the reputation of cheerleaders changed. Instead of a pursuit that 'ranks hardly second' to quarterbacking, cheerleading's association with women led to its trivialisation. By the 1950s, the ideal cheerleader was no longer a strong athlete with leadership skills; it was someone with 'manners, cheerfulness, and good disposition'. In response, boys pretty much bowed out of cheerleading altogether, because they didn't like to be associated with what was becoming 'a girl's activity'. Cheerleading in the 1960s consisted of cutesy chants, big smiles and revealing uniforms. There were no gymnastic tumbling runs, no complicated stunting. Cheerleading was, in other words, transformed, maybe we can say de-masculinised and feminised. But cheerleading has also been transformed again. According to Wade (2012), cheerleaders now, still mostly women, pride themselves in being both athletic and spirited, a blending of masculine and feminine traits. But this may also occur to men, because men seem to be back in the sport. Today cheerleading is a worldwide competitive sport with both gender segregated and co-ed disciplines. Some may argue that cheerleading is on its way to becoming a gender neutral sport, having wandered from a masculine to a feminine sport to what it is today.

Gender stereotyping and inequality in women and men's sport: female coaching and male rhythmic gymnastics

The general under-representation of female coaches and women's lack of opportunities to coach males are revealed in several countries. Remedial actions and initiatives to increase the number of female coaches seem to have been attempted without dramatic success (Fasting *et al.*, 2013). One explanation given by Norman (2010) is that the lack of female coaches is due to the fact that sport is a patriarchal institution dominated by hegemonic masculinity. As an example she mentions that 'the ideology or we could add the stereotyping of men being "better" coaches is manipulated into common sense consciousness, and so even women perceive reality through this thinking' (p. 509). Coaching can, in other words, be considered as both a sex-typed and a gender-stereotyped job or position. Coaching can be seen as a task that requires certain personality characteristics and skills that traditionally have been defined as masculine. When females occupy a top-level coaching position it is a way of gender bending which challenges the coaching role as exclusively male.

LaVoi and Dutove (2012) focus on the fact that over the last few years most efforts have attempted to increase the number of female coaches by focusing on improving knowledge skills and confidence (individual level), developing a support system (interpersonal), and by creating an old girls' network (interpersonal and organisational levels). Individual-centred strategies are, however, limited. Barriers at all of these levels are related to the gender order in society at large, and are likely to be the result of the global dominance of males over females (Connell and Messerschmidt, 2005).

Men's rhythmic gymnastics (RG) is interesting because it is one of the two sports in which men cannot compete in the Olympics. It is strongly associated with femininity. However, there are several countries in which men compete in this sport, both individually and in a team. It is most popular in Asia, particularly in Japan. It emerged in Japan from stick gymnastics. In spite of the fact that there are Men's RG World championships, the international federation does not recognise men's RG. Men are, however, not eligible to participate in any major competition.

Spain has one of the best male rhythmic gymnasts. In an article written after the last summer Olympics Milena Popova (2012, para. 3–6) wrote:

> Why do we not see men's rhythmic gymnastics in the demonstration sports? Partly, gymnastics appears to suffer from a governing body that is painfully conservative.... Women being allowed to do 'men's things' is 'rightfully' celebrated as a great accomplishment for equality, but hardly any questions are being asked about men's absence from certain fields.... Yet if we want true equality, we need to challenge the dinosaurs of sport such as the International Gymnastics Federation, to treat both genders equally across different variations in the sport and to encourage participation from all.

In another article, Irene Kamberidou and colleagues (2009, p. 220) wrote that:

> Despite gender stereotypes that depict this Olympic sport as unacceptable for the image of masculinity, the male body aesthetic, including masculine gender role identity, the rising involvement of boys and men in this sport throughout the globe can no longer be ignored.

With reference to Kimmel, the author reminds us that men also have a gender and are subject to gender stereotyping, distinctive social expectations, social inequalities and exclusions. They also question whether, if the international gymnastic federation officially recognises men's RG, and subsequently mixed groups and mixed pairs, will this signal the beginning of a process that will eventually break down the structurally secured gender segregation system of competitive sports, which often seems to reinforce gender stereotypes.

Strategies for equality in sports

Concerning strategies towards gender equality in sports, three strategies are often mentioned: equal treatment, positive or affirmative action and gender mainstreaming. Equal treatment is rooted in the idea that women and men should be treated the same. In effect this often has meant that women have been treated the same as men. But treating women and men the same is not the same as treating women and men equally. Sometimes one has to treat people differently in order to treat them equally. A major weakness with equal treatment is that it does not lead to equal outcomes (Rees, 2002). In other words this is not a strategy that would always be effective in relation to gender equality. But if women and men had been treated more equally in sport in the past, we would perhaps not have had the gender differences that we have today, and sport might have been less dominated by gender stereotyping which reinforces gender inequality. On the other hand, in relation to breaking gender stereotypes, there is also a chance that this will not happen with equal treatment, because it may actually reinforce the gender stereotypes.

Positive action is often based on the idea that even if there are similarities between women and men there are also differences. On the premise that men and women are different, it seeks to accommodate or make up for those differences, but it always seems to be construed as deficits in women by arranging, for example, women only training courses etc. Some positive action measures therefore are designed to assist women to become more like men. The problem with such actions is that they leave the mainstream unaffected so the sources of women's disadvantage remain intact. Another positive action is preferential treatment, for example, quotas or positive discrimination. In relation to breaking gender stereotypes it is thinkable that some forms of positive actions, for example quotas, may be more successful, for example if it leads to more women in top-level positions in coaching, demonstrating that women can also be successful in such kind of jobs.

The latest strategy is gender mainstreaming, which since 2000 seems to have been adopted as a strategy in most European countries. The essential element in the definition of gender mainstreaming is its accent on policy processes. It is about organising procedures, routines, responsibilities and capacities for the incorporation of a gender perspective. Gender mainstreaming is defined the following way:

> Gender mainstreaming is the (re)organisation, improvement, development and evaluation of policy processes, so that a gender equality perspective is incorporated in all policies at all levels and at all stages, by the actors normally involved in policy-making.
>
> (Council of Europe, 2004, p. 12)

Gender mainstreaming seeks to identify the ways in which existing systems and structures are institutionally sexist. It should neutralise the gender bias, and it is an approach to produce policies and processes that seek to benefit men and women equally. It also focuses on systems and structures that produce deficiencies and disadvantages.

In this definition of gender mainstreaming, a gender equality perspective is mentioned. To have a gender equality perspective means that gender, as a social construction, is discussed or taken into account in descriptions, explanations and interpretations of the world. One can therefore say that a gender perspective refers to an attitude in which one recognises that sexual discrimination, stereotyped division of roles between men and women, and prejudice have their origin in gender and that they are socially constructed. In the long run a gender mainstreaming approach should lead to the diminishing of gender stereotypes, with the result that the power relationships between women and men should become more equally distributed.

It is very unlikely that gender mainstreaming will succeed in a society where no traditional equality policy exists and where there are no instruments or actors to implement it. This may be particularly relevant for sport, because if you live in a country that does not try to mainstream gender in society at large, it may be difficult to do it for non-governmental organisations (NGOs), such as sport organisations. A difficulty for the implementation of gender mainstreaming in general lies in the fact that men are always presented as being the norm. Therefore, the risk of policies accidentally reinforcing gender inequalities and thereby gender stereotypes is a real one, since people may repeat the socially constructed gender patterns.

Due to the strong connection between sport and masculinity, and the dominance of men in sport it may be particularly difficult to implement gender mainstreaming in sport compared to many other areas in society. It may therefore be relevant to ask how it is in Europe today; do all countries have an equality policy which includes strategies such as positive actions and/or gender mainstreaming, and if so, is it implemented and eligible for sport organisations? In 2011 the Council of Europe did a study attempting to answer this question. Twenty-six countries participated in the study (Fasting, 2011). The results revealed that about half of the countries practice neither gender mainstreaming nor positive actions. The most common tool was collection of gender-segregated statistics, which was mentioned by 21 of the countries. The study revealed huge differences between the different European countries in this area, and concluded the following:

• In many countries there is not much of a focus on strategies used to reach gender equality in sport.
• There is a lack of knowledge about gender, gender equality and gender mainstreaming in some countries.

- There is a need for education, consciousness raising concerning gender, equality and gender mainstreaming in administration both in government and sport organizations (Fasting, 2011, p. 25).

In this chapter, I have shown how gender stereotyping may reinforce gender inequality in sport. Two examples were discussed: when elite-level coaching is looked upon as a masculine activity, i.e. a job for men, and the fact that men are not allowed to compete in the feminine sport of rhythmic gymnastics. However, this may change because gender and thereby gender stereotyping, i.e. our perceptions of what is feminine and masculine, can change over time. This was illustrated by showing how the perception of ice skating and cheerleading have changed from being a masculine to a feminine to a more gender-neutral sport. Accordingly breaking the gender stereotypes in sport may lead to a more gender equitable sport. This may be done using different strategies, and future research should focus on studying and comparing both theoretical and practically the impact of undoing gender and/or redoing gender in sports.

References

Carroll, L., Gilroy, P. J. and Ryan, J. (2002). Counseling transgendered, transsexual, and gender-variant clients. *Journal of Counseling and Development*, 80, 131–139. doi:10.1002/j.1556–6678.2002.tb00175.x.

Claringbould, I. and Knoppers, A. (2008). Doing and undoing gender in sport governance. *Sex Roles*, 58(1–2), 81–92. doi:10.1007/s11199–007–9351–9.

Coakley, J. (2009). *Sports in society: Issues and controversies*. New York: McGraw-Hill.

Connell, R. W. (1987). *Gender and power: Society, the person, and sexual politics*. Stanford: Stanford University Press.

Connell, R. W. (2009). *Gender*. Cambridge: Polity.

Connell, R. W. and Messerschmidt, J. W. (2005). Hegemonic masculinity: Rethinking the concept. *Gender and Society*, 19, 829–859. doi:10.1177/0891243205278639.

Council of Europe (2004). Gender mainstreaming: Conceptual framework, methodology and presentation of good practice. Retrieved from www.coe.int/t/dghl/standardsetting/equality/03themes/gender-mainstreaming/EG_S_MS_98_2_rev_en.pdf.

Deutsch, F. M. (2007). Undoing gender. *Gender and Society*, 21, 106–127. doi:10.1177/0891243206293577.

European Commission (2014). Gender equality in sport: Proposal for strategic actions 2014–2020. Retrieved from http://ec.europa.eu/sport/events/2013/documents/20131203-gender/final-proposal-1802_en.pdf.

Fasting, K. (2011). *Gender mainstreaming in European sport*. Report delivered to the Council of Europe, November 2011.

Fasting, K. and Sand, T. S. (2013). *Gender in top-level coaching roles: Presentation of an ongoing research project*. Paper presented at 'Women in Coaching', seminar at Malmö University, 31 January 2013.

Fasting, K., Sand, T. S. and Knorre, N. (2013). European female sport students as future coaches? *European Journal for Sport and Society*, 10, 307–323.

Hofmann, A. R. (2011). Women challenge the IOC in court: The case of ski jumping [Power point slides]. Retrieved from www.playthegame.org/fileadmin/image/PTG2011/Presentation/Wednesday/Annette_Hofmann-Play_the_Game.pdf.

Kamberidou, I., Tsopani, D., George, D. and Nikolaos, P. (2009). Question of identity and equality in sports: Men's participation in men's rhythmic gymnastics. *Nebula*, 6, 220–237.

Laurendeau, J. and Adams, C. (2010). 'Jumping like a girl': Discursive silences, exclusionary practices and the controversy over women's ski jumping. *Sport in Society: Cultures, Commerce, Media, Politics*, 13, 431–447. doi:10.1080/17430431003588051.

LaVoi, N. M. and Dutove, J. K. (2012). Barriers and support for female coaches: An ecological model. *Sports Coaching Review*, 1, 17–37. doi:10.1080/21640629.2012.695891.

Lorber, J. (1994). *Paradoxes of gender*. New Haven: Yale University Press.

Lorber, J. (2005). *Breaking the bowls: Degendering and feminist change*. New York: W. W. Norton & Company.

McKenna, W. and Kessler, S. (2006). Transgendering: Blurring the boundaries of gender. In K. Davis, M. Evans and J. Lorber (eds), *Handbook of gender and women's studies* (pp. 342–356). London: Sage.

Messner, M. A. (2002). *Taking the field: Women, men, and sports*. Minneapolis: University of Minnesota Press.

Norman, L. (2010). Bearing the burden of doubt: Female coaches' experiences of gender relations. *Research Quarterly for Exercise and Sport*, 81, 506–517. doi:10.1080/02701367.2010.10599712.

Paoletti, J. B. (2012). *Pink and blue: Telling the boys from the girls in America*. Bloomington: Indiana University Press.

Pilcher, J., and Whelehan, I. (2004). *50 key concepts in gender studies*. London: Sage.

Pfister, G. (2000). Doing gender: Die Inszenierung des Geschlechts im Eiskunstlauf und im Kunstturnen [Doing gender: The staging of sex in figure skating and gymnastics]. In J. R. Norber (ed.), *Studier i idrott, historia och samhälle. Tillägnade professor Jan Lindroth pa has 60-arsdag* (pp. 170–201). Stockholm: HLS.

Pfister, G. (2005). 'Das Geschlecht läuft immer mit': Frauen und Langstreckenlauf im medizinischen Diskurs ['The sex is always running': Women and long-distance running in medical discourse]. In J. Buschmann and S. Wassong (eds), *Langlauf durch die Olympische Geschichte. Festschrift Karl Lennartz* (pp. 373–405). Cologne: Carl und Liselott Diem Archiv.

Pfister, G. (2010). Women in sport: Gender relations and future perspectives. *Sport in Society: Cultures, Commerce, Media, Politics*, 13, 234–248. doi:10.1080/17430430903522954.

Rees, T. (2002) *A new strategy: Gender mainstreaming*. Paper presented at the 5th European Women and Sport Conference in Berlin, 18–21 April 2002.

Popova, M. (2012, October 8). Where are the male rhythmic gymnasts? Retrieved from www.huffingtonpost.co.uk/milena-popova/where-are-the-male-rhythm_b_1764398.html.

Wade, L. (2012, 31 December). The manly origins of cheerleading. Retrieved from www.huffingtonpost.com/lisa-wade/cheerleading-history_b_2372103.html.

West, C. and Zimmerman, D. H. (1987). Doing gender. *Gender and Society*, 1, 125–151. doi:10.1177/0891243287001002002.

West, C. and Zimmerman, D. H. (2009). Accounting for doing gender. *Gender and Society*, 23, 112–122. doi:10.1177/0891243208326529.

Chapter 2

Reflections on Muslim women and sport

Tansin Benn, Gertrud Pfister and
Haifaa Jawad

Muslim women from the Middle East approached Margaret Talbot in the late 1990s, when she was President of the International Association of Physical Education and Sport for Girls and Women (IAPESGW), asking for the Association's help to challenge stereotypes and barriers to their progress in the field. She worked ceaselessly to promote and support efforts around the world to promote and follow this mission through. Hence it was decided to use material, with the kind permission of the publisher Routledge, from the book *Muslim Women and Sport*, edited by T. Benn, G. Pfister and H. Jawad (2011), for this chapter in her *Festschrift*. It was one outcome from a study week in Oman in 2008 that Margaret inspired and chaired and is a tribute to her support for this complex and highly sensitive area of gender studies in sport and physical education.

Introduction

The issue of women, sport and empowerment remains on the agenda of global social change. The concepts of women's empowerment, gender mainstreaming, gender equality and gender equity have been identified as key drivers for promoting women's quality of life. The increased emphasis on the position of women and sport during the last half century has now been embedded in the broader context of globalisation. A record of this can be found in sequential United Nations policy documents, as well as proceedings from the 17 quadrennial IAPESGW world congresses. These documents track increased global attention to women's rights and have served to facilitate a greater interest and participation in women's sport. IAPESGW has, historically, supported the involvement of girls and women in physical education and sport since its inception in 1949. A half century later, in 1999, IAPESGW, through its members and leaders, responded to requests to work more closely with, and for, Muslim women in physical education and sport. The strategic initiative involved acknowledging and combating negative stereotypes of Muslim women (held predominantly in the West but also in other parts of the world) as oppressed and virtually invisible in the sports arena, and bringing forth understanding, through knowledge exchange, about the diverse experiences of Muslim girls and women in and through physical education and sport internationally. One forum created was in locating the IAPESGW World Congress in Alexandria, Egypt in 2001, under Margaret's Presidency. This provided a world platform from which to facilitate an international agenda for the discussion of challenges and opportunities for Muslim girls and women in sport, alongside wider women and sport issues. Such efforts continue, for example in the Al-Sinani *et al.* (2013) publication which is the first to explore gender equity in physical education across four Gulf countries.

During the following 2005 IAPESGW World Congress in Edmonton, Canada, two important events coincided, the opening keynote by the then President, Professor Margaret Talbot, and a seminar on Muslim women in sport. The former raised concerns about the exclusion of Muslim girls and women from physical education and sport, while the latter identified contested views concerning the participation of Muslim women in the Olympic Games. As a result of subsequent discussion between a group of scholars with mutual interest in facilitating the participation of Muslim women in sport, a commitment to pursue an opportunity for extended dialogue at an international level was agreed. Dr. Tansin Benn, then an Executive Board member of IAPESGW, and later President 2009–2013, was invited by the group to coordinate a study group initiative. Eventually, under the aegis of IAPESGW and with the generous support of Sultan Qaboos University, a study week on 'Improving opportunities for Muslim girls and women in physical education and sport' took place in Oman in February 2008. The result of intense debate and discussion resulted in the 'Accept and Respect' Declaration as well as the book *Muslim Women and Sport* (2011a), edited by T. Benn, G. Pfister and H. Jawad, from which much of the material for this chapter is taken. The book provided new insights into religious, cultural and social influences on the lives of women through the life experiences of Muslim women, told through their own voices and focused on sport and physical education across 14 countries: Bahrain, Bosnia and Herzegovina, Denmark, Germany, Iran, Iraq, Morocco, Oman, Palestine, South Africa, Syria, Turkey, UK and United Arab Emirates.

Muslim women and sport

Approximately one-fifth of the world's population, 1.3 billion people, are followers of Islam, the second largest global religion. Muslim people live on every continent, in around 57 countries, in different social, political and economic situations (Esposito and Mogahed, 2007, p. 3). It is claimed that Islam is the fastest growing religion in the history of the world (FAIR, 2015) but life experiences within Islam are diverse. Countries such as Iran are Islamic countries governed by Sharia Law; others, such as Syria and

Turkey, have Muslim majority populations but separate religion from State; other Islamic groups are part of the diaspora that positions Muslim people as a minority in predominantly non-Muslim countries. In spite of the number and worldwide occurrence of Muslims, their diverse cultures and conditions of life are little known amongst non-Muslims, and even less is understood about the body cultures and physical activities of Muslim girls and women. Public attention to date has focused on top-level athletes at the Olympic Games or fatwas, by religious conservatives, on Muslim women who choose to wear sports clothing considered to be unislamic (lacking in modesty). One example was the case of tennis player Sania Mirza who, despite her popularity with the Indian population, was once the centre of controversy and opposition from fundamental religious groups. Threats led to her travelling with body guards and it was reported in 2008 that she had considered withdrawing from playing in India, despite her love of her country, because of religious controversy (www.all-about-tennis.com/sania-mirza.html, accessed 9 December 2009). Such examples highlight the need to focus on authentic experiences of Muslim women from within different cultures, and listen to their personal sport-related histories of living in diverse contexts around the world because:

> Today we are trying to live ever closer to the lives about which we write ... we are trying to show not that we can live those lives but that we have lived close enough to them to begin to understand how the people who live those lives have constructed their worlds.
>
> (Denzin and Lincoln, 2000, p. 1058)

'Women, Islam and sport' constitutes a contested area where issues of power intersect, for example, in gender relations and politics; where tensions arise between religious and secular values; and where answers need to be found between universal human rights, which can deny the significance of cultural distinctiveness, and cultural relativity, which can unacceptably justify inhumane activities on the grounds of long-held cultural traditions.

The term 'Muslim women' is used to include all women who have committed themselves to the Islamic faith. Although the use of 'Islamic women' is becoming popular in everyday usage, it is a term normally reserved for those who are related to, empathetic with, or belonging to, political Islamic organisations. Therefore, the term 'Muslim women' is used here to be as inclusive of Islamic faith followers as possible. Waljee (2008, p. 99), in her research on transitions in the lives of Muslim women in Tajikistan, critiques academia dominated by Western researchers who do not treat as equal the accounts of women already redefining their roles in complex political, economic and cultural contexts:

Western (even feminist) conceptualisations of gender relations will always remain at best incomplete and at worst misguided. To gain a better understanding of what is played out in such relations it is crucial to pay more attention to political, economic and cultural context so as to understand how communities have historically dealt with imposed ideologies that are diametrically opposed to their values.

Muslim women are often marginalised in accounts of the Muslim world (Runnymede Trust, 1997; Richardson, 2004). Fears of radicalism and stereotypes of Muslim people as 'other' have accelerated in the West with the growth of Islamophobia following the terrorist attacks of 9 September 2001. This has resulted in a fruitless polarisation of values related to how people live their lives (Allen and Nielsen, 2002; Commission on British Muslims and Islamophobia, 2004; Esposito and Mogahed, 2007; Fekete, 2008). In this dialogue Muslim women are often positioned as oppressed, victimised and disadvantaged.

The authors do not intend to suggest that Muslim women are homogeneous. But religion is a defining and important aspect of identity to those who regard themselves as Muslim. Hargreaves (2000, p. 68) wrote of the 'progressive sense of global Islam in the international Muslim women's sports movement, which grows in strength and effectiveness'. For many, Islam is a way of life, a set of principles, values and beliefs, a shared frame of reference that gives meaning and purpose to everyday living. Research into life experiences of Muslim women in sporting contexts addresses the contested discourses and practices between religion and sport but also between the diversity of personal, local and international contexts. This is where sporting and educational institutions are culturally constructed by subtle nuances of cultural and religious dynamics, as well as political, social and economic factors.

Body culture and Islamic concern for modesty is one theme that permeates work in the area of Muslim women and sport. For example, the hijab (commonly used to refer to head-covering) has become a global symbol of religious identity with many meanings for both the wearer and the observer. It is seen by some as essential to religious observance, by others as a political statement and by others as a repressive imposition. Body culture in the dominant sporting world often demands high visibility of men's and women's bodies in accordance with the dress code regulations of international sports federations. Some Muslim women may participate when the dress code is flexible and allows body covering but are excluded when flexibility does not exist. Similarly, in schools, particularly in diaspora Muslim communities in Western countries, dependent on state political persuasions, school-based physical/sport education policy and practice can accommodate or deny religiously motivated requests concerning dress (see Benn et al. (2011b) and Dagkas et al. (2011) for an English case study). There are countries that make the hijab compulsory and others that deny citizens the right to wear it in public. These positions remove individuals' freedom of choice. The relatively rare participation of Muslim women in sporting activities means they are often labelled as marginalised and they become the subjects of struggle for feminists with common aims and different worldviews, such as Western and Islamic feminists.

A group of feminists have viewed the exclusion from the Olympic Games of Muslim women from Islamic countries' teams as discriminatory (Hargreaves, 2000). Such views certainly defend the rights of women who wish to compete in the mainstream sporting context but who are barred politically or culturally from doing so. In such cases it is important to have somebody who pleads their case. On the other hand, viewing all Olympic non-attendance by women from Islamic countries as discriminatory also ignores, denies or fails to respect the rights of those Muslim women who have embodied their faith in ways that lead them to prefer participation in physical activity in more private ways. For example, some choose to participate in events organised to provide a more Islamically appropriate environment that manages their faith need for body modesty and women-only environments. Sport institutions are themselves socially constructed, contested and changeable. See also Benn and Ahmed (2006) for insights into the British Muslim Women's Futsal team that attended the 2005 Women's Islamic Games in Tehran, Knez et al. (2014) for insider perspectives of the influence of Qatar's successful 2022 World Cup Football bid on women, Miles and Benn (2014) for a study on Muslim women's issues regarding recreational sport provision in one UK university and Dagkas et al. (2014) for wider international perspectives.

Islamic feminism offers a way to understand and empower Muslim women from inside the religion by recognising that a faith-based approach is the only way forward for many women (and men). Islamic feminists counter that the suppression experienced by some Muslim women does not reflect gender relations in early Islam and has come about by an Islam 'interpreted for them by men' (Waljee 2008, p. 99). 'Islamic feminism ... explicates the perspective of women (and men) who, although committed to Islam as an essential part of their identity, don't hesitate to criticise and challenge the Islamic patriarchal authority' (Jawad, 2009 p. 2). Through reinterpretation of Islamic texts from a female perspective these feminists have helped Muslim women to re-enter a more public life, pursuing equality within an Islamic framework (Jawad, 1998, 2009; Wadud 2006). Such interrogation has also helped Muslim women in sport to distinguish religious from cultural barriers through understanding that nothing in Islam precludes participation in physical activity (Al-Ansari, 1999; Daiman, 1994; Sfeir, 1985). Islamic feminists are giving legitimacy to social action by Muslim women who are creating new agendas, for example in living more public lives, entering the workplace and contributing more visibly in their communities.

Muslim scholars, practitioners and leaders are marginalised in the scientific community. Much of the research and academic writing in the field of women in sport and physical education is produced in the USA, some parts of Europe and Australia. This constitutes a problem of invisibility and marginalisation for people who are living on the periphery of expanding scientific knowledge, a problem acknowledged by many writers, for example Tinning (2006, pp. 369, 373) who recognises the risk of a 'distorted vision', and Knez et al. (2014) for an extended discussion on insider/outsider researchers. The dominance of English-language literature is one of the reasons for the distorted vision and why the voices of few are much more audible than the voices of the majority of the world's population. The core problem is that Western academic frameworks are at risk of legitimising and generalising what counts as knowledge from an ethnocentric position that fails to recognise the lens through which such work is created. This is not to deny that all researchers have ethnocentric perspectives and particular lenses through which worldviews are formed, but it becomes problematic when other ways of seeking to know and understand the world in which we live are marginalised or treated as inferior. Increased sensitivities are required in a globalised world as researchers strive to cross cultural boundaries in endeavours to increase knowledge and understanding. For example, the limitations in international studies on 'gender' are criticised by Waljee (2008, p. 87), who suggests that restricted models of gender analysis such as access, outcomes and performance can be misinterpreted by those 'outside' the situation studied in a way that can 'fail to address, or find wanting, cultural and religious specificity and economic realities of nations in transition, or different cultural norms that frame gender relations'. One attempt to overcome this was the IAPESGW/Oman 2008 international study week (www.iapesgw.org) that focused on listening to women's issues from Europe, the Middle East and the Far East; crossing cultural boundaries by being together, and learning from each other. One outcome was a consensus on the final 'Accept and Respect' Declaration (www.iapesgw.org), which has given leverage to lobbyists around the world to improve access and opportunities for Muslim girls and women around the world. The 'Accept and Respect' Declaration is as follows:

1   Islam is an enabling religion that endorses women's participation in physical activity.
2   We affirm the importance of physical education and physical activity in the lives of all girls and boys, men and women.
3   We emphasise the importance of good quality programmes of physical education and sport in school curriculum time, especially for girls.
4   We emphasise the desirability, in places where many children have limited access to school, of providing other ways of helping children to learn the physical skills and confidence they need to practise sport.

5   We recommend that people working in the sport and education systems Accept and Respect the diverse ways in which Muslim women and girls practise their religion and participate in sport and physical activity, for example, choices of activity, dress and gender grouping.

6   We urge international sport federations to show their commitment to inclusion by ensuring that their dress codes for competition embrace Islamic requirements, taking into account the principles of propriety, safety and integrity.

7   We recommend national governments and organisations include in their strategies for the development of sport and physical education, structures and systems that encourage women to take positions in teaching and research, coaching, administration and leadership.

Underpinning the Declaration was the intention to increase awareness that women have different religious preferences for sporting participation and key to improving life chances is listening to the diverse voices and choices of women in their specific situations. Significant to the process and outcome was the need to reaffirm the important distinctions between Islam the religion, and cultural overlays that can damage life chances and understanding in the world. 'Accept and Respect' has become a catch-phrase for fighting other areas of discrimination.

The Declaration has been used to reach people interested or engaged in policy and practice of physical education, from schools to universities, in community provision and elite-level sport. A major success area has been with sports governing bodies, many of which have changed their clothing policy to be more inclusive, for example beach volleyball, football and weightlifting. It is a Declaration created with and for Muslim women whose religious belief and situational realities may lead them to choose a path of modest dress codes and/or sex-segregation for sports participation, as well as for those who choose not to wear the hijab. It is for Muslim and non-Muslim people who live together in many countries of the world and who want to understand each other's worldview more fully and to stand in solidarity for the right of personal choice. Simply, the Declaration is about 'Accepting and Respecting' the voices and choices of others.

A major characteristic of researchers and practitioners able to work across cultural boundaries in our ever more globalised world is a 'global mindset':

> People with global mindsets have the ability to continually expand their knowledge; have a highly developed conceptual capacity to deal with the complexity of global organizations; are extremely flexible; strive to be sensitive to cultural diversity; are able to intuit decisions with inadequate information; and have a strong capacity for reflection.... A global mindset thinks and sees the world globally, is open to

exchanging ideas and concepts across borders, is able to break down one's provisional ways of thinking. The emphasis is placed on balancing global and local needs, and being able to operate cross-functionally, cross-divisionally, and cross-culturally around the world.

(Marquardt, 2000, p. 4)

All women have been the subject of prejudice and discrimination in the sporting world. Indeed the modern Olympics started in 1896 as a male preserve where women were deemed fit only to crown the heads of the victors. Today there is hardly a sport, or even an event within a sport, for example athletics, that is not open to women. Where women rarely compete against men for valid physiological reasons, they are now accepted as officials in men's competitions at the highest level. Research across a range of disciplines has slowly brought about change from an excluding to an including discourse (Pfister, 2000), but this has been a journey led predominantly by Western academics and it has largely ignored cultural differences and knowledge of people's lives beyond Western societies. While many of the barriers Muslim women face are similar to those of all women, such as social and economic forces, there are important faith-based and cultural differences situated in distinctive contexts which are significant in shaping people's priorities and preferences for their lives in the twenty-first century.

The premise of all the efforts to increase opportunities for Muslim girls and women internationally is that physical activity is beneficial in human development, health and fulfilment; and that within the religion of Islam, women's participation in physical activity is encouraged. It is also acknowledged that some girls and women live in challenging cultural, economic and political situations that deny them life chances in terms of education, freedom to move and equality of opportunity to contribute to their society (Sfeir, 1985). Progress and increased knowledge sharing has shown that some Muslim women have been agents of change, role models for others and pioneers in the area of physical activity in their respective countries and regions, which is in contrast to the dominant discourses of the West.

Diversity, religion and sporting cultures

From gathering Muslim Women's accounts of the sporting experiences across countries in *Muslim Women and Sport*, and wider research, it has become evident that ways in which faith and sporting identities are managed cover a wide spectrum of positive and negative encounters of Muslim women in sport-related activities. There are athletes for whom religion is a private aspect of their lives, who see no need for adoption of hijab and non-conventional sports clothing, as exemplified by the women Olympians in North Africa. There are other participants whose 'embodied-faith' necessitates the adoption of hijab and whose religious identity is compromised by sports governing bodies and political regulations that ban the wearing of the hijab, for example in Turkey. For others, there are times, when engaged in playing sport, that young women prioritise their national identity over religious identity. Most women physical education teacher training students in Oman regarded modest Islamic dress and gender segregated sports spaces as a religious requirement and Omani cultural expectation, although there were some exceptions to this as a small number of Omani women stepped into the international women's sporting arena.

Diverse attitudes towards physical activity prevail amongst Muslim women in European countries. For example, in Denmark and Germany current discourses of immigration, assimilation, integration and inclusion ensure political goodwill towards immigrant populations. Sporting opportunities are many and the climate for participation is positive, but the structures and practices are culturally designed by and for a Westernised/European understanding of social relations and body culture. This can create inevitable conflicts for some participants and providers of sporting environments in disapora situations.

Diverse situations for women's participation in international sport prevail in different countries, for example in Iran, gender segregated sporting structures have led to a separate but active women's sport movement alongside the required all-female infrastructure of sports coaches, coaches and judges/referees (Koushkie Jahromi, 2011). In contrast in countries that have undergone relatively recent modernisation processes, for example Morocco, there have been struggles endured for the acceptance of women's rights and sporting opportunities alongside those of men, with success to Olympic level (El Faquir, 2011). Women's sport in the Arab Gulf countries is in its infancy with differences in and between the countries that relate to urban/rural lives, socioeconomic conditions and cultural traditions (Knez et al., 2014). While Bahrain led the region in the provision of sporting opportunities for women at university level (Al-Ansari, 2011), other countries in the region still have no university-level teacher training or sport provision. In the UAE physical activity opportunities are making a difference in the lives of young people with intellectual disabilities, but public acceptance of this disadvantaged group is recent (Gaad, 2011).

It is a positive note that most countries of the world have a commitment to the provision of physical education for girls and boys within their education systems, at least in theory, although this is not yet a global phenomenon (Hardman and Marshall, 1999, 2005; MINEPS, 2013). In some countries there can still be barriers to participation for those girls who wish to adhere to Islamic requirements for modesty in their schools. In addition to this desire, other barriers may also be present, such as a hostile climate, poor or inappropriate facilities, inflexible policies, lack of teacher understanding, cultural/parental resistance, lack of student motivation and an increasing body and faith consciousness of the girls (Benn et al., 2011b).

A major factor in determining opportunities for women in physical activities and playing sports is a country's 'sporting culture'. Where there is a long history of modern sport,[1] albeit a male-dominated model of sport, it has been integrated into the infrastructure of school and community provision, such as in Germany and Denmark. It is the relatively recent numbers and patterns of immigration that have raised new challenges in Europe for inclusion of people with different beliefs, values, expectations and needs in their sport discourses and practices. In many of the Muslim countries modern sport is not rooted in traditions but arrived with colonialism and alongside Westernisation projects with migrant workers. Globalisation processes such as commercialisation, internationalism and politicisation have led to Western models of sport becoming part of the global sports business, screened, and available worldwide, on a daily basis, for example the Olympic Games (Benn and Dagkas, 2013).

The culture of commercially popular elite sport today has an aura of spectacle, glamour and wealth, but is also criticised for exploitation (including of women), cheating, gambling and drug abuse (Bale and Christensen, 2004). While there is criticism, rarely do critics touch issues related to complex overlaps between religious and secular values, and the inevitable difference in value-positions. High achievers in modern sport are frequently considered as role models for aspiring, or even participating, sportspeople. However, the spectacle, consumerism, fanaticism and inappropriate behaviour that surrounds many sports and sporting 'heroes' could be seen as the antithesis of an Islamic lifestyle, increasing the challenge of inclusion efforts.

Despite the challenges, sporting opportunities have given many women the self-determination, confidence and perseverance to resolve multiple complexities in and between religious beliefs, gender relations, body and sporting cultures. Such personal attributes can be lost where shifting balances of political power leave women relatively powerless. The atrocities suffered by girls and women in periods of instability, such as the wars of Bosnia and Herzegovina, Iraq and Syria, lead to instability with women's pursuits such as sport, marginalised in the traumas of life crises, although it also has the power to help maintenance and reconstruction of identities (Ibrahimbegovic-Gafic, 2011). The power of sport should not be underestimated.

Recommendations

In any research and policy action to support increased opportunities for Muslim girls and women to participate in physical activities, recognition of situation is essential to relevance and appropriateness since there will be different priorities and aspirations. For example, while some women may aim at top-level competitions, others participate in physical activities to maintain health and others are uninterested. It should be regarded, as a principle, that sport and physical activities – their conditions, contents and aims – must be oriented to the needs of these different groups.

Schools, sport organisations/clubs, youth centres or women's groups should develop concepts and programmes which follow the principles of equal rights, equal opportunities and inclusion, as well as acceptance and tolerance. The following guide lines make sense in sport programs for Muslim women in Western as well as in Islamic countries:

Women, who choose to wear the hijab and adhere to strict gender sensitive religious requirements, may be encouraged to participate in sport if:

- only females take part in these activities;
- the course leaders are female;
- boys and men have no access to the facilities when used by females;
- clothes are accepted which cover the body;
- separate changing and showering facilities are available;
- the sports facilities are within easy reach of the girls' and women's homes;
- the sports courses take place in the afternoon or early evening;
- participants may bring their friends or acquaintances;
- male family members are supportive of the sporting activities of their daughters, sisters or mothers;
- the activities are significant and meaningful for the groups, which may differ in their expectations;
- activities offered are oriented, in particular, towards health and fitness;
- culturally valued movement forms, such as traditional dance, can be integrated.

Furthermore, women should be made familiar with a variety of physical activities in order to give them a chance of choosing the activity which best fits into their lives.

In addition, in Western countries it may be helpful, in some cases, if the courses are run by a woman from the same cultural background. The question remains, however, whether it is better to organise physical activity/ sports courses exclusively for ethnic minority groups or whether immigrant women should be integrated into multi-ethnic groups. On the one hand, it is important not to isolate immigrants, whilst on the other hand, it makes sense to encourage the preservation of ethnic groups in order to strengthen cultural identity and offer a 'safe haven'. Therefore, both opportunities of doing sport should be available.

Girls and women can be empowered in and through sport, but there is still much to be done in order to provide sports for females and to motivate females to take part in sports. At least some initiatives do exist which work not only for, but above all with, minority girls and women for their empowerment.

At local levels Muslim women are negotiating change and opportunities for themselves in arenas of physical activity, in line with Henry's (2007) concept of 'situated ethics'. Local initiatives are commendable, but these can only become universal with the widespread dissemination of knowledge and understanding to facilitate the provision of opportunities for girls and women to participate in physical activities and sport.

Through a process of exchanging experiences, listening and negotiating, the architects of the 'Accept and Respect' Declaration reached a consensus. The Declaration stands between universal human rights that ignore cultural difference and cultural relativity that may accept discriminatory behaviour justified in cultural and religious terms. 'Accept and Respect' was a product of post-modern 'situated ethics' (Henry, 2007, pp. 317, 319) where 'absolute standards are rejected in favour of the requirements of a particular situation', in full recognition of the fact that 'consensus has limits and ... some groups will almost invariably stand outside the consensus achieved, but that consensus is an on-going constructer upon mutual respect and dialogue'. Through the Declaration, and the research and practice evidenced in *Muslim Women and Sport* and subsequent studies identified in this chapter, negative stereotypes of Muslim women are challenged, awareness of difference is increased and solidarity of support for the rights of all women in sport is entrusted to 'accepting and respecting' the voices and choices of others.

Margaret Talbot was a champion for the cause of increasing opportunities for Muslim girls and women to participate in sporting activities at every level. She was an inspiration for many of us, Muslim and non-Muslim, who took up the challenge, a person of vision for a better world with the skills and wisdom to steer and support, always putting the needs of others before her own.

Note

1 Modern sport started towards the end of the nineteenth century in Europe with the formalisation of national, then international rules and regulations that enabled competition to take place. Many sports governing bodies were formed between the 1870s and 1890s. This development was part of major societal changes, particularly industrialisation and the spread of ideas and lifestyles internationally with ideologies such as Athleticism, Olympism and Imperialism.

References

Al-Ansari, M. (1999). *Women, Sport and Islam. Historical and Future Implications for the New Millennium.* Unpublished paper, Department of Physical Education, University of Bahrain.

Al-Ansari, M. (2011). Women in Sports Leadership in Bahrain. In T. Benn, G. Pfister, and H. Jawad (eds), *Muslim Women and Sport* (pp. 79–91). London: Routledge.

Al-Sinani, Y., Benn, T., Al-Ansari, M. and Gaad, E. (2013). Exploring Provision and Practice of Physical Education and Gender Equity across Four Arab Gulf Countries. *International Sports Studies,* 35(2), 3–21.

Allen, C. and Nielsen, J. S. (2002). *Summary Report on Islamophobia in the EU after 11 September 2001.* European Monitoring Centre on Racism and Xenophobia, Centre for the Study of Islam and Christian–Muslim Relations. Department of Theology. University of Birmingham, UK.

Bale, J. and Christensen, M. (eds) (2004). *Post-Olympism? Questioning Sport in the Twenty-First Century.* Oxford: Berg.

Benn, T. and Ahmed, A. (2006). Alternative Visions: International Sporting Opportunities for Muslim Women and Implications for British Youth Sport. *Youth and Policy,* 92, 119–132.

Benn, T. and Dagkas, S. (2013). The Olympic Movement and Islamic Culture: Conflict or Compromise for Muslim Women? *International Journal of Sport Policy and Politics,* 5(2), 281–294.

Benn, T., Pfister, G. and Jawad, H. (eds) (2011a). *Muslim Women and Sport.* London: Routledge.

Benn, T., Dagkas, S. and Jawad, H. (2011b). Embodied Faith: Islam, Religious Freedom and Educational Practices in Physical Education. *Sport, Education and Society,* 16(1), 17–34.

Commission on British Muslims and Islamophobia (2004). *Islamophobia, Issues, Challenges and Action.* Report by the Commission on British Muslims and Islamophobia. Stoke-on-Trent, UK: Trentham Books.

Dagkas, S., Benn, T. and Jawad, H. (2011). Multiple Voices: Improving Participation of Muslim Girls in Physical Education and School Sport. *Sport, Education and Society,* 16(2), 223–239.

Dagkas, S., Benn, T. and Knez, K. (2014). Religion, Culture and Sport in the Lives of Young Muslim Women: International Perspectives. In J. Hargreaves and E. Anderson (eds), *Handbook of Sport, Gender and Sexuality* (pp. 198–206). London: Routledge.

Daiman, S. (1994). Women, Sport and Islam. *Sport,* 2 (May–June), 14–15.

Denzin, N. and Lincoln, Y. (eds) (2000). *Handbook of Qualitative Research* (2nd edition). London: Sage.

El Faquir, F. (2011). Women and Sport in North Africa: Voices of Moroccan Athletes. In T. Benn, G. Pfister and H. Jawad (eds), *Muslim Women and Sport* (pp. 236–248). London: Routledge.

Esposito, J. L. and Mogahed, D. (2007). *Who Speaks for Islam? What a Billion Muslims Really Think.* New York: Gallup Press.

FAIR (2015). Forum Against Islamophobia and Racism, www.fairuk.org/intro.htm. Accessed 2 June 2015.

Fekete, L. (2008). *Integration, Islamophobia and Civil Rights in Europe.* London: Institute of Race Relations.

Gaad, E. (2011). A Case Study on the United Arab Emirates: Women, Disability and Sport. In T. Benn, G. Pfister and H. Jawad (eds), *Muslim Women and Sport* (pp. 210–222). London: Routledge.

Hardman, K. and Marshall, J. (1999). *World-Wide Survey on the State and Status of Physical Education in Schools.* Conference Proceedings, World Summit on Physical Education, Berlin, 3–5 November 1999. Berlin: ICSSPE/CIEPSS.

Hardman, K. and Marshall, J. (2005). *Update on the Status of Physical Education World-Wide.* 2nd World Summit on Physical Education. Magglingen: ICCSPE/CEIPSS.

Hargreaves, J. (2000). *Heroines of Sport: The Politics of Difference and Identity.* London: Routledge.

Henry, I. (2007). *Transnational and Comparative Research in Sport: Globalisation, Governance and Sport Policy.* London: Routledge.

Ibrahimbegovic-Gafic, F. (2011). Experiences of War in Bosnia and Herzegovina and the Effects on Physical Activities of Girls and Women. In T. Benn, G. Pfister and H. Jawad (eds), *Muslim Women and Sport* (pp. 225–235). London: Routledge.

Jawad, H. (1998). *The Rights of Women in Islam: An Authentic Approach.* Basingstoke: Macmillan Press.

Jawad, H. (2009). Islamic Feminism: Leadership Roles and Public Representation. *HAWWA – Journal of Women of the Middle East and the Islamic World,* 7(1), 1–24.

Knez, K., Benn, T. and Al-Khalid, S. (2014). World Cup Football as a Catalyst for Change: Exploring the Lives of Women in Qatar's First National Football Team – A Case Study. *International Journal of the History of Sport,* 31(14), 1755–1773.

Koushkie Jahromi, M. (2011). Physical Activity and Sport for Women in Iran. In T. Benn, G. Pfister and H. Jawad (eds), *Muslim Women and Sport* (pp. 109–124). London: Routledge.

Marquardt, M. (2000). *Successful Global Training: Business Skills.* Alexandria, VA: ASTD.

Miles, C. and Benn, T. (2014). A Case Study on the Experiences of University-Based Muslim Women in Physical Activity during Their Studies at One UK Higher Education Institution. *Sport, Education and Society,* 21(5), 109–124. Published online 11 August 2014.

MINEPS V (2013). *Report by the International Council of Sports Science and Physical Education (ICSSPE),* www.icsspe.org/content/mineps-v-2013-0. Accessed 31 October 2014.

Pfister, G. (2000). *Contested Her-story: The Historical Discourse on Women in the Olympic Movement.* 2000 Pre-Olympic Congress Sports Medicine and Physical Education, International Congress on Sport Science, 7–13 September 2000, Brisbane, Australia.

Pfister, G. (2003). Women and Sport in Iran: Keeping Goal in the Hijab? In G. Hartmann, I. Tews and G. Pfister (eds), *Sport and Women: Social Issues in International Perspective* (pp. 207–223). London: Routledge.

Richardson, R. (2004). *Islamophobia: Issues, Challenges and Action.* Stoke-on-Trent, UK: Trentham Books.

Runnymede Trust (1997). *Islamophobia: A Challenge for Us All*. Report of the Runnymede Trust Commission on British Muslims and Islamophobia. London.

Sfeir, L. (1985). The Status of Muslim Women in Sport: Conflict between Cultural Tradition and Modernization. *International Review for the Sociology of Sport*, 30, 283–306.

Tinning, R. (2006). Theoretical Orientations in Physical Education Teacher Education. In D. Kirk, D. Macdonald and M. O'Sullivan (eds), *The Handbook of Physical Education* (pp. 369–385). London: Sage.

Wadud, A. (2006). *Inside the Gender Jihad: Women's Reform in Islam*. Oxford: Oneworld Publications.

Waljee, A. (2008). Researching Transitions: Gendered Education, Marketisation and Islam in Tajikistan. In S. Fennell and M. Arnot (eds), *Gender Education and Equality in a Global Context* (pp. 87–101). London: Routledge.

Chapter 3

Women, sport and policy

Darlene A. Kluka and Anneliese Goslin

Introduction

The status of women in society has been at the centre of conversations for decades. The concepts of women's empowerment, gender mainstreaming, gender equality and gender equity have been identified through these conversations as key drivers for promoting women's quality of life (Malhotra *et al.*, 2002). According to the World Bank (Malhotra, *et al.*, 2002), the promotion of women's empowerment as a development goal is based on a dual argument: that social justice is an important aspect of human welfare and is intrinsically worth pursuing and that women's empowerment is a means to other ends (including access to equitable sport and physical activity opportunities). The increased emphasis on the position of women during the last several decades has now been embedded in the broader context of global development and should no longer be regarded as an isolated effort. It builds on considerable international consensus, policies and declarations relative to women's position that has developed since the World Population Conference, Bucharest, 1974 (United Nations, 1974); International Conference on Population, Mexico City, 1984 (United Nations, 1984); World Conference to Review and Appraise the Achievements of the UN (United Nations) Decade for Women: Equality, Development and Peace, Nairobi, 1985 (United Nations, 1985); World Summit for Children, New York, 1990 (United Nations, 1990); World Conference on Human Rights, Vienna, 1993 (United Nations, 1993); and International Conference on Population and Development, Cairo, 1994 (United Nations, 1994) with its resulting Program of Action. Rationales for supporting holistic women's empowerment in society have further been articulated in policy statements developed from several high-level conferences such as the Beijing Platform for Action in 1995 (resulting from the UN 4th World Conference on Women in Beijing), the UN Beijing + 5 Declaration and resolution in 2000, the Cairo Program of Action (resulting from the UN International Conference on Population and Development in 1994), the UN Millennium Declaration and Millennium Development Goals in 2000 and the UN Convention on the Elimination of All Forms of Discrimination Against Women (CEDAW) in 1979. The common line of argumentation in all of these policy documents is that it is through the process of social inclusion of women that systems are modified and institutions and societies can be transformed.

The UN Millennium Development Goals (MDGs) were born from the Millennium Declaration – an unprecedented global consensus reached in 2000 by 189 member states of the United Nations. In the declaration, these nations collectively undertook to advance a global vision for improving the condition of humanity throughout the world in the areas of development and poverty eradication, peace and security, protection of the environment and human rights and democracy. In particular, the advancement of women's right to gender equality was recognised as critically necessary for progress. The declaration pledged to combat all forms of violence against women and to implement CEDAW. It recognised the importance of promoting gender equality and women's empowerment as an effective pathway to combat poverty, hunger and disease and for stimulating truly sustainable development (UNIFEM, 2003). The Millennium Declaration renewed the commitments regarding gender equality made at previous world conferences since 1974. Eight of the commitments set out in the Millennium Declaration resulted in the MDGs: to eradicate extreme poverty and hunger, reduce child mortality, improve maternal health, combat HIV/ AIDS, malaria and other diseases, ensure environmental sustainability and develop a global partnership for development (UNIFEM, 2003).

Parallel to these initiatives, involvement in physical activity and sport and creating genuine access and opportunities for girls and women has also become a widely shared goal in global and regional agendas of gender equality/equity. The global women's movement over the past half century has developed the perspective that females are enhanced as human beings when they develop their intellectual and physical abilities. This assertion of women's rights has served to solidify women's interest in sport. A human rights-based understanding of sport and physical activity has been present since the beginning of the United Nations. With the established framework of human rights, a number of UN intergovernmental, international and national policy or normative frameworks on women, gender equality and sport have been developed. These policies, processes and frameworks have laid the foundation for the continuing efforts to achieve a just and equitable world of sport for women. Selected documents critical to the issue of equality for women in sport are listed in Table 3.1 in a timeline that does not claim to be comprehensive, but provides a valuable overview.

Table 3.1 Timeline of selected global and regional conferences, declarations and policy documents relevant to women's position in society and sport

Date	Conferences, policies, declarations, frameworks, resolutions
1948	Universal Declaration of Human Rights (UN)
1974	World Population Conference, Bucharest (UN)
1976	MINEPS I, Paris (UNESCO)
1978	International Charter of Physical Education and Sport (UNESCO)
1979	Convention on the Elimination of All Forms of Discrimination Against Women (CEDAW) (UN)
1984	International Conference on Population, Mexico City (UN)
1985	World Conference to Review and Appraise Achievements of the UN Decade For Women: Equality, Development and Peace, Nairobi (UN)
1988	Moscow Declaration, MINEPS II, Moscow (UNESCO)
1989	Convention on the Rights of the Child (UN)
1990	World Summit for Children, New York (UN)
1993	World Conference on Human Rights, Vienna (UN)
1994	Brighton Declaration on Women and Sport, 1st World Conference on Women and Sport, 'Women, Sport and the Challenge of Change' (IWG)
1994	Cairo Program of Action, resulting from International Conference on Population and Development, Cairo (UN)
1994	Women and Sport Working Group (IOC)
1995	Beijing Platform for Action, resulting from 4th World Conference on Women, Beijing (UN)
1996	Manila Declaration, 1st Asian Conference on Women and Sport (ICHPER-SD)
1996, 2000, 2004, 2008, 2012	IOC resolutions: 1996, 2000, 2004, 2008, 2012 (see 2012 below)
1998	Windhoek Call for Action, 2nd World Conference on Women and Sport, 'Reaching out for Change' (IWG)
1999	Berlin Agenda for Action, 1st World Summit on Physical Education
1999	Declaration of Punta del Este, MINEPS III, Uruguay (UNESCO)
2000	Helsinki Spirit Declaration, EWS conference, 'Women, Sport and Culture: How to Change Sports Culture'
2000	Millennium Development Goals (UN)
2000	Beijing + 5 Declaration (UN)
2001	Asian Women and Sport Action Plan, 1st Asian Conference on Women and Sport (IWG)
2002	Montreal Communique, 3rd World Conference on Women and Sport, 'Investing in Change' (IWG)
2002	Sport as a Tool for Development and Peace: Towards Achieving the United Nations Millennium Development Goals, UN Inter-Agency Task Force on Sport for Development and Peace

Table 3.1 Continued

Date	Conferences, policies, declarations, frameworks, resolutions
2002	Policy on disabled women and girls participating in sport (ASCOD)
2002	Resolution on Women and Sport (European Parliament)
2004	Declaration of Athens, MINEPS IV, Athens (UNESCO)
2005	UN International Year of Sport and Physical Education
2005	Beijing + 10 Declaration
2005	Magglingen Commitment for Physical Education, 2nd World Summit on Physical Education
2006	Kumamoto Commitment, 4th World Conference on Women and Sport, 'Participating in Change' (IWG)
2006	UN Action Plan on Sport for Development and Peace
2006	UN Convention on the Rights of Persons with Disabilities
2008	Accept and Respect Declaration, international study week, IAPESGW/Sultan Qaboos University, Oman
2008	Shafallah Declaration, Doha, Qatar
2009	Kigali Declaration on Gender Equity in Sports for Social Change (AKWOS)
2009	Stellenbosch Importance Statement (IAPESGW)
2010	Sydney Scoreboard, 5th World Conference on Women and Sport, 'Play, Think, Change' (IWG)
2010	Beijing + 15 Declaration
2010	Toronto Charter for Physical Activity: A Global Call for Action
2012	Los Angeles Declaration, 5th World Conference on Women and Sport (IOC)
2013	'Adelante Muchachas' Declaration, IAPESGW/INDER Conference, 'Moving Together towards a Better World', Cuba
2013	Declaration of Berlin, MINEPS V, Berlin (UNESCO)
2014	Brighton Plus Helsinki Declaration on Women and Sport, 6th World Conference on Women and Sport, 'Lead the Change, Be the Change' (IWG)

Rationale for global and regional sport policies and declarations

Intelligence and energy appear to be evenly distributed throughout the world, but access, opportunity, investment and effective organisations are not. The modern world is, at this time, unequal, unstable and unsustainable. The great mission of the twenty-first century is to move neighbourhoods, nations and the world towards integrated communities of shared access, shared opportunities, shared responsibilities and a shared sense of genuine belonging, based on the essence of sustainable community; that our common humanity is more important than our interesting differences. According to the timeline of conferences, policies and declarations presented in Table 3.1, there is a continuing need for more enlightened government policies, more monitoring and evaluation of policies, more competent and honest public administration and management, and more investment of money to benefit all people in all sectors of society. The role of government in many countries, its laws, regulations, programmes, grants and policies, is essential in advancing the common good. There is evidence that more effective government can produce better living conditions and more social justice. In many areas of the world, however, regardless of the quality of government, a critical difference is also being made by citizens working as individuals through nongovernmental nonprofit organisations (NGOs). An NGO is any group of private citizens who join together to advance the public good. The content of this chapter focuses on sport policies and declarations that have been created by government and NGOs that are devoted to gender mainstreaming.

In the era of globalisation, there has become a need to join sport globally. The modern Olympic Games and sport-specific world championships have become increasingly visible and participated in by men and some women. Many ministries have been designed to provide leadership, policy direction and financial assistance for the development of sport at national and international levels (Sport Canada, 1984). The role of men's and boys' participation in sport has been clearly defined in many countries, but the role of those with disabilities and all women continue to be marginalised or missing from the picture. Several regions of the world have collaborated and created policies and declarations that include cultural contexts as well. The position of girls and women in sport cannot be divorced from broader generic policies on girls and women in society and a number of policies and declarations on women and sport resulting from broader generic policies on girls and women. The section that follows explores the timeline of policies and declarations and provides an explanation and analysis of selected global and regional policies and declarations that influence the position of women and girls in society through sport and physical activity.

Global sport policies and declarations

From the timeline presented in Table 3.1 it is evident that policies and declarations are driven and advocated by global sport organisations dedicated to women and girls. Selected contributions of organisations are highlighted below.

United Nations

During the past 65 years, the United Nations (UN) has provided member states with policy statements, resolutions and frameworks that have sought to benefit those who participate in sport. Several of the resolutions, although not mentioning girls and women specifically, imply their inclusion with the terms 'everyone' or 'all'. Since the initiation of the United Nations in 1948, sport and physical activity have been considered a human right. The Universal Declaration of Human Rights of 1948 contains a framework for inclusion: 'Everyone has the right to rest and leisure...' (Article 24); 'Education shall be directed to the full development of the human personality...' (Article 26); and 'Everyone has the right to freely participate in the cultural life of the community...' (Article 27) (United Nations, 1948b).

In 1976 the United Nations Educational, Scientific and Cultural Organisation (UNESCO) created an international platform that initiated intellectual and technical exchange in the field of physical education and sport with the aim of articulating a coherent international strategy for physical education and sport. This global platform emerged in the form of the International Conference of Ministers and Senior Officials Responsible for Physical Education and Sport (MINEPS) and was first held at UNESCO headquarters in 1976. MINEPS I initiated an international strategy for developing physical education and sport as essential aspects of education, a dimension of culture and a key component in the harmonious formation of humans as proposed in the Universal Declaration of Human Rights. MINEPS, as a global platform, assists in guiding the implementation of effective policies and practices globally and provides overall direction of UNESCO's international physical education and sport programme. An important legacy of MINEPS I was the recommendation to create the Intergovernmental Committee for Physical Education and Sport (CIGEPS). The mandate and aim of CIGEPS were to promote international cooperation, drive government action in the areas of physical education and sport and as a mechanism to ensure implementation of recommendations of future MINEPS conferences. MINEPS I was further instrumental in the development of the seminal International Charter of Physical Education and Sport. The mandate, aims and legacy of MINEPS I lived through the MINEPS II (Moscow Declaration, 1988), MINEPS III (Declaration of Punta del Este, 1999), MINEPS IV (Declaration of Athens, 2004) and MINEPS V (Declaration of Berlin, 2013).

UNESCO, as an organ of the United Nations, supports the teaching of physical education and sport, underpinned by the International Charter of Physical Education and Sport that provided a framework for UNESCO's decade of commitment to physical education and sport. At the same time, UNESCO established the International Fund for the Development of Physical Education and Sport (FIDEPS) to aid and implement the statements and aims of the Charter. The Charter contains ten Articles that extend Articles 24, 26 and 27 of the Universal Declaration of Human Rights, referring to the right to rest and leisure, education and participation in cultural activities. The ten Articles declare that one of the essential conditions for the effective exercise of human rights is that everyone should be free to develop and preserve his or her physical, intellectual, and moral powers, and that access to physical education and sport should consequently be assured and guaranteed for all human beings.

The Charter further declares that the fulfilment of the right to opportunity and the appropriate structures for practising physical education and sport will enable social responsibility (UNESCO, 1978).

In 1979, the Convention on the Elimination of All Forms of Discrimination Against Women (CEDAW) focused on the issue of discrimination against girls and women in sport and physical education. Articles 10 and 13 mandate member states of the United Nations to take appropriate action to eliminate discrimination against women in the areas of education, including providing the same opportunities as their male counterparts to actively participate in sport and physical education (United Nations, 1979).

In 1989, the Convention on the Rights of the Child provided support for the concept of sport and physical education as a human right. Article 29(1) of UN Resolution 44/25 declares that a child's education should include 'the development of the child's personality, talents and mental and physical abilities to their fullest potential' (United Nations, 1989).

The report from the 4th World Conference on Women in 1995, which produced the Beijing Platform for Action, included significant policy recommendations on women and sport. One of the planks of the platform supported accessible recreational and sport facilities at educational institutions, the formation of gender-sensitive programmes for girls and women throughout the lifespan in education and community environments, and the establishment and maintenance of programmes in the education system, in places of work, and in communities so that the equivalent of what was offered for boys and men was also offered for girls and women.

A follow-up to the 1995 Platform for Action was a review of progress in 1999 (United Nations, 1999). The Commission on the Status of Women, responsible for global policymaking on gender equality, focused its review on progress made in the areas of sport and physical activity. In its report conclusions 1999/17(l) appealed to governments, the UN system and society to support women in sport and physical activity on a regular basis, having positive effects on women's health throughout the lifespan, and to guarantee that women have equal opportunity to practise, use facilities and compete in sport. The outcome of the review supported the assurance of equal opportunities for girls and women at national, regional and international levels in access, training, competition, prizes and financial benefits (United Nations, 2000b).

In 2002, the UN Inter-Agency Task Force on Sport for Development and Peace met to promulgate a more cohesive approach to the use of sport-related initiatives in the pursuit of development goals. The task force report, Sport as a Tool for Development and Peace: Towards Achieving the United Nations Millennium Development Goals, provided an overview of the increasing role that sport plays in many UN policies and programmes. The report indicates that sport programmes must be based on the 'sport for all' model, ensuring that all groups are given access and opportunity to participate, particularly those who gain additional benefits, such as women, people with disabilities and the young (United Nations, 1999).

The General Assembly of the UN, in 2004, adopted a resolution (58/5) that provided an historical 'first' to the UN 'International Year of...'. The resolution declared 2005 as International Year of Sport and Physical Education and invited governments, nongovernmental agencies, UN agencies and other sport-related stakeholders to join together throughout the world so that sport and physical education opportunities could blossom for the people of the world.

The Secretary General of the UN, in 2006, presented a UN Action Plan on Sport for Development and Peace as part of a report on sport for development (United Nations, 2006a). The plan included the need for the development of a global framework to strengthen a common vision, defined priorities and further raised awareness to promote and mainstream easily repeated sport for development and peace policies and included specific reference to women's involvement in sport and development.

Within the framework of persons with disabilities, which includes women and girls, a Convention on the Rights of Persons with Disabilities (United Nations, 2006b) was held. Resolution 61/106, Article 30, provided a policy framework that supports the right of persons with disabilities to participate in mainstream and disability-specific sporting activities at every level and to have equal access to training, venues, services and resources. Children with disabilities also have the right to equal access, including those in school systems.

The women and sport voice

Within the established frameworks of the UN human rights and sport for development and peace, substantive progress has been made at international and regional levels. Prioritisation of these resolutions, however, had seemingly made little impact on the issue of women and sport until 1995 with the adoption of the Beijing Platform for Action at the 4th World Conference on Women when equality issues in sport and physical education had come to the forefront alongside other rights of women. The women and sport voice had joined the chorus of gender mainstreaming through the United Nations, particularly through behind-the-scenes efforts of WomenSport International and Women's Sports Foundation (USA) members attending the conference (Oglesby, 2007). Outside the UN system, the women and sport movement was beginning to mobilise globally with the Brighton Declaration of 1994 generally accepted as the seminal declaration on gender equality in sport.

Brighton Declaration, 1994

In May, 1994, the 1st IWG (International Working Group) World Conference on Women and Sport themed, 'Women, Sport and the Challenge of Change', was held in Brighton, England. This conference was unique and evolved from the desire to bring together a variety of organisations and countries to share ideas and experiences from within the global women and sport movement. This historical conference presented a forum for an international perspective on women and sport, where governmental and nongovernmental organisations had an opportunity to recognise and value diversity through women and sport. The specific focus of the conference involved the issue of how to accelerate the process of change that would rectify the imbalances women face in participation and involvement in sport at all levels. Three culminating results came from the conference: the Brighton Declaration on Women and Sport, the International Working Group on Women and Sport and the International Strategy on Women and Sport. The Brighton Declaration involves ten principles relating to:

1 Equity and equality in society and sport;
2 Facilities that meet the needs of women;
3 School and junior sport increased opportunities;
4 Developing participation in sport for girls and women;
5 High performance sport opportunities for girls and women;
6 Leadership in sport through an increase in the quality and number of women coaches, referees and decision makers;
7 Education, training and development that address gender equality;
8 Sports information and research on women and sport;
9 Resources allocated for women and women's programmes; and
10 Domestic and international cooperation between governmental and nongovernmental agencies, policies and programs involving women and sport (IWG, 1994).

The Brighton Declaration continues to serve as a reference point for future declarations on gender equality in sport through the most recent conference, 2014, with the Brighton Plus Helsinki 2014 Declaration on Women and Sport as the legacy of the 6th IWG World Conference on Women and Sport 'Lead the Change, Be the Change'.

International Working Group on Women and Sport (IWG)

At the Brighton conference, it also became evident that there was a need for an international women and sport strategy (Oglesby, 2007). The rationale behind an international strategy was that by sharing good practice, change could be accelerated towards a more equitable sport culture. The strategy had four key elements: (1) Brighton Declaration on Women and Sport; (2) international coordination mechanisms; (3) regular conferences and opportunities for information exchange; and (4) an international working group on women and sport (IWG). A significant objective of the IWG was to secure adoption of the Brighton Declaration by as many influential decision makers as possible.

Windhoek, Namibia was selected as the site for the IWG 2nd World Conference on Women and Sport in 1998 (Women's Sports Foundation, 1998). One of its significant results was the launching of the Africa Women in Sport Association which was conceptualised in Brighton. This second conference was entitled 'Reaching Out for Change'. With the theme reflecting thoughts of women reaching out to other sectors of society, the Windhoek Call for Action with its 11 principles resulted from the conference and built upon the Brighton Declaration as advocate for the promotion of sport as a means to realise broader goals in health, education and women's rights.

The 3rd IWG World Conference on Women and Sport occurred in Montreal, Canada in 2002. 'Investing in Change' provided a significant document for the women and sport movement. It resulted in 'The Montreal Toolkit' (Montreal Communique), a reference manual that proposed that realising broader goals of health, education and women's human rights involved multifaceted action plans, including information and advocacy campaigns as well as the integration of sport into community development. Conference legacies from Montreal also included amongst others a recommendation to the IWG to present an official report of the 2002 World Conference on Women and Sport to the 2004 MINEPS IV Conference. The Commission III Women and Sport Recommendations document was a milestone for MINEPS IV (UNESCO, 2004).

The 4th IWG World Conference on Women and Sport was held in Kumamoto, Japan in 2006 as 'Participating in Change'. The Kumamoto Commitment, as the legacy of the 4th IWG World Conference on Women and Sport expressed participants' commitment to establishing a collaborative global network in order to realise gender equality in and through sport.

The 5th IWG World Conference on Women and Sport occurred in Sydney, Australia in 2010 under the theme 'Play, Think, Change'. The Sydney Scoreboard emerged as a legacy from this conference and emphasises female leadership in sport to increase women's participation and representation on sports governing boards globally (Sydney Scorecard, 2010).

The mandate of the IWG to organise regular international conferences to advocate the position of women and sport continued in 2014 in Helsinki with the 6th IWG World Conference on Women and Sport. The theme of this conference proposed 'Lead the Change, Be the Change'. The conference legacy declaration 'Brighton Plus Helsinki' called upon role players in sport to develop a sporting culture that enables and values the full involvement of women in every aspect of sport and physical activity.

IOC Resolutions (1996–2012)

The International Olympic Committee (IOC), after its general assembly in 1996, vowed to hold an International Women and Sport Conference once every four years, under the aegis of the IOC Commission on Women and Sport. The first conference, held in Lausanne, Switzerland, acknowledged that the Olympic ideal will not be fully realised without equality for women within the Olympic Movement. The resolution called upon the IOC, International Federations (IFs) and national olympic committees (NOCs) to consider the issue of gender; the IOC to elevate its Working Group on Women and Sport to the status of an IOC commission; and the IOC to designate 1996–2000 quadrennial as the 'Olympiad for Women' (IOC, 1996).

The 2nd IOC World Conference on Women and Sport was held in Paris, France. The resulting resolution called for several strategies and actions, such as encouraging the minimum representation of at least one woman representative in national delegations at world and regional assemblies and that the IOC, IFs and NOCs set their own forward targets for future female representation in sport governing structures through 2020, and provide access and opportunity for women to be educated and trained for leadership positions.

At the end of the 3rd IOC World Conference on Women and Sport, held in Marrakech, the Morocco Resolution which was adopted, reaffirmed equality in representation in sport governing structures and encouraged education for female leadership opportunities. The resolution also asked that athletes serve as role models and mentors for young girls and women to facilitate growth and development and contribute to promote diversity, peace and human understanding.

The 4th IOC World Conference on Women and Sport was held in Jordan near the Dead Sea. This conference produced the Dead Sea Jordan Plan of Action focusing on six major areas of interest and action plans on gender equality, governance, women, sport and the MDGs, empowerment through education and development as well as women, sport and the media.

The 5th IOC World Conference on Women and Sport (2012) in Los Angeles, USA, produced the Los Angeles Declaration that called upon the Olympic Movement to review the existing targets of at least 20 per cent women in decision making positions by 2005 that were not achieved and set a minimum target for all sport governing bodies to be 40 per cent by 2020. Although the IOC made valuable contributions to gender issues to their present state, scholars, however, have stated that the IOC has moved too slowly and has not taken a proactive global leadership role in many of the issues involved in the women and sport movement (Corbett, 2000; Talbot, 2004).

Declarations of the International Association of Physical Education for Girls and Women (IAPESGW) (2008–2015)

IAPESGW focuses on the importance and values of physical education and sport in the lives of girls and women worldwide. Through its regular quadrennial international conferences since 1949, IAPESGW has evolved into an organisation that has begun to locate physical education and sport for girls and women in a broader social and political context under the leadership of one of its presidents, Margaret Talbot (Kluka, 2007). IAPESGW, as a signatory of the Brighton Declaration in 1984 and its solidarity with the position of women and sport, facilitated and produced a number of significant declarations. In 2008 the 'Accept and Respect' Declaration emerged from a joint international study week in Oman when IAPESGW and Sultan Qaboos University partnered. The Accept and Respect Declaration was the first that specifically affirmed the value of physical education and sport in the lives of Muslim girls and women, urging national and international sport federations to be culturally sensitive to Muslim customs, particularly in dress. The IAPESGW Stellenbosch Importance Statement in 2009 urged governments, national and international organisations to recognise the vital importance of sport and physical education in positively contributing to the education, health and well-being of girls and women. The 2013 IAPESGW/INDER Adelante Muchachas Declaration was produced in Cuba as a legacy of the 16th International IAPESGW conference under the theme "Moving Together towards a Better World". The Cuba Declaration urged governments to work harder to fulfil the MDGs and recognise the reality of physical activity across the lifespan, particularly in the lives of girls and women from birth to death, as central to universal education goals.

Declaration of the International Council for Health Physical Education, Recreation, Sport and Dance (ICHPER-SD)

ICHPER-SD, in partnership with Manila Sports Commission and Philippine Women's Sports Foundation, produced the Manila Declaration on Women and Sport in 1996. This Declaration is discussed in more detail under the section on regional sport policies and declarations.

Regional sport policies and declarations

It is notable that the following policies and declarations, although regional in nature, have addressed similar issues involving gender mainstreaming in and through sport, but in some instances may have actually been ahead of global policies and declarations. Of particular note is the assertiveness of the European Union (EU) in establishing benchmarks and monitoring progress relative to gender mainstreaming.

Manila Declaration on Women and Sport, 1996

A significant step forward on the position of women and sport was taken in Manila in 1996 when the Philippine Sports Commission, the Philippine Women's Sports Foundation and the International Council for Health Physical Education, Recreation, Sport and Dance (ICHPER-SD) Girls and Women in Sport Commission hosted the 1st Asian Conference on Women and Sport. Sixteen Asian nations were represented. The Brighton Declaration was adapted and called the Manila Declaration, with principal amendments to respect cultural matters. A covenant was also designed which each country's representative committed to by signing (Kluka, 1996).

Helsinki Spirit, 2000

The European Women and Sport network (EWS) met in Helsinki, Finland for its fourth EWS conference with the theme, 'Women, Sport and Culture: How to Change Sports Culture'. The result of the conference was the Helsinki Spirit Declaration. Recommendations were presented to be dealt with by the network in the future (EWS, 2000), amongst others that women's role as a resource for sports culture and decision making be strengthened and that the awareness and value of equality in sport be increased. It also called for the Berlin Agenda for Physical Education and the Declaration of Punta del Este (MINEPS III) be implemented and monitored.

Council of Europe Resolution, 2002

The Council of Europe, in an unprecedented move, took a strong stance on the prevention of sexual harassment and abuse of women, young people and children in sport. This was a significant resolution by government, as the topic is one that seldom reaches the governmental level (Council of Europe, 2002).

African Sports Confederation of Disabled (ASCOD) policy on disabled women's and girls' participation in sport, 2002

Constitutionalised as a non-profit organisation and recognised by the Supreme Council of Sports in Africa in 1992, ASCOD created a policy relative to participation of women and girls with disabilities in sport and recreation. It specifically focused upon women and girls with disabilities and the need for access to facilities and equipment, the need for equitable funding for programmes, competent coaches, as well as the development of an action plan to promote, develop and provide equal opportunities for both women/girls and men/boys (ASCOD, 2002).

European Parliament Resolution on Women and Sport, 2002/2280 (INI)

Building upon previous global declarations, the European Parliament Resolution on Women and Sport was institutionalised by members of the European Parliament in the form of actions that specifically pertained to women and sport (European Parliament, 2002). This Resolution called on the Committee of Ministers to promote women's sport and women's participation in sport and promote greater awareness and participation of women in leadership positions, and equal prize money, with a special chapter on women with disabilities and sport.

Another substantive contribution was the EU's White Paper on Sport (2007) and its accompanying action plan that highlighted the need to encourage gender mainstreaming into all of the EU's activities that relate to sport. Its authors also encouraged gender issues as mainstream items in all sport-related activities, focusing on access and opportunities for immigrant and ethnic minority women, in addition to access for women to decision making positions in sport and media coverage. Although the European Parliament has no jurisdiction in sport specifically, it serves as a compass for the directionality of its member states. The implementation of policies, frameworks, resolutions and declarations is left up to each member state. There is additional incentive placed by the Parliament for member state compliance, as funding has been tied to initiatives relating to the abovementioned issues.

Asian Women and Sport: Doha Conference Resolutions, 2003

The 2nd Asian Conference on Women and Sport, held in Doha, Qatar, 2003, adopted the Doha Conference Resolutions, which sought to persuade all governmental organisations and NGOs to actively support women and sport (2nd Asian Conference on Women and Sport, 2003).

European Women and Sport (EWS): Paris Call for Action, 2005

The EWS held a significant conference in 2005 in Paris, France, building upon the Brighton Declaration, the Helsinki Spirit recommendations, the Athens declaration of UNESCO on women and sport 2001, and its own ability to promote gender equality in sport through its network (EWS, 2005).

Asian Women and Sport: Yemen Challenge, 2005

At its 3rd Asian Conference on Women and Sport in Yemen (2005), delegates underscored the importance for the Asia Women and Sport (AWS) group to collaborate with the Olympic Council of Asia to promote and develop women in sport in Asia.

International and regional role players

Internationally, there have been several organisations whose leadership has been in the forefront of gender mainstreaming through sport. Some have genuinely proven to be leaders and key role players, while others have proven to be key role players who are central to the issue of gender mainstreaming, equality and equity in and through sport. The role players presented below have been and continue to be involved in international and regional efforts in the women and sport movement.

International role players

International Association of Physical Education and Sport for Girls and Women (IAPESGW)

IAPESGW was established in 1949 by Dorothy Ainsworth, the Director of Physical Education at Smith College (Northampton, Massachusetts, USA). IAPESGW's Executive Board has grown to reflect the major regions of the world (North America, South America, Africa, Asia, Europe, Australia and the Middle East). Although initially linked to the philosophy of Western culture, there has been an increasing attempt by organisational leadership to recognise, understand, preserve and introduce leadership and initiatives that differ from exclusively Western thinking (Kluka, 2007). IAPESGW has done valuable work in the field of Muslim women and sport that is reflected in the 'Accept and Respect' Declaration (2008), under the leadership of then President, Tansin Benn, with support of a Past President, Margaret Talbot. IAPESGW has worked consistently since its inception to advocate for the status of women and sport in society, primarily through members who are school-based professionals in physical education and professionals in physical education and sport policy and research at universities around the world.

United Nations (UN)

The UN has had a rich history as a central role player in the global movement of women and development, particularly the role of women and sport in the past two decades. Its role and impact on policymaking and advocacy on women and sport is evident from Table 3.1. The UN has joined in partnerships with the IOC and the World Health Orgasnisation (WHO) as well as having formal and informal working relationships with International Council of Sports Science and Physical Education (ICSSPE), ICHPER-SD, IWG and WomenSport International (WSI), particularly in the areas of women, sport and development. The United Nations Decade for Women was successful in gaining attention for the role of women in national and regional development with a number of women's development concerns being legislated during the Decade in order to promulgate women's rights.

International Council of Health, Physical Education, Recreation, Sport and Dance (ICHPER-SD)

The International Council for Health, Physical Education, Recreation, Sport and Dance (ICHPER-SD) was an outgrowth of an idea first conceived in 1950 by the Board of Directors of the American Association for Health, Physical Education, and Recreation (AAHPER) and founded in Rome, Italy, in 1958. The first Girls and Women in Sport Commission was established by President Doris Corbett in 1992, with Darlene Kluka appointed as its first director. This Commission was the first to have a region of the world amend the Brighton Declaration with its own declaration, the Manila Declaration. Those selected to initially lead regionally included Josefina Bauzon (Southeast Asia), Meelee Leung (Hong Kong/Asia), Joan Fry (Australia), Maria Beatriz Rocha Ferreira (Brazil/South America), Phyllis Love (USA/North America), Wilhemena Ikulayo (Nigeria/Africa), Mona Alansari (Bahrain/Middle East) and Claudette Jones (Caribbean).

International Council of Sport Science and Physical Education (ICSSPE)

The International Council of Sport Science and Physical Education (ICSSPE) was founded in Paris, France in 1958 under the name 'International Council of Sport and Physical Education'; the name was changed to include 'Sport Science' in 1982. Although the Council is not specifically focused on women, its aims contribute to the awareness of human values inherent in sport and physical activity, to improve health and physical well-being, and to develop physical activity, physical education and sport in all countries (ICSSPE, 2008). It was one of the first international organisations to use its position statement on women and sport as a pillar of good governance, under the leadership of its first woman president, Gudrun Doll-Tepper and three members of its Executive Board (Margaret Talbot, Anita White, Darlene Kluka) (ICSSPE minutes, 1997).

UK Sports Council

The decade of the 1990s brought policy of the Sports Council, later named the United Kingdom (UK) Sports Council, more sharply into focus with the publication of a strategy document, referred to as New Horizons (Sports Council, 1991). The strategy was the first to make reference to equal opportunities for all through sport despite race, gender, age, ability, social class or religious belief (Houlihan and White, 2002). Policy statements were released that defined the principle of sports equity and represented a paradigm shift from targeting specific groups in sport development to humanitarian initiatives that had the potential to change the structure and culture of sport. The decision to thread the concept of sports equity through the whole of sport development was at that time an unprecedented concept globally (White, 1997a). Specifically, the women and sport policy crafted by the Sports Council in 1993 linked the status quo with policy objectives and action steps required by NSFs, the mass media, local government, sport managers, educators and the Sports Council to achieve the objectives. This initiative was led by Anita White, staff member working for the Council.

WomenSport International (WSI)

At the 1993 North American Society for the Sociology of Sport (NASSS) Conference, it was decided by several of those in attendance, some who were also IAPESGW members, to form a new organisation, WomenSport International, that served advocacy efforts. Celia Brackenridge, Kari Fasting, Marion Lay, Elizabeth Darlison and Barbara Drinkwater founded the group. WSI continues to be an evidence-based advocacy group committed to creating and supporting actions that bring about increased opportunities and positive changes for women and girls in all levels of involvement in sport and physical activity/education. The organisation has proven to be pivotal in several areas of the women and sport movement and has provided a series of position statements regarding issues of sexual harassment and the female athlete triad. Most recently, Carole Oglesby prepared a document, on behalf of WSI, entitled 'Women 2000 and

Beyond: Women, Gender Equality and Sport' to promote the goals of the Beijing Declaration and the Platform for Action.

International Working Group on Women and Sport (IWG)

One of the key results of the Brighton conference in 1994 was the establishment of the IWG. It was originally composed of senior women decision makers from sport throughout the world. Some of the main aims of the IWG focus on the assessment of the impact of the seminal Brighton Declaration and other global declarations on the status of women and sport as well as organising quadrennial world conferences to keep the advocacy for equality of women in sport alive.

International Olympic Committee (IOC)

The IOC is the nexus from which directionality of sport takes place globally. By 1995 the IOC had initiated a Working Group on Women and Sport; by 2004 the Working Group had been advanced to the IOC Commission on Women and Sport that meets annually and serves to monitor women's participation in the Olympic Games and chart progress in the appointment/election of women to decision making positions in the Olympic Movement. Anita de Franz (USA) served as its first chair. In February 2007 the IOC adopted a consensus statement on 'sexual harassment and abuse in sport' (IOC, 2007).

Regional role players

Having global declarations, frameworks and policies relating to gender mainstreaming through sport is insufficient to reach grassroots levels for transformation. Regional organisations also play vital roles in the institutionalisation of transformation relative to women and sport issues. The Sports Association of Arab Women (SAAW), African Women in Sport Association (AWSA), Asian Women and Sport Group (AWS) and European Women and Sport Group (EWS) represent several regions of the world. It is not within the scope of this chapter to discuss their valuable contributions in detail. Suffice it to state that their contributions are at various levels of success, but structures have been established to serve as conduits in the women and sport movement.

Assessment of impact of global sport policies and declarations on women and sport

Declarations, policies, resolutions and calls for action on women and sport are produced on a regular basis. Assessment of the impact of these policies on the position of women and sport in global and national societies, as well as audits on management processes to implement policies is, however, done less regularly. Initiatives to scientifically assess the impact of policies can be grouped into proactive and reactive assessments. In the reactive category, the Sydney Scoreboard and the Analysis and Review of International Working Group on Women and Sport Progress Reports 1994–2010 (Anita White Foundation, 2012) are found. *The Brighton Declaration: A Management Audit of Process Quality* (Kluka, 2008b) is in the category of proactive assessments. The IWG report presents a quantitative and qualitative content analysis and review of global progress made in addressing issues related to women and sport since the 1st IWG World Conference on Women and Sport in Brighton (1994) to the 4th IWG World Conference in Helsinki (2006). The Kluka (2008) audit focused on the effectiveness of management processes of Brighton Declaration signatories and resulted in a management rubric that can be applied proactively to guide management processes to optimally achieve the objectives and goals of global and regional policies documents.

Conclusion

What began at the global level, in 1948 with the Universal Declaration of Human Rights and accelerated by the Brighton Declaration on Women and Sport in 1984, evolved into global and regional declarations, policies, resolutions and calls for action to advocate the fair and equitable position of girls and women and sport. Influential global and continental role players unite efforts in this regard to keep momentum in the efforts to 'enable and value the full involvement of women in every aspect of sport' (IWG vision statement, 2007).

Commentary

As early as 2002, Gilmore, Pool and Charvat declared that the ultimate best practice in social change governance was to manage the desired change by means of quality management processes. In order to achieve gender mainstreaming in global and regional sport organisations, a rubric has been designed by the authors of this chapter that has been based upon available literature and international standards (ISO 9001, 2000). This rubric can form the theoretical basis in the description of the institutionalisation of equity in sport organisations. We hope that this rubric is helpful as a management audit of process quality for sport organisations.

Table 3.2 Audit process quality and sporting organisations

	Statement			
	1 Not in place	2 Somewhat in place	3 In place, but not fully implemented	4 In place and fully implemented

Management process design

Our organisation has developed a specific management process to achieve gender equity

Our organisation designed this management process in collaboration with internal stakeholders

Our organisation designed this management process in collaboration with external stakeholders

A specific person within our organisation has the authority to implement the process

A specific person within our organisation maintains the management process relevant to gender equity in sport

The words 'gender equity in sport' appear in our planning documents and strategies

Our organisation made a public high-profile commitment to the principles of gender equity in sport

Our organisation has a management review process in place to monitor gender equity in sport

Our organisation's management system generates decisions and actions to improve the effectiveness of gender equity

continued

Table 3.2 Continued

Statement	1 Not in place	2 Somewhat in place	3 In place, but not fully implemented	4 In place and fully implemented
Our organisation examines feedback on the implementation process of gender equity				
Our organisation takes regular corrective action regarding gender equity based on feedback from external stakeholders				
Our organisation has strategic sessions to plan our management process regarding gender equity				
Our organisation plans how to provide resources for the implementation process of gender equity				
Our organisation plans how to provide information for the management process				
Our organisation plans how to monitor our management process performance relative to gender equity				
Our organisation develops records to support our management process of gender equity				
Implementing the management process				
Our organisation develops documents that can be used to implement the management process of gender equity				
Our organisation provides infrastructure to manage the implementation of gender equity				

Our organisation ensures that top management apply the management process for gender equity

Our organisation regularly evaluates the performance criteria of the management system for gender equity

Our organisation regularly commissions research on gender equity

The term 'gender equity in sport' appears on our organisation's website

New staff members are formally familiarised with the role and value of gender equity in our organisation

Gender equity in sport is mentioned in the foundation documents of our organisation relative to gender mainstreaming

Supporting the management process
Our organisation regularly identifies the training and awareness needs of our members and our staff regarding gender equity

Our organisation delivers appropriate training programmes on how to manage the implementation of gender equity

Our organisation delivers appropriate awareness programmes on gender equity

Monitoring and controlling the management process
Top management of our organisation regularly mentions the importance of gender equity in gender mainstreaming campaigns

continued

Table 3.2 Continued

Statement	1 Not in place	2 Somewhat in place	3 In place, but not fully implemented	4 In place and fully implemented
Our organisation has baseline information on the status of gender equity in our organisation				
Our organisation has valid information on the progress of the implementation of gender equity				
Our organisation can provide reliable qualitative management process information on the implementation of gender equity				
Our organisation monitors the management process of gender equity				
Our organisation only monitors the quantitative outputs of gender equity				
Our organisation evaluates the effectiveness of training programmes related to the management of gender equity				
Our organisation evaluates the effectiveness of awareness programmes related to the management of gender equity				

Our organisation creates methods to evaluate the impact of gender equity

Records of the effectiveness of gender equity are accessible to the public

Records of the effectiveness of gender equity are only accessible to members or staff of our organisation

Our organisation defines acceptable levels of competency for staff involved in the implementation management of gender equity

Improving the management process
Our organisation has a management process improvement strategy regarding gender equity implementation

Our organisation takes corrective actions whenever feedback on our management processes fail to achieve planned results regarding gender equity

References

2nd Asian Conference on Women and Sport. (2003). Notes taken from Kluka collection.

AKWOS (Organisation of Kigali Women in Sports) (2008). Kigali Declaration. Retrieved February 2, 2015 from www.akwos.org.

Anita White Foundation (2012). *Analysis and Review of the International Working Group on Women and Sport Progress Reports 1994–2010.* Chichester.

ASCOD (American Sports Federation of Disabled). (2002). Retrieved March 15, 2012 from www.ascod.org.

AWISA (African Women in Sport Association). (2005). Background information about AWISA . Retrieved April 26, 2012 from www.awisa.org.

Brighton Declaration on Women and Sport. (1994). International Working Group on Women and Sport. Retrieved August 15, 2013 from www.icsspe.org.

Casablanca Conference. (2007). Gender equity in sport for social change: Creating power and impact for gender equity in sport for social change. Report of the Conference in Casablanca, May 19–22, 2013.

Corbett, D. R. (2000). Professional issues in sport science. 'How can sport science professionals help bridge the increasing chasm between socio-economic and cultural groups?' ICSSPE Pre-Olympic Congress. Retrieved March 15, 2012 from www.icsspe.org/index.php?m=12&wert=3200PHPSESSION.htm.

Council of Europe. (2002). Enactment of Parliament on Women and Sport. Retrieved March 6, 20012 from www.councilofeurope.

Doll-Tepper, G. (2000). Foreword, in D. A. Kluka, C. Melling and D. Scoretz (eds), *Women, sport and physical activity: Sharing good practice.* Berlin: ICSSPE.

European Union. (2007). White paper on sport. Retrieved February 26, 2012 from www.europeanunion.gov.eu.

European Women in Sport. (2000). Meeting proceedings. Retrieved March 1, 2013 from www.ews.org.

European Women in Sport. (2005). Meeting proceedings. Retrieved March 1, 2012 from www.ews.org.

European Women in Sport. (2008). Meeting proceedings. Retrieved March 1, 2013 from www.ews.org.

Gilmore, T., Pool, I. and Charvat, B. J. (2002). *Using catalytic mechanisms to drive and institutionalise change.* Cambridge, MA: Harvard University John F. Kennedy School of Government.

Houlihan, B. and White, A. (2002). *The politics of sports development.* London: Routledge.

IAPESGW (International Association of Physical Education and Sport for Girls and Women). (2007). President's notes.

ICHPER-SD (International Council of Health, Physical Education, Recreation, Sport and Dance) (1996). Manila Declaration on Women and Sport. Girls and Women in Sport Commission. ICHPER-SD Women and Sport Commission Archives.

ICHPER-SD (International Council of Health, Physical Education, Recreation, Sport and Dance). (2000). Archives. Retrieved March 1, 2013 from www.ichpersd.org.

ICSSPE (International Council of Sport Science and Physical Education). (2008). History. Retrieved March 1, 2013 from www.icsspe.org.

IOC (International Olympic Committee). (1996). Declaration on Women in Sport. Lausanne, Switzerland. Retrieved March 10, 2012 from www.olympic.org.

IOC (International Olympic Committee). (2000). Declaration on Women in Sport. Lausanne, Switzerland. Retrieved March 10, 2012 from www.olympic.org.

IOC (International Olympic Committee). (2004). Declaration on Women in Sport. Lausanne, Switzerland. Retrieved March 10, 2012 from www.olympic.org.

IOC (International Olympic Committee). (2007). Consensus Statement on Sexual Harassment and Abuse in Sport. Retrieved August 1, 2016 from www.sportlaw. ca/wp-content/uploads/2011/03/em-IOC-Consensus-Statement-on-Sexual-Harassment-and-Abuse-in-Sport.pdf

IOC (International Olympic Committee). (2008). From Marrakech to the Dead Sea: Tangible progress for women in sport. Lausanne, Switzerland. Retrieved March 20, 2013 from www.olympic.org.

ISO (International Standards Organization). (2000). ISO Survey 2000. Geneva, Switzerland.

IWG (International Working Group). (1994). Proceedings. Retrieved January 5, 2013 from www.iwg-gti.org/index.php?id=7.

IWG (International Working Group). (1998). Proceedings. Retrieved January 5, 2012 from www.iwg-gti.org/index.php?id=7.

IWG (International Working Group). (1999). Proceedings. Retrieved January 5, 2012 from www.iwg-gti.org/index.php?id=7.

IWG (International Working Group). (2000). Proceedings. Retrieved January 5, 2012 from www.iwg-gti.org/index.php?id=7.

IWG (International Working Group). (2002). Montreal Toolkit. Retrieved February 6, 2013 from www.iwg-org.

IWG (International Working Group). (2006). Proceedings. Retrieved January 5, 2012 from www.iwg-gti.org/index.php?id=7.

IWG (International Working Group). (2007). Proceedings. Retrieved January 5, 2013 from www.iwg-gti.org/index.php?id=7.

Kluka, D. A. (1996). Personal notes from 1st Asian Conference on Women and Sport, Manila.

Kluka, D. A. (2000). Epilogue, in D. A. Kluka, C. Melling and D. Scoretz (eds), *Women, sport and physical activity: Sharing good practice*. Berlin: ICSSPE.

Kluka, D. A. (Fall, 2007). President's message. IAPESGW Newsletter, 2.

Kluka, D. A. (2008a). *Directory of sport science: Women and sport*. Berlin: ICSSPE.

Kluka, D. A. (2008b). *The Brighton Declaration: A management audit of process quality*. Published doctoral thesis. University of Pretoria, South Africa.

Malhotra, A., Schuler, S. R. and Boender, C. (2002). Measuring women's empowerment as a variable in international development. Background paper prepared for the World Bank Workshop on Poverty and Gender: New Perspectives.

Oglesby, C. (2007). *Women, gender equality, and sport: Women 2000 and beyond*. New York: United Nations Division for the Advancement of Women.

Sport Canada. (1984). Sport policies. Retrieved March 20, 2013 from www. canadianheritage.gc.ca/progs/sc/pol/femmes-women/1_e.cfm.

Sports Council. (1991). *Sport in the Nineties: New horizons*. London: Sports Council.

Sports Council. (1993a). *Black and ethnic minorities and sport: Policy and objectives*. London: Sports Council.

Sports Council. (1993b). *Women and sport: Policy and frameworks for action.* London: Sports Council.

Sports Council. (1993c). *People with disabilities and sport: Policy and current/planned action*. London: Sports Council.

Sports Council. (1993d). *Young people and sport: Frameworks for action.* London: Sports Council.

Talbot, M. (2004). EWS report on conference. Retrieved March 20, 2013 from www.wsff.org.uk/docs/ews_web_report.doc.

UN (United Nations). (1948a). United Nations Charter. Retrieved June 5, 2013 from www.un.org/documents/instruments/docs_en.asp?year=1969.

UN (United Nations). (1948b). Universal Declaration of Human Rights. Retrieved June 5, 2013 from www.un.org/documents/instruments/docs_en.asp?year=1969.

UN (United Nations). (1979). CEDAW Resolution 34/22. Retrieved August 28, 2013 from www.un.org/documents/instruments/docs_en.asp?year=1989.

UN (United Nations). (1989). Convention on the Rights of the Child Resolution 44/25. Retrieved August 28, 2013 from www.un.org/documents/instruments/docs_en.asp?year=1999.

UN (United Nations). (1995). Report of the 4th World Conference on Women. Beijing, September 4, 1995. Retrieved October 6, 2013 from www.womens sportsfoundation.org.

UN (United Nations). (1999). Commission on the Status of Women Report E/1999/27E/CN.6/1999/10. Retrieved August 20, 2013 from www.un.org/documents/instruments/docs_en.asp?year=1999.

UN (United Nations). (2000a). Further action and initiatives to implement the Beijing Declaration and Platform for Action Outcome Document (A/RES/S-23/3). Retrieved August 20, 2013 from www.un.org/documents/instruments/docs_en.asp?year=2000.

UN (United Nations). (2000b). Outcome document of the 23rd special session of the General Assembly on 'Women 2000: Gender equality, development and peace for the twenty-first century', 10 June 2000. Retrieved November 20, 2013 from www.un.org/documents/instruments/docs_en.asp?year=2000.

UN (United Nations). (2006a). Sport for development and peace: The way forward (A/61/373). Retrieved August 20, 2013 from www.un.org/documents/instruments/docs_en.asp?year=2000.

UN (United Nations). (2006b). Convention on the right of persons with disabilities Resolution 61/106. Retrieved February 28, 2013 from www.un.org/documents/instruments/docs_en.asp?year=2000.

UN (United Nations). (2006c). Sport as a means to promote education, health, development and peace Resolution 60/9. Retrieved February 28, 2013 from www.un.org/documents/instruments/docs_en.asp?year=2000.

UN (United Nations). (2008). Women 2000 and beyond: Women, gender, equality and sport. New York: Division for the Advancement of Women of the United Nations Secretariat.

UNIFEM (United Nations Development Fund for Women). (2003). Pathway to Gender Equality: CEDAW, Beijing and the MDGs. Retrieved November 16, 2013 from www.un.org/documents/instruments/docs_en.asp?year=2000.

UNESCO (United Nations Educational, Scientific and Cultural Organization). (1978). International Charter of Physical Education and Sport. Retrieved January 2, 2013 from http://unesdoc.unesco.org/ulis/index.html.

UNESCO (United Nations Educational, Scientific and Cultural Organization). (2002). Dakar Framework for Action, Education for All: Meeting our collective commitments. Retrieved October 20, 2013 from http://unesdoc.unesco.org/ulis/index.html.

UNESCO (United Nations Educational, Scientific and Cultural Organization). (2004). 4th International Conference of Ministers and Senior Officials Responsible for Physical Education and Sport, MINEPS IV, Athens, Greece. Retrieved August 25, 2013 from www.minepsiv.gr/pdf.%2111.pdf.

White, A. (1997a). The growth of the international women and sport movement, in Proceedings of the 2nd Scientific International Conference for Women's Sport: Woman and child, a future vision from a sport perspective. Alexandria, Egypt: University of Alexandria.

White. A. (1997b). Towards gender equity in sport: An update on Sports Council policy development, in A. Tomlinson (ed.), Gender, sport and leisure: Continuities and challenges. Aachen, Germany: Meyer & Meyer.

Women's Sports Foundation. (May, 1998). Women's Sports Foundation Newsletter. Retrieved August 25, 2013 from www.womenssportsfoundation.org.

Women's Sports Foundation. (2003). Campaign for coverage. London: UK Sport.

Women's Sports Foundation. (December, 2007). Women's Olympic sports initiatives. Retrieved December 31, 2013 from www.womenssportsfoundation.org.

Women's Sports Foundation. (January, 2008). Indicators of progress. Retrieved January 20, 2013 from www.womenssportsfoundation.org.

Chapter 4

How gender order is enacted in physical education

The French *didactique* research approach

Chantal Amade-Escot

Introduction

This chapter is about the issues of gender and the French *didactique* research. Its aim is to give a literature overview of the scope, conceptual framework and findings of this body of academic knowledge in physical education (PE) referring to Margaret Talbot[1] as a particularly significant researcher in the field. Through her research (Talbot, 1986, 1993, 2001) and her commitment as Chairwoman of the International Association of Physical Education and Sport for Girls and Women (IAPESGW) and as Vice-President for Education in the International Council of Sport Science and Physical Education (ICSSPE), Margaret Talbot fought continually to defend quality PE for girls (and boys) over diverse geographical and cultural areas. She inspired numerous scholars and I am greatly honoured to pay a tribute to her internationally renowned advocacy of inclusive opportunities for all children in PE.

In the 1990s, at a time when not much attention was being given in France to gender issues except the seminal work of Annick Davisse and Catherine Louveau (1991), Margaret Talbot's thoughts about gendered PE was an important contribution to the French reflection and my own research work which is rooted, for over 40 years, in the 'French *didactique*', a field of research that has a special focus on students learning through classroom interactions (Amade-Escot, 2006). In the early 2000s I initiated with a group of doctoral students a research program[2] with the aim of investigating gender issues in day-to-day PE settings through a fine-grained analysis of the gendered content taught and learned and how it emerges from the situated interactions. This research programme, which is reviewed here, has to owe a debt of gratitude for Margaret Talbot's academic contribution to gender studies in PE.

In this chapter I highlight how PE *didactique* research relies on Margaret Talbot's advocacy for gender equality. Drawing on sociological and pedagogical research, this ethnographic approach focuses on classroom interactions and sheds light on how gendered content is co-constructed through didactical transactions. The overarching findings provide a rich portrayal and in-depth understanding of how girls' and boys' engagement in PE interplays with teacher's supervision in relation to the knowledge content at stake. Most of this research was presented at ARIS Congresses (French 'Association for Research on Intervention in Sport and Physical Education') or in French journals, and thus is little known in the Anglo-American PE research community. After a brief overview of gender research in PE at the end of the 1990s, the chapter presents the conceptual framework that undergirds the *didactique* research over the last 15 years. Attention, then, turns to its major findings which describe how gendered contents are developed within the enacted curriculum. Finally, the conclusion sketches some implications for research and teacher education.

Overview of gender research in the PE classroom at the end of the 1990s

During the 1990s a large body of researchers in Western countries established that PE curricula are generally 'male-oriented' and thus contribute to the social construction of gendered bodies and minds (for reviews, Flintoff and Scraton, 2006; Penney, 2002). 'PE is seen as one of the most sex-differentiated subjects on the school curriculum that contributes to the social construction of homogeneous gendered categories' (Flintoff and Scraton, 2006, p. 768). Students' social relations about what behaviour is appropriate as a girl or a boy are constructed through more or less implicit but permanent processes. PE teachers display gender-biased perceptions and provide gender-biased explanations to their students. They interact more often with boys than girls, and the content and the language of their verbal interactions indicate stereotypical attitudes. In a word, PE lessons often convey to girls that they are weaker, less enthusiastic and less skilled than boys (Davisse, 1991; Evans *et al.*, 1996; Griffin, 1985; Kirk, 2003; Scraton, 1992; Talbot, 1986, 1993; Wright, 1996, 1997). These assumptions, however, do not explain in depth how day-to-day lessons impact gendered learning. Informed by the reflection initiated in France by Annick Davisse (1991) and Nicole Mosconi (2003), the idea that the social construction of gender in the classroom is deeply interwoven with didactical interactions emerged and was at the heart of the line of research I initiated with a group of doctoral students, using the French *didactique* framework to conduct empirical studies:

> To understand how teachers act with girls and boys in the classroom, fine-grained analysis of everyday classroom life and didactical interactions needs to be addressed. The differences and even the inequalities of treatment between students according to gender (but also according

to their social origin, as well as their standing of excellence in the class) go through very tiny and almost invisible facets that cannot be seen without a very detailed analysis, including the didactical viewpoint.

(Mosconi, 2003, p. 38, our translation)

This assumption leads us to initiate studies to look at how gendered content is produced through didactical transactions, defined as the set of pedagogical interactions whose purpose is to leverage students learning in the domain-specific content knowledge and knowing at stake in a learning environment. The *didactique* perspective, thus, attempts to characterise precisely, in the everyday life of the class, how boys and girls differently construct their knowledge through actions and discourses in which they are involved. One may say that *didactique* research has some links with Jane Wright's perspective of discourse analysis in gender studies (1993, 1997). At the end of the 1990s, evidence exists that a fine-grained analysis of student and teacher interactions related to PE contents can further the studies conducted in the English-speaking area with the purpose of better understanding the situated processes involved in the production of a gendered curriculum and the maintenance of gender order in the gym.

Observing didactical transactions to investigate the dynamics of student gendered learning in PE

In the French-speaking world of educational research, the terms 'didactics, didactic, didactical' do not convey the pejorative meaning they may have in the English language.

On the contrary to what is usually thought, the *didactique* tradition does not promote a subject-matter centred model, but studies the way in which the subtleties of knowledge content are organised and presented to students, how they interpret them, what forms of teacher/ students interactions are developed concerning the unit of knowledge at stake, in order to have a better understanding of the teaching/learning process.

(Amade-Escot, 2006, p. 347)

As a new academic field of research, the French *didactique* arose in the late 1970s. Allal (2011, p. 331) indicates that

researchers in didactics have developed a coherent, well-integrated set of concepts. Starting with the definition of the didactical system as a triadic relation between teacher, student, and knowledge, they have analysed the didactic transposition of knowledge and the embodiment of knowledge in classroom situations.

In PE, the *didactique* approach of gender issues emerged in the early 2000s. At that time, in PE as well as in other subject didactics, very little research existed on the theme. Ingrid Verscheure's master's thesis (2001), which focused on the differential dynamics of gendered knowledge construction in PE classrooms (Verscheure and Amade-Escot, 2004), opened up a new line of research in the field: How does knowledge content embedded in learning environments offer (or not) equal opportunities to girls and boys? How do teacher and students deal with the official curriculum in day-to-day practices? How do they jointly construct the gendered context and the learning outcomes of their relationships?

Key concepts used to analyse gender issues from a didactical standpoint

To capture in detail the curriculum in motion in classroom settings, the *didactique* approach draws on the idea that the knowledge taught and learned, and all meaning making associated are co-produced by teacher and students in culturally situated institutions. The analysis takes into account simultaneously the teacher, the students and the particular situatedness of knowledge content as interrelated instances. Teachers' and students' practices are theoretically seen as 'joint action' (Blumer, 1969). However, joint action does not mean that participants (teacher and students) have the same goals or the same agendas. Negotiations and transactions occur between them and are related to the gendered facets of each particular piece of content at stake. These transactions should be described in detail to better understand the gendered dynamics of the whole process. Looking at classroom practices as being organically cooperative actions between participants, the didactical framework supports the idea, shared by most learning theorists, that student learning occurs within the unavoidable tension between active agents and the cultural, institutional and historical contexts that are more or less monitored by the teacher.

Three interrelated concepts are used to convey gender analysis of didactical transactions: (1) 'differential didactical contract', which accounts for students' various trajectories of learning (Verscheure and Amade-Escot, 2007); (2) 'gender positioning', which helps understanding how individuals (particularly students) engage themselves in the practice (Amade-Escot *et al.*, 2012); (3) 'teachers' practical epistemology', which allows for the gendered facets of the knowledge that teachers privilege when teaching physical activities (Amade-Escot, 2013). A brief description of this system of concepts is presented below.

Differential didactic contract

The concept of didactic contract is used to account for the evolution of student learning through classroom interactions (Amade-Escot, 2006). This concept should be understood not as a formal contract but as an implicit attempt to find a common understanding between teacher and students about the knowledge content at stake. The need for common backgrounds in order to make communication possible between people has been brought to light by many social sciences (linguistics, symbolic interactionism, ethnomethodology, micro sociology, etc.). It draws attention to the fact that social interaction consists of a continuous process of interpretation and definition of both the context and the meanings. The didactic contract is a specification of this phenomenon within the teaching/learning process when classroom interactions involve a domain-specific knowledge (Amade-Escot, 2006; Schubauer-Leoni, 1996). Actually, the meaning that each student attributes to the situation in which she/he is involved may differ among students; symmetrically the teacher may interact differently with each of them. These transactional relations are at the heart of the 'differential didactic contract' which is:

> not implicitly negotiated with all the students of the classroom but with some groups of students which have diverse standings in the classroom. These standings are related to diverse hierarchies of excellence and are partially attributable to students' social origins.
>
> (Schubauer-Leoni, 1996, p. 160, our translation)

This concept carries on the idea of subtle differences emerging from in-situ teacher and student joint actions. Thus deciphering the implicit transactions and the evolution of mutual gendered expectations related to the content to be learned in PE lessons helps in better understanding student gendered learning.

Gender positioning

The *didactique* approach focuses on how teacher and students co-construct gendered knowledge considering that knowledge itself is transformed through the pedagogical acts of conveyance and appropriation which characterise the dynamics of the differential didactic contract. The study of this evolving process leads us to formulate the concept of 'gender positioning', borrowed from 'positioning theory' (Harré and van Langenhove, 1999). 'Positions' according to Harré and van Langenhove (1999) are not fixed but fluid and can change from one moment to the next, depending on the context through which the various participants take meaning from the interaction. Extending this idea to students' participation in PE practices, we argue that the concept of 'gender positioning' (Amade-Escot *et al.*, 2012; Verscheure *et al.*, 2014) is an alternative to the one of gender role in educational research which disregards the transactional aspect of the construction of gender difference in everyday classroom life. The concept helps in reconsidering how gendered contents are enacted in the classroom. However, looking at the transactional dimension of teaching and learning implies necessarily to account for teacher practice.

Teacher's practical epistemology

The concept of 'teacher practical epistemology' belongs to the *didactique* framework (Amade-Escot, 2013; Sensevy, 2007). It should be understood less as a knowledge base than as a tropism of action which influences the ways teachers set up learning environments and supervise student learning. Teacher epistemology 'is practical because it is – in large measure – produced by and for practice' (Sensevy, 2007, p. 38). That is why the components of any learning tasks as well as any form of teacher discourse or action document her/his practical epistemology. Moreover, when teaching, the teacher gives the students directions that reveal what counts as knowledge and appropriate ways of practicing in a specific social practice while other aspects are underestimated or ignored (Amade-Escot, 2013). For example, forms of masculinities may be valued by teachers while others are underestimated. In her doctoral thesis, Ingrid Verscheure (2005) has shown how the facets of any particular content in PE volleyball can express (or not) subtle forms of gender stereotypes and how they impact the differential didactic contract. 'Since the demands of every sport involve a particular balance between force and skill, it can be suggested that the more it is force that is decisive, the more a physically dominating hegemonic masculinity can be publicly celebrated' (Whitson, 1994, p. 363). Following this author, we claim that the content of PE lessons verbally and non-verbally privileged by teachers when teaching physical activities is linked to her/his practical epistemology (Amade-Escot, 2013; Amade-Escot *et al.*, 2015; Elandoulsi, 2011; Verscheure, 2009; Vinson, 2013). Broadly speaking, the concept of teacher practical epistemology helps in characterising in detail the gendered content valued in each particular learning environment and over the lessons and the unit.

Brief outline of the method

The research design is based on the observation of a series of PE lessons in various physical activities that belong to the national PE curriculum, but have, according to literature, various gendered connotations (as examples: dance or gymnastics which convey a feminine connotation; football which conveys a masculine one; badminton or volleyball which are considered as more 'gender-neutral'). To avoid bias, teachers are selected after an in-depth pre-research interview concerning their willingness to implement an equal-gendered PE curriculum. The data collection included observation and teacher interviews for each lesson. Narrative records of teacher and student joint action during the observed lessons are established from the transcripts of all observations, discourse and interviews (for a development, see Amade-Escot et al., 2015; Verscheure and Amade-Escot, 2007). They account for the temporal features of the learning process in which the content learned by each student evolves over the lessons in relation to the dynamics of the differential didactic contract.

To sum up, the *didactique* research on gender in PE relies on a conceptual construction and a methodological design that allows deciphering in detail the gendered dynamics of student learning during PE practices.

Overview of the findings

Over the last 15 years a substantial number of studies were carried out using the concepts and method presented in the above sections (Aguado, 2011; Amade-Escot, 2005; Amade-Escot et al., 2002, 2015; Bennour, 2014; Costes, 2003; Costes and Amade-Escot, 2005; Desmurs and Verscheure, 2009; Elandoulsi, 2011, 2012; Elandousi and Abdouli, 2014; Elandoulsi and Amade-Escot, 2013; Uchan, 2002; Uchan and Amade-Escot, 2004; Verscheure, 2005; Verscheure and Amade-Escot, 2004, 2007, 2011; Verscheure et al., 2013, 2014; Vinson, 2013; Vinson and Amade-Escot, 2014; Vinson and Dugal, 2013; Vinson and Elandoulsi, 2015). This body of research on gender inequalities in PE highlights how teacher and student joint action has subtle consequences in terms of student learning and the maintenance of gender order in the gym. This section reviews the major findings of this line of research, which mostly concerns the secondary level of schooling even though recent studies have extended the theme to primary schools (Desmurs and Verscheure, 2009; Verscheure et al., 2011, 2013, 2014). The studies concern two cultural areas: France and Tunisia. The findings underscore that gendered content in PE should be considered as an emergent outcome, a by-product co-constructed by teacher and students through a process of situated action, negotiation and intersubjective interpretation more often than not unbeknown to the participants. These findings expand, as well as they nuance, the findings established by other researchers. First, they demonstrate the incredible diversity of student gendered learning trajectories. Second, they shed light on three interwoven topics at the heart of the co-construction of these unequal learning trajectories through differential processes that involve student gender positioning and teacher practical epistemology.

The incredible diversity of gendered learning trajectories

All studies confirm that gender-biased curriculum and interactions play an important role in PE classrooms. Above and beyond these conclusions, the *didactique* approach, however, brings into light the relational dimension of a complex process which nuances some assertions hitherto provided. Girls and boys interact differently with the learning environment due to their gendered identities, but their interpretation of the content at stake and of teacher action and privileging lead to additional effects (Aguado, 2011; Amade-Escot, 2005; Amade-Escot *et al.*, 2015; Bennour, 2014; Costes, 2003, Elandoulsi, 2011; Uchan, 2002; Verscheure, 2005; Verscheure and Amade-Escot, 2007, 2011; Verscheure *et al.*, 2014; Vinson, 2013). The fine-grained analysis of didactical transactions demonstrates that student-diverse learning trajectories result from a co-constructed process between teacher and students about the specific content embedded in an evolving learning environment. Ingrid Verscheure (2005, 2009) demonstrated that the multiple micro-social interactions affect classroom practices in ways that explain how gendered learning is achieved. Each student occupies a unique niche within the differential didactic contract, each of them interprets the learning environment provided by the teacher in ways that influence their gender positioning all along didactical transactions. Reciprocally the content of teacher–students interaction varies in relation to what the teacher values when supervising each of them. This interwoven process is at the heart of gendered learning. For example, when teachers attempt to challenge the gender-stereotypical forms of the volley-ball attack, giving all students the opportunity to perform using a range of tactical responses, some boys transform the way they perform from a stereotypical masculine attack (using invariably a spike or a power hit on the ball whatever the specific circumstances of the game) to more effective attacks which exploit the game context, either by spiking or by placing the ball in an open space. In the same learning environment, however, others boys do not change their stereotypical masculine attack. Similarly, in settings where teachers value forms of hegemonic masculine attack, some girls grasp opportunities, under their own agency, to improve their tactical awareness and performance above and beyond the teacher's gendered expectations (Verscheure, 2009). Moreover, Uchan (2002) in gymnastics, as well as Aguado (2011) in dance, pointed out how students (girls as well as boys) convey their cultural experience in the subject that allows them to improve, while others do not modify their stereotypical forms of participation or non-participation (see also Amade-Escot *et al.*, 2015; Verscheure and Amade-Escot, 2011).

These considerations support the idea of a less one-directional explanation than the direct effect, although important, of gender-biased curriculum and teacher gender-biased interactions on student learning. They point out a relational process related to the transactional dimension of gender inequities in day-to-day classroom life. Actually, students participate in the production of the enacted curriculum as demonstrated by Doyle (1992). Each of them interprets the specific expectations embedded in the instructional environment and the perspectives the teacher conveys when teaching. As learning in most physical activities involves a particular balance between force and skill, students may activate the one or the other dimension. Some of them thus use systematically stereotypical masculine forms of actions while others use stereotypical feminine ones whether they are girls or boys; and others use a wider range of actions from one moment to the next, depending on the context through which they take meaning from the interaction. These forms of participation should not be considered as dichotomous; they should be understood as the two poles of a continuum of potential forms of gendered engagement. Following Ann Hall (1985), who considers the need to view gender in sport as a system of social relations rather than dichotomous categories, student gender positioning, in our studies, is interpreted from the recurrent and variable forms of student actions and associated discourses during classroom interactions over time and during lessons.

From the findings it appears that gender positioning when learning is not fixed but fluid and may (or not) evolve. But our studies suggest also that learning environments which allow and promote gender sensibility in achieving the goal of the task at hand help students (girls and boys) to attune to a situation and thus construct more holistic understandings and ways of knowing the content to be learned (Aguado, 2011; Amade-Escot *et al.*, 2015; Elandoulsi, 2011, 2012; Uchan, 2002; Uchan and Amade-Escot, 2004; Verscheure, 2005; Verscheure and Amade-Escot, 2004, 2007; Verscheure *et al.*, 2014). Notwithstanding, implementing a gender-responsive approach is not an easy thing! Despite the best intentions of teachers who attempt to challenge gender stereotypes in their class, some teaching may have unexpected outcomes.

Unexpected outcomes of a 'gender-sensitive' classroom

Interestingly, the *didactique* approach uncovered unexpected outcomes when teacher willingness to promote a more equal teaching does not enhance equal learning. A study at a lower middle school illustrates this critical issue (Costes and Amade-Escot, 2005). The data were collected during a football unit in a mixed class (12th grade). The teacher strongly desires to 'create equal conditions to help girls' learning in this very masculine game'. Her objectives were that students: (1) 'extend their ability in performing a collective attack'; (2) 'favour social relationships among girls and boys and among low and high skilled students'; and (3) develop a 'fair sense of playing together' (pre-research interview). Throughout the unit, the teacher enforced three rules within a three-on-three modified football game:

(a) The first rule limits the number of contacts with the ball each boy is allowed during one attack (teacher's assignment: 'no more than three hits'). This rule is intended 'to support a collective game inside the mixed team of three players', and 'to prevent boys from monopolizing the ball' (post-lesson, interview).
(b) The second rule requires the attackers to hit the ball at least once before crossing the central line with the aim at 'increasing exchanges inside the mixed team'.
(c) The last rule requires all defenders to reduce the defending pressure: 'when defending on girls, stay at an arm length from ball holder' (teacher's assignment). This third rule aims at giving time to girls when kicking the ball to partners or when shooting.

The in-depth analysis of didactical transactions during four consecutive lessons where students play this modified football game brings to light that most girls and low-skilled boys do not benefit educationally from the situation. The three modified rules initially aimed at favouring girls' learning have unexpected effects on low-skilled students (girls and boys) who interpret the didactic contract in ways that allow them to progressively disengage. The first rule, which limits the number of contacts allowed for all boys, jeopardises the learning of low-skilled boys. The second rule, which obliges all three attackers to have played the ball at least once before crossing the central line, limits the participation of low-skilled students (girls as well as boys) because most of them interpret this rule as the core demand of the didactic contract. Therefore after having crossed the central line they often stop their engagement in the game, in particular, when defenders become more active. The last modified rule, which reduces the defensive pressure on girls, has a positive effect on girls' control of the ball and their decision making, and even more for three high-skilled girls.

To conclude, the qualitative analysis of the didactical transactions over studies highlights the uniqueness of student positioning within the didactic contract and thus gives an insight on the incredible diversity of gendered learning trajectories in a class. The findings ascertain the relational process through which gendered content is co-constructed in the classroom. They also suggest possible links between student skill level and student gender positioning. Furthermore, however, teacher willingness appears in itself insufficient to promote a gender sensitive curriculum. As per Margaret Talbot (1993), the didactical approach underlines the dialectical relationship between agency and constraint in everyday PE. Three relational and interwoven topics, which impact the dynamics of the differential didactic contract, have been identified.

Topics that influence student gendered learning

Three interwoven topics, related to teacher practical epistemology, influence the dynamics of the differential didactic contract: (1) the teacher's appraisal of student ability in the subject; (2) the knowledge facets privileged by the teacher when teaching; and (3) the non-verbal dimension of classroom interactions. All three topics have an impact on student gender positioning because of the relation dimension of didactical transactions.

Teacher's appraisal of student ability

To investigate how student gendered learning may be connected with teacher's appraisal of their standard of excellence (Bennour, 2014; Costes, 2003; Elandoulsi, 2011) teachers were asked to indicate the level of excellence they attribute to each of their students in the subject (pre-research interview). These studies state that student gender positioning during didactical transactions is influenced by the teacher's differential expectations in relation to the skilfulness attributed to each. Each student (girls and boys) do not benefit from the same attention and supervision (Amade-Escot et al., 2015; Bennour, 2014; Costes, 2003). High-skilled students, whether they are girls or boys, benefit more from teacher higher expectation (at times due to extra interactions) than low-skilled students (Bennour, 2014; Elandoulsi, 2011). But, since girls are generally perceived to have lower skill and lower fitness levels than boys, girls are generally less challenged (Amade-Escot, 2005; Bennour, 2014; Elandoulsi, 2011, Verscheure, 2005; Verscheure and Amade-Escot, 2011; Vinson, 2013). Benevolence to middle-skilled and low-skilled girls, however, was observed in some settings where teachers are willing to support their learning (Amade-Escot et al., 2015; Elandoulsi, 2011; Verscheure, 2009; Vinson and Elandoulsi, 2015). From these studies, student learning trajectories appear not only gender-dependant but connected to the teacher's initial appraisal of their ability in the subject taught. Additionally gender-biased appraisal is often expressed through verbal and non-verbal interactions that may amplify stereotypical expectations.

To sum up, high-skilled boys and, to a lesser degree, high-skilled girls who activate a masculine positioning benefit from specific interactions from their teacher that enhance their performance (Bennour, 2014; Elandoulsi, 2011; Verscheure, 2005, 2009). Lower-skilled girls as well as lower-skilled boys are most often under-challenged in their learning (Costes and Amade-Escot, 2005) or even disadvantaged in some settings. From these conclusions, it is confirmed that PE contexts are often powerless in challenging gender stereotypes.

Knowledge facets privileged by teachers

As stated earlier in this chapter, learning tasks in PE may be achieved through various actions that are gender sensitive. These actions may be recurrently valued (or not) by the teacher. As examples, in volleyball attacks, a teacher may privilege a power spike or an efficient tactical hit of the ball in the defender open space (Verscheure, 2009); in gymnastics, either the acrobatic facet of the element, or the aesthetic one, or a combination of both facets may be elected by a teacher in accordance with her/his practical epistemology (Amade-Escot *et al.*, 2015; Elandoulsi, 2011; Uchan, 2002; Uchan and Amade-Escot, 2004). Among the various knowledge facets that can be valued by the teacher when teaching – even though *à leur insu* ['without their knowing it'] – some may fall within stereotypical masculine or feminine ways of performing. Notwithstanding, any teacher's privileging expresses what counts as learning experience in PE. Thus facets of knowledge privileged by teachers impact students' gender positioning in relation to the actual context through which the participants make meaning from the interactions (Amade-Escot *et al.*, 2015). Following Messner (2011), one can say that the didactical approach uncovers, when focusing on teacher privileging, the 'soft essentialism' that subtly undergirds classroom interactions.

The particular role of teacher's non-verbal discourse

Recent studies investigate the semiotic functions of teacher non-verbal discourse within the dynamics of the differential didactic contract. The underlying thesis is to consider that teacher gesture conveys gendered expectations that, over the lessons, are less controlled than teacher verbal discourse (Vinson, 2013; Vinson and Amade-Escot, 2014; Vinson and Dugal, 2013; Vinson and Elandoulsi, 2015). The analysis of didactical transactions through the fine-grained lens of the body gestures used by teachers when monitoring students (forms of demonstration, forms of body manipulation, body distances, deictic gestures, and so forth) extends the findings established through the discourse approach (Wright, 1993, 1997). In a word, beyond the context of verbal interactions the studying of non-verbal interactions brings to light a very subtle process of differentiation between girls and boys in the gym. Martine Vinson (2013) demonstrates how the gesture used by a male and a female teacher when teaching badminton (a subject considered as gender 'neutral' in the literature) expresses what count as student learning. The design of the study was replicated in gymnastics in Tunisia (Vinson and Elandoulsi, 2015). In both subject-content and in both countries, the body language (within each cultural area) expresses in depth what is unknowingly valued and privileged by teachers in terms of their practical epistemology as well as in terms of what kind of performance is expected from girls and boys in the gym (Vinson and Amade-Escot, 2013; Vinson and Dugal, 2013; Vinson and Elandoulsi, 2015). The findings demonstrate that body gestures addressed to girls consist of demonstrations and body manipulations within an intimate body distance. Using these gestures, teachers progressively reduce the learning environments to some molecular sport techniques. As a consequence, girls cannot experiment under their own initiative the different facets of the knowledge embedded in the task. On the contrary, teachers offer boys greater opportunities to develop rich and meaningful contents. Within a format of personal and social body distances teachers use numerous deictic gestures to indicate strategic goals to boys. Their demonstrations are more analogic than detailed and focus on strategic actions (i.e. to show/indicate the open space where to put the shuttlecock). Boys are thus stimulated and sustained in developing their own experiences. In a word, an important autonomy is given to boys and they are allowed to express their own agency, while girls are more directed to the smallest content elements.

This recent line of research should be furthered to deepen the role of the interwoven process of body language and teacher discourse when monitoring students in the gym. Nevertheless, it confirms how PE is an important means through which bodies are inscribed in and produce gender differences which contribute to the marginalisation of girls and lower-skilled boys in ways that show their body as lacking those qualities associated with the straightforward masculine one.

Conclusion

The *didactique* research reviewed in this chapter ascertains that students gendered learning trajectories depend on how teacher and students bring forward together actions that are very specific to the subject content taught and very specific to what each participant values through implicit and ongoing transactions. This approach confirms that gender issues in PE are co-constructed over a subtle process at the basis of the production of gender order in PE, which more often than not 'pays a tribute to masculinity'. Since the beginning of the 2000s, this research program supports the theoretical idea that teaching and learning are situated actions and that PE practices offer thus resources and opportunities, but also constraints that limit gender educational benefits. Underscoring the relational process involved in the production of PE gendered content and the marginalisation of girls and lower-skilled boys, the didactic approach suggests paying greater attention to teacher and students joint action related to the knowledge content at stake through classroom verbal and non-verbal interactions.

From various aspects this research expands and extends the reflection opened by Margaret Talbot (1993) when she pointed out the dialectical relationship between agency and constraint. What the didactic approach brings forward is that gendered learning trajectories are plural, divided and unstable, however related to the curriculum enactment. Expanding the knowledge on gender issues in the gym, thanks to the fine-grained analysis of didactical transactions, the *didactique* research provides crucial insights that potentially can improve changes in PE practices. Margaret Talbot drew our attention to the fact that without challenging the social and cultural ideologies of women and sport, and without an explicit anti-sexist pedagogy, gender equity in PE will remain an aspiration (1986, 1993). Her support for curriculum innovation should be undoubtedly advanced, as should the understanding of PE contexts through research: How are decisions made? How do individuals resist, accommodate, implement or drive change? (Talbot, 1993).

The *didactique* research clearly states that teacher practical epistemology is a by-product of teacher and students didactical joint action (Amade-Escot, 2013). Thus changes in teaching PE should not only rely on the increase of teacher awareness of gender inequalities, but should implement also specific strategies for teacher education including the observation and criticism of teacher's own contributions to student gendered learning (Elandousi and Abdouli, 2014; Verscheure *et al.*, 2013, 2014). From the findings reviewed here the need for a specific focus on the enacted pedagogical content knowledge appears decisive in helping teachers in identifying previouly unrecognised forms of gendered supervision they used, and to envision their possible transformations. However, teachers should not and cannot be solely responsible for such transformative change. Margaret Talbot considers that a major obstacle for changes is related to the increased masculinisation of the teaching of PE (1986). As a researcher in *didactique* I would add that without a focus through research and teacher education on the conditions that promote a more holistic and anthropological view of knowledge in PE, it will be difficult to challenge the current gender order in the gym.

Notes

1 I met Margaret Talbot in the mid-1990s when I was involved in the European Women and Sport network as a representative for France. Her work and dedication as a feminist scholar in promoting equality and quality physical education was a source of inspiration for my own work as a teacher educator and a researcher in the field of sport pedagogy.

2 Initiated at Toulouse University, the research programme was expended through the nomination of young doctors as scholars, first at the University of Franche-Comté, and more recently at Limoges University and the University of La Manouba in Tunis. This group of researchers furthers the reflection and the review in this chapter is based on their work.

References

Aguado, F. (2011). *Etude des contrats didactiques différentiels en danse contemporaine en EPS au sein de l'atelier chorégraphique.* Unpublished master's thesis. University of Toulouse.

Allal, L. (2011). Pedagogy, didactics and the co-regulation of learning: a perspective from the French-language world of educational research. *Research Papers in Education*, 26(3), 329–336.

Amade-Escot, C. (2005). Interactions didactiques et difficultés d'apprentissage des filles et des garçons en EPS. In L. Talbot (ed.), *Pratiques d'enseignement et difficultés d'apprentissage* (pp. 61–74). Ramonville Ste Agne: Erès.

Amade-Escot, C. (2006). Student learning within the didactique tradition. In D. Kirk, M. O'Sullivan and D. Macdonald (eds), *Handbook of research in physical education* (pp. 347–365). London: SAGE Publications.

Amade-Escot C. (2013). L'épistémologie pratique des professeurs et les recherches sur l'intervention. Perspectives pour de futurs dialogues. In B. Carnel and J. Moniotte (eds), *Intervention, recherche et formation: quels enjeux, quelles transformations?* (pp. 37–58). Amiens: Université de Picardie and ARIS.

Amade-Escot, C., Elandoulsi, S. and Verscheure, I. (2012, September). Gender positioning as an analytical tool for the studying of learning in physical education didactics. European Conference on Educational Research, Cádiz, Spain.

Amade-Escot, C., Elandoulsi, S. and Verscheure, I. (2015). Physical education in Tunisia: teachers' practical epistemology, students' positioning and gender issues. *Sport, Education and Society.* doi.10.1080/13573322.2014.997694.

Amade-Escot, C., Uchan, K. and Verscheure, I. (2002, December). La question des inégalités de genres en éducation physique et sportive, pertinence de l'approche didactique. 2nd Biennial ARIS, Rennes, France.

Bennour, N. (2014). L'engagement disciplinaire productif des élèves dans l'action didactique conjointe en gymnastique. Etudes de cas dans deux établissements contrastés en Tunisie. Unpublished doctoral dissertation. University of Toulouse.

Blumer, H. (1969). *Symbolic interactionism: perspective and method.* Berkeley, Los Angeles, London: University of California Press.

Costes, L. (2003). Dynamiques différentielles des apprentissages en Football: une étude selon le sexe et le niveau d'habileté en classe de 6ème. Unpublished master's thesis. University of Toulouse.

Costes, L. and Amade-Escot, C. (2005, January). Effets de l'intervention différenciée de l'enseignant selon le sexe des élèves sur les dynamiques d'apprentissage des filles et des garçons dans une activité connotée masculine: le football. Colloque International ARIS-AFRAPS, Catholic University of Louvain, Belgique.

Davisse, A. (1991). Au temps de l'école: l'éducation physique et sportive des filles. In A. Davisse and C. Louveau (eds), *Sports, école et société: la part des femmes* (pp. 174–263). Paris: Actio.

Davisse, A. and Louveau, C. (1991). *Sports, école et société: la part des femmes.* Paris: Actio.

Desmurs, L. and Verscheure, I. (2009, May). Differential dynamic of the teacher's interventions confronted to the gender difference in PE: the weight of social and cultural education or the transmission of a hidden curriculum. AIESEP World Seminar, Besançon, France.

Doyle, W. (1992). Curriculum and pedagogy. In P. W. Jackson (ed.), *Handbook of research on curriculum* (pp. 486–516). New York: Macmillan.

Elandoulsi, S. (2011). *L'épistémologie pratique des professeurs: effets de l'expérience et de l'expertise dans l'enseignement de l'appui tendu renversé en mixité. Analyse comparée de 3 enseignants d'éducation physique et sportive en Tunisie.* Unpublished doctoral dissertation. University of Toulouse.

Elandoulsi, S. (2012, October). Effets de l'expérience et de l'expertise des enseignants d'éducation physique sur le curriculum en acte et les trajectoires d'apprentissage d'élèves contrastés: le cas de l'enseignement de la gymnastique en mixité en Tunisie. 6th World Congress of the Mediterranean Society of Comparative Education, Hammamet, Tunisia.

Elandousi, S. and Abdouli, I. (2014, July). Analyse des pratiques des enseignants stagiaires et co-construction de la différence des sexes. 8th Biennial ARIS, Geneva, Switzerland.

Elandoulsi, S and Amade-Escot, C. (2013, August). Position de genre et apprentissage en EPS. Le cas de l'enseignement de l'ATR en gymnastique en Tunisie. AREF Congress, Montpellier, France.

Evans, J., Davies, B. and Penney, D (1996). Teachers, teaching and the social construction of gender relations. *Sport, Education and Society*, 1(2), 165–185.

Flintoff, A. and Scraton, S. (2006). Girls and physical education. In D. Kirk, M. O'Sullivan, and D. Macdonald (eds), *Handbook of research in physical education* (pp. 767–783). London: SAGE Publications.

Griffin, P. S. (1985). Teachers' perceptions of and responses to sex equity problems in a middle school physical education program. *Research Quarterly for Exercise and Sport*, 56, 103–110.

Hall, A. (1985). Knowledge and gender: epistemological questions in the social analysis of sport. *Sociology of Sport Journal*, 2(1), 25–42.

Harré, R. and van Langenhove, L. (1999). *Positioning theory: moral contexts of intentional action.* Oxford: Blackwell.

Kirk, D. (2003). Student learning and the social construction of gender in sport and physical education. In P. Silverman and C. Ennis (eds), *Student learning in physical education: applying research to enhance instruction* (pp. 67–81). Champaign, Ill.: Human Kinetics.

Messner, M. A. (2011). Gender ideologies, youth sports, and the production of soft essentialism. *Sociology of Sport Journal*, 28(2), 151–170.

Mosconi, N. (2003). Rapport au savoir et division socio-sexuée des savoirs à l'école. *La lettre de l'enfance et de l'adolescence*, 51, 31–38.

Penney, D. (2002). *Gender and physical education: contemporary issues and future directions.* London: Routledge, Falmer.

Schubauer-Leoni, M. L. (1996). Etude du contrat didactique pour des élèves en difficulté en mathématiques. Problématique didactique et/ou psychosociale. In C. Raisky and M. Caillot (eds), *Au-delà des didactiques, le didactique* (pp. 159–189). Bruxelles: De Boeck.

Scraton, S. (1992). Shaping up to womanhood: gender and girls' physical education. Milton Keynes: Open University Press.

Sensevy, G. (2007) Des catégories pour décrire et comprendre l'action didactique. In G. Sensevy and A. Mercier (eds), *Agir ensemble. L'action didactique conjointe du professeur et des élèves* (pp. 13–49). Rennes: Presses Universitaires.

Talbot, M. (1986). Gender and physical education. *British Journal of Physical Education*, 4(1), 120–122.

Talbot, M. (1993). A gendered physical education: equality and sexism. In J. Evans (ed.), *Equality, education and physical education* (pp. 74–89). London: Falmer Press.

Talbot, M. (2001). The case for physical education. World summit on Physical Education, Berlin, 39.

Uchan, K. (2002). Contrats didactiques différentiels selon les genres: le cas de l'apprentissage de l'ATR en 4ème. Unpublished master's dissertation. University of Toulouse.

Uchan, K. and Amade-Escot, C. (2004). Les contrats didactiques différentiels filles et garçons au collège: le cas de l'appui tendu renversé. In M. Loquet and Y. Léziart (eds), *Cultures sportives et artistiques* (pp. 161–170). Rennes: ARIS.

Verscheure, I. (2005). Dynamique différentielle des interactions didactiques et co-construction de la différence des sexes en Education Physique et Sportive: Le cas de l'attaque en volley-ball en lycées agricoles. Unpublished doctoral dissertation. University of Toulouse.

Verscheure, I. (2009). Modalité de direction d'étude et apprentissage de l'attaque en volley-ball: quels effets de genre? *eJRIEPS*, 18, 122–155.

Verscheure, I. and Amade-Escot, C. (2004). Dynamiques différentielles des interactions didactiques selon le genre en EPS. Le cas de l'attaque en volley-ball en seconde. *Revue STAPS*, 66, 79–97.

Verscheure, I. and Amade-Escot, C. (2007). The gendered construction of physical education content as the result of the differentiated didactic contract. *Physical Education and Sport Pedagogy*, 12(3), 245–272.

Verscheure I. and Amade-Escot, C. (2011, January). Variation des savoirs enseignés en éducation physique et sportive selon le genre: analyse comparée de l'action didactique conjointe du professeur et des élèves en volley-ball, football et gymnastique. 2nd International Colloquium ARCD, Université Lille, France.

Verscheure I., Deforêt, L. and Poggi, M. P. (2013, August). Le difficile changement des pratiques à l'école élémentaire. Analyse d'une situation 'neutre' du point de vue du genre en éducation physique. AREF Congress , Montpellier, France.

Verscheure I., Deforêt, L and Poggi, M.-P. (2014, July). Lorsque les inégalités de genre se construisent en classe: analyse d'une situation d'apprentissage visant l'équité pour accompagner le changement des pratiques. ARIS Colloquium, Genève, Suisse.

Verscheure, I., Elandoulsi, S. and Amade-Escot, C. (2014). Co-construction des savoirs selon le genre en EPS: études de cas en volley-ball. *Recherches en Didactiques – Les Cahiers Théodile*, 18, 133–154.

Verscheure, I., Robin, E. and Poggi, M.-P. (2011, June). Health Education in Physical Education in elementary school: the influence of the teacher's gender. AIESEP World Congress, Limerick, Ireland.

Vinson, M. (2013). Sous la dynamique non verbale des interactions didactiques, le genre. Analyse de l'action conjointe du professeur et des élèves: deux études de cas. Unpublished doctoral dissertation. University of Toulouse.

Vinson, M. and Amade-Escot, C. (2014). Sous la dynamique non verbale des interactions didactiques, 'l'impensable du genre': analyse en classe d'éducation physique. In I. Collet and C. Dayer (eds), *Que nous apprends le genre? Enjeux et paradoxes de l'éducation-formation* (pp. 219–245). Bruxelles: De Boeck, Raisons Educatives.

Vinson, M. and Dugal, J. P. (2013, August). Le non verbal et la construction du genre en EPS: une analyse didactique. Symposium 'Genre et éducation', AREF Congress, Montpellier, France.

Vinson, M. and Elandoulsi, S. (2015). Curriculum et construction différentielle des savoirs selon le genre en EPS. *Questions Vives*, 22. doi:10.4000/questions-vives.1636.

Whitson, D. (1994). The embodiment of gender: discipline, domination and empowerment. In S. Birrell and S. Cole (eds), *Women, sport and culture* (pp. 353–371). Champaign, Ill.: Human Kinetics.

Wright, J. (1993). Regulation and resistance: the physical education lesson as speech genre. *Social Semiotics*, 3(1), 23–56.

Wright J. (1996). The construction of complementarity in physical education. *Gender and Education*, 8(1), 61–80.

Wright, J. (1997) The construction of gendered contexts in single sex and co-educational physical education lessons. *Sport, Education and Society*, 2(1), 55–72.

Chapter 5

Adapted physical activity
Developments from an international perspective

Gudrun Doll-Tepper

Introduction

Integration and inclusion have become keywords in almost all areas of society, and in particular in education, physical education and sport. The aim of this chapter is to describe and comment on historical and current developments of these areas with a special emphasis on adapted physical activity, a cross-disciplinary area of research and practice which is still relatively young. Although inclusion not only addresses issues related to persons with disabilities in various contexts, but also – in a broader sense – all individuals who are lacking equal access and participation, for example because of their gender, socio-economic, religious and cultural backgrounds, sexual orientation, ethnicity, the focus here is placed on developments and approaches towards including persons with disabilities into physical education and sport.

It is obvious that this process of inclusion is ongoing. It is, however, also important to look back and identify the origins, obstacles and milestones in order to better understand the current situation of the "inclusion movement" and to develop and implement strategies for the future.

Historical overview

Since the 1950s the term 'adapted physical education' has been used to describe a specialization area within teaching/education that has a focus on children and youth with a disability participating in physical education in special schools (see Doll-Tepper, 2003; Sherrill and DePauw, 1997).

During these early years, emphasis in the education of persons with a disability was placed on differences between them and their 'able-bodied' counterparts, making it necessary to develop specific curricula and teaching methods for these individuals, almost all of them being taught in special schools or special classes. During the 1970s, based on approaches developed by Canadian sport scientists, a new term was introduced, 'Adapted Physical Activity', covering a much broader spectrum of physical activities and sport for persons with a disability (see DePauw and Sherrill, 1994). Over the past decades, many professionals around the world have used both terms. Many different definitions exist, they have changed over time based on changes in the understanding and roles of persons with a disability in all areas of society, including physical education and sport. In particular, new approaches in adapted physical education were developed in the 1970s, as a result of new legal requirements stipulating that education and physical education of children and youth with a disability must be offered in integrated/inclusive settings. Key words of these processes were 'equal access', 'integration/inclusion', 'movement success' and 'empowerment/self-actualization' (see Sherrill, 1996).

In this context, it is important to refer to international developments highlighting the changes of the status of persons with a disability in society. The year 1981 was proclaimed as the 'United Nations Year of Disabled Persons' and was the starting point for the 'UN Decade of Disabled Persons' from 1983 to 1992. Another important initiative was the publication of the 'International Classification of Impairment, Disability and Handicap' (ICIDH) by the World Health Organization in 1980, a classification system which was revised in 2001 to become the International Classification of Functioning, Disability and Health, commonly known as ICF (see WHO, 2001).

Over the last three decades there has been a gradual change in the conceptualization of disability which is reflected in the new classification system of the WHO (see Üstün et al., 2001). 'Disability is now understood to be a complex phenomenon that manifests itself at the body, person or social levels' (Üstün et al., 2001: 5). The revision process from ICIDH to ICF was

> based on the principle that disability is a universal trait of human being and not a unique identifier of a social group. The principle of universalism entails that all human beings have, either in fact or potentially, some limitation in functionality at the body, person or social level associated with a health condition.
>
> (Üstün et al., 2001: 9)

The new model reflects these aspects (see Figure 5.1).

From a socio-cultural perspective, it is important to note that disability and its social construction vary from society to society and attitudes towards persons with disabilities are very diverse. There appears to be an enormous variation across cultures which is reflected in recent studies (see Üstün et al., 2001: 11ff.). However, from a global perspective, it is important to stress that there is a trend towards changing the use of language when describing persons with a disability. Terms such as 'the disabled', 'invalid', 'sufferer' etc. are being replaced by 'persons with a

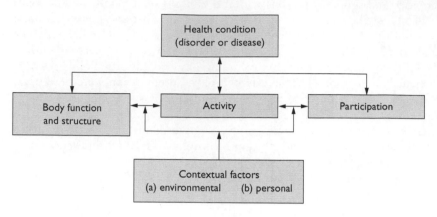

Figure 5.1 Conceptualization of disability.
Source: Üstün *et al.*, 2001: 8.

disability'. In many countries around the world, education of children with and without disabilities was based on a dichotomous approach, which led to education in two different settings: regular schools and special schools. As a consequence, physical education also took place in separate institutional settings. In the context of discussions on the state and status of physical education worldwide (see Hardman and Marshall, 2001) the importance of physical education as an integral part of education was highlighted. Physical education as a right for all children, including those with a disability, was unanimously agreed upon during the 'World Summit on Physical Education', held in Berlin, Germany, in 1999. The Berlin Agenda for government ministers states: 'All children have the right to: (1) the highest level of health; (2) free and compulsory primary education for both cognitive and physical development; (3) rest, leisure, play and recreation' (Doll-Tepper and Scoretz, 2001: 115). At the UNESCO World Conference of Ministers and Senior Officials responsible for physical education and sport (MINEPS III) held in Punta del Este, Uruguay, the Berlin Agenda was adopted. Both MINEPS IV 2004 in Athens, Greece, and MINEPS V 2013 in Berlin emphasized the rights of children and youth to full and inclusive participation in physical education and sport.

A milestone document was proclaimed in 2006, 'The Convention of the United Nations on the rights of persons with disabilities', which is currently being implemented in many countries around the world. Two articles of the Convention are in this context highly relevant:

•   Article 24 Education, and
•   Article 30 Participation in cultural life, recreation, leisure and sport.

Article 24 emphasizes the right of persons with disabilities to access an inclusive, quality and free primary and secondary education on an equal basis with others in the communities in which they live. Article 30(5) refers to participation of persons with disabilities on an equal basis with others in recreational, leisure and sporting activities. Two options are mentioned:

- participation in mainstream sporting activities at all levels, and
- participation in disability-specific sporting and recreational activities.

In addition, this chapter also contains a special paragraph regarding the access to and participation in play, recreation and leisure and sporting activities, also in the school system, for children with disabilities.

This brief overview of selected initiatives on the international level clearly indicates remarkable societal changes which have had an impact on the education and physical education of individuals with a disability, in particular, with regard to the educational system/institution (special education/inclusive education), to the training and in-service training of professionals and increased efforts in research based both on disciplinary and inter-/crossdisciplinary approaches.

Since the 1990s several new programmes in the area of adapted physical activity/education have been introduced. These include 'The Erasmus Mundus Master's Degree in Adapted Physical Activity', coordinated by KU Leuven (until 2016), the newly introduced 'International Master's Programme of Adapted Physical Activity' (starting 2015), jointly organized by KU Leuven and Palacky University Olomouc, and the 'European University Diploma in Adapted Physical Activity', currently coordinated by Haaga-Helia University Vierumäki. University programmes in many countries around the world offer professional training in this particular area of expertise, leading to bachelor, master's and doctoral degrees.

Research has addressed many aspects of physical education for persons with a disability with changing emphasis on different disabilities and issues related to their physical education. Many definitions of disability exist, they are 'socially constructed and thus vary by language, culture, environment, and time' (Sherrill, 2004: 1). And Squair and Groeneveld (2003: 45), in their chapter on 'Disability Definitions' state:

> Society's understanding of disability has been shaped by a medical community that emphasizes the physical and mental functioning of the individual. With this approach, people with a disability are grouped according to their etiology (the medical cause, or description of their condition.

These authors make a distinction between:

- mental health
- mental illness
- physical disabilities
- sensory disabilities
- learning disabilities
- developmental disabilities.

Despite the classification system of WHO (2001) past and current research in physical education has predominantly addressed issues related to these different disabilities and it is therefore unavoidable to mention these 'categories' of disability.

Concepts of physical education for persons with a disability

The early concepts of teaching physical education for individuals with a disability were focusing on specific disability and health-related problems, mostly practiced in segregated settings such as special schools or special classes. In her article 'Early Research Concerns in Adapted Physical Education, 1930–1969', Pyfer (1986) states that almost all research articles published at that time had a descriptive design and/or included comparative studies, focusing on issues such as:

- incidence, evaluation, or correction of posture problems;
- the value of physical education for asthmatics, mildly, moderately, severely and profoundly mentally retarded, learning disabled and developmentally delayed;
- specific problems in children with Down's syndrome, deaf individuals and obese children.

Early concepts of physical education for students with disabilities were based on the main motives of researchers to prove the effects of physical activity programmes on persons with a disability. Many of these research projects dealt with comparisons of various factors of behaviour in individuals with and without disabilities, so-called 'normal' persons.

In an analysis of research trends in the period 1970–1990, Broadhead (1986) carried out an in-depth review of literature; he distinguished three research thrusts:

- evaluating performance;
- lessening restrictive environments;
- effective programming.

These were important research issues, especially in North America, but also in several European countries, and the interest in evaluating performance of persons with a disability led to the development of a great number of assessment tools, such as the 'Bruininks–Oseretzky Test of Motor Proficiency' (Bruininks, 1974), the 'Test of Gross Motor Development' (Ulrich, 1985), to name but a few. Similar developments occurred in other parts of the world, for example in Germany, where specific motor assessment tools, such as the 'Body Coordination Test for Children'/Körperkoordinationstest für Kinder (KTK) (Schilling and Kiphard, 1974), were introduced in order to identify the developmental stage of children with motor, learning and behavioural difficulties. The underlying approach was a search for differences rather than for similarities in individuals with and without disabilities. Sherrill (1976/1981/1986) was one of the first to emphasize the need for physical education for all children, including those with a disability, from the setting in which it was practiced (see Sherrill and DePauw, 1997). During the 1970s and 1980s in many countries – based on new legal requirements – new concepts were developed which emphasized the similarities between children with and without disabilities rather than their differences. However, many programmes existed that aimed at offering exercises, games and play specifically tailored to the needs of children with a disability. Many of these programmes were closely linked to therapeutic approaches, for example therapeutic swimming/adapted aquatics, therapeutic dance activities and psychomotor skill acquisition. An example of such an approach is the concept of psychomotor education for children with a disability, developed by E. J. Kiphard in Germany. Emphasis was placed on a holistic approach, embracing all the different spheres of the personality of the individual, the aims being to broaden the children's experience, to raise their level of performance, to intensify their enjoyment of life, to build up their self-confidence and to give them strength. Three areas of competence were distinguished:

- personal competence;
- environmental competence;
- social competence (see Kiphard, 1979).

Physical education lessons in regular and special schools following this concept experienced great success in Germany and it has led to the inclusion of this concept into school curricula for physical education, particularly for primary schools.

In the United States a variety of different approaches were developed, such as the I CAN curriculum (Wessel, 1976, 1983), the project ACTIVE (Vodola, 1973, 1976, 1978), Data Based Gymnasium Curriculum (Dunn, 1980, 1983), the Project UNIQUE (Winnick and Short, 1982, 1984, 1985) and many more (see Sherrill and DePauw, 1997: 73). It is interesting to note that mainstream physical education during these years had little interest in disability. Physical education for children with disabilities was rather seen as an element of special education and as a therapeutic treatment. However, the training of special educators did not always include physical education, making it therefore difficult to provide children with disabilities in special schools/classes with quality physical education. New approaches during the 1980s and 1990s were based on increased research findings and closer links between regular physical education and adapted physical education. Integration and inclusion became key words in this educational process in which children with disabilities were increasingly educated in regular school settings.

Great impact on how to teach children with a disability was PL 94–142, the Education for All Handicapped Children Act, passed in the USA in 1975. Similar developments occurred in other countries to address many new issues related to physical education of children with and without disabilities. A large number of studies was carried out by researchers in the sport science sub-disciplines of exercise physiology, exercise science, biomechanics and sport pedagogy: more recently, other sub-disciplines such as sport psychology, sport sociology and sport medicine deal with issues of physical education/adapted physical education and they study aspects of sport participation of persons with different kinds of disability including physical disabilities, such as amputation, cerebral palsy and spinal cord injuries, intellectual disabilities, deafness, visual impairments, hyperactivity, asthma, diabetes and obesity.

Special emphasis is currently put on the exclusion/inclusion issue because there is general agreement – worldwide – that persons with disabilities have fewer choices in participating in physical education and sport due to various barriers, such as architectural and attitudinal barriers (see DePauw and Doll-Tepper, 2000; Hodge et al., 2012).

New concepts of physical education are based on research that focuses on accepting diversity of individuals in the education process and on studying attitudes of students and teachers towards the integration or inclusion of persons with a disability in physical education. Research in this area has been carried out in different parts of the world, for example DePauw and Goc Karp (1990) in the USA, Downs and Williams (1994) in England and Doll-Tepper et al. (1994) in Germany, and shows to what extent stereotyped attitudes exist towards including persons with a disability in physical education. In a survey of Doll-Tepper et al. (1994) it was found that physical education teachers did not hold a favourable attitude towards including children with disabilities in their physical education classes. They indicated that there had been no preparation in their teacher training and therefore they did not have the necessary knowledge and skills to practice inclusive physical education. A demand for changing physical education teacher preparation was expressed, but still has not yet been implemented on a global scale. In terms of different concepts that currently exist it is also important to mention various approaches preferring either physical education or sport education which have an impact on the education of children with a disability as well.

Margaret Talbot (2001: 39) defines physical education using the following characteristics: physical education

- aims to develop physical literacy and integrated development of the whole person;
- is a systematic introduction to and progression through the skills and understandings required for life-long involvement in physical activity and sport.

Other publications (Penney *et al.*, 2004) emphasize the importance of sport education in physical education, in which social learning and personal development through sport are highlighted and in which skills like team-working and leadership should be developed by the children and youth.

In addition, an interesting debate arose a few years ago based on an article by Whitehead (2001) about 'physical literacy'. What is 'physical literacy' and how can it be taught to children of different age and skill levels? Whitehead (2001) notes that the concept of physical literacy has been used already for some years and that it was used in a flyer of the United Kingdom Sports Council in 1991. 'Physical Education creates literacy in movement, which is as vital to every person as in verbal expression itself' (UK Sports Council 1991, Publicity leaflet). Whitehead (2001: 6) raises a number of issues that need to be clarified before an attempt to create a definition can be made:

> First, is the concept universal, or is it culturally grounded? Should we be trying to describe a physically literate individual in the UK, or anywhere in the world? Secondly, is the concept age related? Should we refer to an end state achieved by an adult, or do we need to create a concept that can be unpacked at different stages of life – infancy, childhood, adolescence, adulthood, old age? Thirdly, where do the physically challenged fit in – those with a physical and/or another disability? And fourthly, how far should we include, what could be called for short, dexterity? Should we confirm ourselves to movement involving larger muscle groups, otherwise known as gross motor skills?

In addition, in her conclusion she raises a number of important issues culminating in the question: 'How does the concept of Physical Literacy affect what is and might be the practice of Physical Education?' (Whitehead, 2001: 8). It seems to be very relevant to introduce this concept of physical literacy into the general debate in physical education and, in particular, regarding physical education of children with a disability.

On the road to inclusive education

Since the 1990s the term 'integration' has been replaced by 'inclusion' in many official documents (for example, the Salamanca Declaration, UNESCO, 1994), especially relevant for developments and changes in education and educational institutions. Inclusion means that all schools and school systems need to be changed structurally in such a way that they provide education for all children, including those with a disability. 'An inclusive school is a place where everyone belongs, is accepted, supports and is supported by his or her peers and other members of the school community in the course of having his or her educational needs met' (Stainback and Stainback, 1990: 3). All persons have a right to education and of equal opportunity for education. Equality has become a basic value and goal as part of changes in society, in particular with respect to people with a disability. The UN-Standard Rules on the Equalization of Opportunities for Persons with Disabilities (1993) state that general education systems in principle are responsible for the education of all children with a disability. Controversial and hot debates have accompanied these recent processes in education, some advocating the existence of special schools, others advocating inclusive education in regular schools. A review of this process clearly indicates tremendous differences between countries, some of them keeping their traditional school system with special schools, others being on their way towards decentralization of education offered by schools and the closure of special schools in countries such as the USA, Canada, Australia, Denmark, Norway, Italy and Germany; the main aim here is the development of a 'school for all' (see Hans and Ginnold, 2000).

> There are some important educational implications in the concept, which have been articulated by those writing extensively about inclusion. First, all students are included not just those with mild disabilities, as was the case with mainstreaming.... Second, the regular classroom is the starting point for instruction, not a reward for good performance elsewhere.
>
> (Reid, 2003: 139–140)

Despite various efforts, for example in the countries of the European Union, implementation has occurred at different rates. Cross-cultural and cross-national communication and cooperation currently speeds up this process and has led to structural changes of the school system and to new approaches in teacher training and preparation. In this context, it is important to highlight the role of international agencies, such as the United Nations Educational, Scientific and Cultural Organization (UNESCO), the International Labour Organization (ILO), the World Health Organization (WHO) and the United Nations International Children's Emergency Fund

(UNICEF). 'It is a UNESCO commission which urges the international community to continue to work on achieving the goals set to make education a right and reality for children before 2015' (Eklindh, 2003: 25).

In order to reach the goal of education for all, it is necessary to:

* promote the right of every child and youth with a disability to express his/her view pertaining to his/her education and life skills...
* identify and disseminate effective practices and stimulate research and studies ... to include such areas as:

  * quality teacher education;
  * school organization including adequate and accessible facilities;
  * curriculum and pedagogy;
  * assistive devices and appropriate materials.

(Eklindh, 2003: 27)

Sander (2004) summarizes the past, current and future developments regarding concepts of an inclusive education and distinguishes five levels:

1 Exclusion: children with a disability were/are excluded from education/school in general. This was the situation for example in the different states of Germany during the eighteenth century.
2 Separation: children with a disability attend special institutions (special schools). This has been the case in Germany since the nineteenth century.
3 Integration: children with a disability can attend regular schools with special education assistance.
4 Inclusion: all children with a disability attend regular schools like their 'able-bodied' counterparts. Heterogeneity and differences are appreciated.
5 Diversity as 'normality': inclusion is practiced in every educational setting, the term inclusion can be omitted.

Current concepts of physical education need to take these aspects into account which have been developed for education. Inclusive physical education is a challenge for the profession who should provide appropriate responses to the broad spectrum of learning needs of children and youth (see Block, 2007).

Inclusive physical education

Amongst adapted physical activity/education professionals a debate has been ongoing since the 1990s over the 'inclusion movement' (see DePauw and Doll-Tepper, 2000). In the context of this debate, it is important to acknowledge that this is primarily a discourse which initially took place in the USA, however, at the World Summit on Physical Education in 1999 in Berlin, it became clear that a similar debate exists in other countries as well. It is obvious that concepts of inclusion exist and some understand it as one universal placement for all. Others define inclusion not as a place or placement, but rather reconceptualize it as an attitude or process (see DePauw and Doll-Tepper, 2000). Block (1999) encouraged us

> to question the efficacy of inclusion and to re-examine the assumptions about general physical education: (a) general physical education programmes are of high quality with individualized instruction; (b) class sizes are similar to general education class rooms, and most typically, developing children are well behaved and motivated; (c) physical educators are willing to take on the challenge of working with children with a disability; and (d) physical educators do and will continue to receive training from adapted physical educators.
>
> (DePauw and Doll-Tepper, 2000: 139)

It is clear that these assumptions need to be examined with regard to the trend towards progressive inclusion and acceptance. 'Inclusion must be seen as a philosophy, a process, and as an attitude' (DePauw and Doll-Tepper, 2000: 140). In order to contribute to changes in society in general and in education, and in particular, in physical education, dialogue needs to be intensified between the professionals in different disciplines and areas of expertise. Comparative studies undertaken by Hardman and Marshall (2001) and by Hardman (2004) show remarkable differences in this process.

> Opportunities for disabled pupils in physical education seem to be increasing but there are regional variations: in central and eastern Europe the level of integration is considerably lower than in the rest of Europe. Problems in realizing integration embrace: the lack of official policy to address and to raise broader awareness of integration issues, shortage of material, resources, a shortage of trained specialist personnel, physical barriers to access, class management inadequacies, programme content and class size.
>
> (Hardman, 2004: 5–6)

Hardman (2004: 13) also reports that

> countries such as England, Sweden, Canada, Australia, Finland and Israel have in place specific programmes to support the inclusion of children with disabilities into physical education. Undoubtedly, these programmes are making progress and are beginning to cater for a much more diverse group of children than ever before.

In his report, Hardman identifies several challenging issues, such as the perceived additional burden for physical education teachers, the lack of driving forces within and from the Education Departments for inclusive physical education and the ongoing debate concerning the role of specialist providers of adapted physical education teachers. He concludes: 'Worldwide there appears to a lack of recognition, mostly from Education itself, of the important role that children with disabilities play in our playgrounds' (Hardman, 2004: 13).

Challenges for research and a call for action

With regard to the role and impact of physical education and sport for children and youth: What do we know? What do we not know? What should we know? These were questions raised and addressed to professionals in physical education and sport coming from different disciplinary backgrounds. One section of the 'First German Children and Youth Sport Report' (Schmidt *et al.*, 2003) dealt with children and youth with disabilities in physical education and sport. With regard to terminology and definition of disability it was made clear that still no global understanding exists and most studies that were included in the survey still followed the former classification system of WHO (impairment, disability, handicap) because the revised classification system ICF had not yet been adopted by researchers. Many studies have focused on inclusive physical education of children with intellectual disability/mental retardation (Bös and Scholtes, 1990; Fediuk, 1988; Streicher and Leske, 1985), of children with visual impairments (Wurzel, 1991) and of children with different disabilities in regular physical education (Scheid, 1995). A generalization of existing research findings is not possible to date due to a lack of empirical research both with regards to physical education for children with disabilities in special schools and in inclusive education settings. Sherrill (2004) listed several constraints related to research and a solid knowledge base. These include:

- constraints specific to areas dominated by poverty and/or war;
- constraints specific to females with disabilities and activity involvement;
- constraints of prejudice, stigmatization and oppression;
- constraints of not realizing trends in attitude research;
- constraints of translation of research into action pedagogy and of dissemination; and
- constraints of not recognizing and teaching specific APA and disability sport knowledge base.

Recently, Haegele *et al.* (2015) published a documentary analysis on research trends in *Adapted Physical Activity Quarterly* from 2004 to 2013.

They found that the two most common topical areas were those in the categories 'psychosocial issues' and 'motor behaviour'. These results were consistent with previous findings; however, they found a large decrease in the number of articles addressing inclusion/programming issues, but expected more research in this area in the future. The ratification of the Convention of the United Nations on the Rights of Persons with Disabilities in many countries around the world has led to increased efforts towards including persons with disabilities in all areas of society, such as in physical education and sport. As part of the implementation process researchers and practitioners are challenged to intensify their cooperation in order to answer questions related to ensuring quality and success of teaching and learning processes in inclusive settings. Questions raised regarding the students are:

- How can children and youth with disabilities participate on an equal basis with their peers in physical education and sport?
- What is the motivation of participants with and without disabilities to take part in inclusive sport programmes?
- What are the attitudes of the participants towards each other?
- What is the impact of inclusive physical education and sport on the individual's self-perception and self-esteem?

Questions raised regarding the teachers and coaches include:

- What kind of professional training is necessary to ensure the acquisition of appropriate skills and positive attitudes towards inclusion?
- What kind of teaching/coaching material is needed, where can it be accessed and who prepares it?
- What kind of assistance is needed and is made available?
- How can the learning process and outcome be measured?

These are just a few topics which are relevant for the implementation of inclusion in various settings. Currently, some research projects also address issues of accessibility and communication, both with regard to school and sport programmes. Systems of sport (separate vs. inclusive structures) are also addressed, in particular, by comparing developments in various countries (see Radtke and Doll-Tepper, 2014).

Finally, it can be stated that tremendous changes have occurred in many countries as far as physical education and sport for persons with disabilities are concerned. This trend towards full and effective participation and inclusion of persons with disabilities as encouraged by the UN Convention can be identified in physical education and sport and is progressing.

However, it seems necessary to call for more action and cooperation at international, national and local levels and to increase efforts to mainstreaming disability issues as an integral part of physical education and sport.

References

Block, M. (1999) Did we jump on the wrong bandwagon? Making general physical education placement work. *Palaestra*, 15(3), 30–36, 55–56.

Block, M. (2007) *A teacher's guide to including students with disabilities in general physical education*. Baltimore, MD: Brooks Publishing.

Bös, K. and Scholtes, U. (1990) Integrativer Sportunterricht von nichtbehinderten und geistigbehinderten Schülern. *Zeitschrift für Heilpädagogik*, 41(4), 246–271.

Broadhead, G. D. (1986) Adapted physical education research trends: 1970–1990. *Adapted Physical Activity Quarterly*, 3, 104–111.

Bruininks, R. H. (1974) Physical and motor development of retarded persons. In N. R. Ellis (ed.), *International Review of Research in Mental Retardation* (pp. 209–261). New York: Academic Press.

DePauw, K. and Doll-Tepper, G. (2000) Toward progressive inclusion and acceptance: myth or reality? The inclusion debate and bandwagon discourse. *Adapted Physical Activity Quarterly*, 17(2), 135–143.

DePauw, K. and Goc Karp, G. (1990) Attitudes of selected college students toward including disabled individuals in integrated settings. In G. Doll-Tepper, C. Dahms, B. Doll and H. von Selzam (eds), *Adapted Physical Activity: An Interdisciplinary Approach* (pp. 149–157). Berlin, Heidelberg, New York, Tokyo: Springer Verlag.

DePauw, K. and Sherrill, C. (1994) Adapted physical activity: present and future. *Physical Education Review*, 17, 6–13.

Doll-Tepper, G. (2003) Adapted physical activity and sport. *Lifelong Learning in Europe*, 4, 47–51.

Doll-Tepper, G. and Scoretz, D. (eds) (2001) *World summit on physical education: proceedings*. Schorndorf: Hofmann.

Doll-Tepper, G., Schmidt-Gotz, E., Lienert, C., Döen, U. and Hecker, R. (1994) *Einstellungen von Sportlehrkräften zur Integration von Menschen mit Behinderungen in Schule und Verein*. Köln: Sport und Buch Strauß.

Downs, P. and Williams, T. (1994) Student attitudes toward integration of people with disabilities in activity settings: a European comparison. *Adapted Physical Activity Quarterly*, 11(1), 32–43.

Dunn, J. M. (1980) *A data-based gymnasium*. Monmouth, OR: Instructional Development Corporation.

Dunn, J. M. (1983) Physical activity for the severely handicapped: theoretical and practical considerations. In R. L. Eason, T. L. Smith and F. Caron (eds), *Adapted physical activity: from theory to application* (pp. 63–73). Champaign, IL: Human Kinetics.

Eklindh, K. (2003) Education for all means all. *Lifelong Learning in Europe*, 4, 24–27.

Fediuk, F. (1988) *Integrierter Sport mit geistig retardierten und nichtretardierten Jugendlichen*. Köln: Sport und Buch Strauß.

Fediuk, F. (1999) *Integrativer Schulsport*. Kassel: Gesamthochschule.

Haegele, J., Lee, J. and Porretta, D. (2015) Research trends in adapted physical activity quarterly from 2004 to 2013. *Adapted Physical Activity Quarterly*, 32(2), 187–205.

Hans, M. and Ginnold, A. (eds) (2000) *Integration von Menschen mit Behinderung. Entwicklungen in Europa.* Neuwied, Kriftel, Berlin: Luchterhand.

Hardman, K. (2004) *An up-date on the status of physical education in schools worldwide: technical report for the World Health Organisation.* Unpublished document on behalf of International Council of Sport Science and Physical Education (ICSSPE).

Hardman, K. and Marshall, J. (2001) World-wide survey of the state and status of school physical education. In G. Doll-Tepper and D. Scoretz (eds), *World summit on physical education: proceedings* (pp. 15–37). Schorndorf: Hofmann.

Hodge, S., Lieberman, L. and Murata, N. (2012) *Essentials of teaching adapted physical education.* Scottsdale: Holcomb Hathaway.

Kiphard, E. J. (1979) *Motopädagogik.* Dortmund: Modernes Lernen.

Penney, D., Clarke, G., Kinchin, G. and Quill, M. (2004) *Sport education in physical education.* London: Routledge.

Pyfer, J. (1986) Early research concerns in adapted physical education, 1930–1969. *Adapted Physical Activity Quarterly,* 3, 95–103.

Radtke, S. and Doll-Tepper, G. (2014) *Nachwuchsgewinnung und -förderung im paralympischen Sport.* Köln: Sportverlag Strauß.

Reid, G. (2003) Moving towards inclusion. In R. Steadward, G. Wheeler and E. J. Watkinson (eds), *Adapted physical activity* (pp. 11–25). Edmonton: University of Alberta Press and Steadward Centre.

Sander, A. (2004) Konzepte einer Inklusiven Pädagogik. *Zeitschrift für Heilpädagogik,* 5, 240–244.

Scheid, V. (1995) *Chancen der Integration durch Sport.* Aachen: Meyer & Meyer.

Schilling, F. and Kiphard, E. J. (1974) *Körperkoordinationstest für Kinder (KTK),* Manual. Weinheim: Beltz.

Schmidt, W., Hartmann-Tews, I. and Brettschneider, W.-D. (eds) (2003) *Erster Deutscher Kinder- und Jugendsportbericht.* Schorndorf: Hofmann.

Sherrill, C. (1976/1981/1986) *Adapted physical education and recreation: a multidisciplinary approach.* Dubuque, IA: Brown.

Sherrill, C. (1996) Individual differences, adaptation, and creativity theory: applications and perspectives. In G. Doll-Tepper and W.-D. Brettschneider (eds), *Physical Education and Sport:Changes and Challenges* (pp. 384–397). Aachen: Meyer & Meyer.

Sherrrill, C. (2004) *Young people with disability in physical education/physical activity/sport in and out of schools: technical report for the World Health Organization.* Unpublished document on behalf of ICSSPE.

Sherrill, C. and DePauw, K. (1997) Adapted physical activity and education. In J. Massengale and R. Swanson (eds), *The History of Exercise and Sport Science* (pp. 39–108). Champaign, IL: Human Kinetics.

Squair, L. and Groeneveld, H. (2003) Disability definitions. In R. Steadward, G. Wheeler and E. J. Watkinson (eds), *Adapted Physical Activity* (pp. 45–64). Edmonton: University of Alberta Press and Steadward Centre.

Stainback, S. and Stainback, W. (1990) Inclusive schooling. In W. Stainback and S. Stainback (eds), *Support networks for inclusive schooling* (pp. 3–24). Baltimore: Paul H. Brookes.

Streicher, W. and Leske, R. (1985) Soziale Integration Geistigbehinderter im Sportunterricht der Grund- und Hauptschule. *Zeitschrift für Heilpädagogik*, 36(7), 477–487.

Talbot, M. (2001) The case for physical education. In G. Doll-Tepper and D. Scoretz (eds), *2001 World Summit on Physical Education: Proceedings* (pp. 39–50). Schorndorf: Hofmann.

UK Sports Council (1991) *The case for sport*. Publicity leaflet.

Ulrich, D. (1985) *Test of gross motor development*. Austin: Pro-Ed.

UNESCO (United Nations Educational, Scientific and Cultural Organization) (1994) Die Salamanca-Erklärung und der Aktionsrahmen zur Pädagogik für besondere Bedürfnisse. www.unesco.at/bildung/basisdokumente/salamanca_erklaerung.pdf (retrieved 30 March 2015).

United Nations (2006) *Convention on the rights of persons with disabilities*. New York.

Üstün, T. B., Chatterji, S., Bickenbach, J. E., Trotter, R. T. and Saxena, S. (2001) Disability and cultural variation: the ICIDH-2 cross-cultural applicability research study. In T. B Üstün, S. Chatterji, J. E. Bickenbach, R. T. Trotter, R. Room, J. Rehm and S. Saxena (eds), *Disability and Culture: Universalism and Diversity* (pp. 3–19). Seattle, Toronto, Bern, Göttingen: Hogrefe & Huber Publishers.

Vodola, T. (1973) *Individualized physical education for the handicapped child*. Englewood Cliffs, NJ: Prentice Hall.

Vodola, T. (1976) *Developmental and adapted physical education: a competency-based teacher training manual*. Oakhurst, NJ: Project Active.

Vodola, T. (1978) *ACTIVE research monograph: competency-based teacher training and individualized-personalized physical activity*. Oakhurst, NJ: Township of Ocean School District.

Wessel, J. A. (1976) *I CAN instructional resource materials: primary skills*. Northbrook, IL: Hubbard.

Wessel, J. A. (1983) Quality programming in physical education and recreation for all handicapped persons. In R. L. Eason, T. L. Smith and F. Caron (eds), *Adapted physical activity: from theory to application* (pp. 35–52). Champaign, IL: Human Kinetics.

Whitehead, M. (2001) The concept of physical literacy. *The British Journal of Teaching Physical Education*, 32(1) Spring, 6–8.

Winnick, J. P. and Short, F. X. (1982) *The physical fitness of sensory and orthopedically impaired youth*. Project UNIQUE final report. Brockport: State University of New York.

Winnick, J. P. and Short, F. X. (1984) The physical fitness of youngsters with spinal neuromuscular conditions. *Adapted Physical Activity Quarterly*, 1, 37–51.

Winnick, J. P. and Short, F. X. (1985) *Physical fitness testing of the disabled: Project UNIQUE*. Champaign, IL: Human Kinetics.

World Health Organization (2001) *International classification of functioning, disability and health*. Geneva: WHO.

Wurzel, B. (1991) *Sportunterricht mit Behinderten und Nichtbehinderten*. Schorndorf: Hofmann.

Chapter 6

Reflections and influences – this way ... this explains my reality

Critical race theory in sport and leisure

Kevin Hylton

Recently I was invited to contribute to the *Routledge Handbook of Theory in Sport Management* (Hylton, 2016). Soon after writing the chapter I was informed of the passing of the international scholar Professor Margaret Talbot OBE with whom I shared many instructive hours as, first, her undergraduate student and then colleague at Leeds Beckett University. The editors were keen to explore how theory should be seen as a critical element in the advancement of sport management and that theory is the basis for our scholarship, teaching, and engagement. As I have been busy in using Critical Race Theory (CRT) since the late 1990s I was asked to reflect upon and write about it in relation to a paper that I wrote in 2005, 'Race, Sport and Leisure: Lessons from Critical Race Theory' (Hylton, 2005). In the chapter I offer an overview of CRT as a framework, my influences in adopting it, and examine developments that have emerged from its use. However, what I omitted to state in the handbook due to the usual constraints of space and readership was the direct influence of Margaret Talbot as a mentor since the 1980s. Routledge have kindly given permission for me to reproduce the chapter in their handbook and this is what I outline below.

As a black undergraduate student with no black counterparts or black lecturers, the dominant epistemologies in sport, leisure, and PE did not empower its readers to focus on the lived experience of black people. Even within Margaret's feminist work she would be the first to agree with other scholars that black women were also excluded in their mainstream anti-patriarchy missives (Birrell, 1989; hooks, 1990; Scraton, 2001; Weekes and Mirza, 1997). As activist scholars we must make space for transformation, however this can be achieved. Margaret's insight made space for me to change how I viewed the sovereignty of established knowledge by offering advice on the marginal status of research on 'race' in the sport, leisure, and PE literatures; her advice to me was: 'If you don't do research in this area ["race"] then no one else will.' As a result of Margaret's influence I am (re)presenting this chapter from the *Routledge Handbook of Theory and Theory Development in Sport Management* because in it I reflect upon my use of Critical Race Theory, encountered as a result of being encouraged by Margaret Talbot, and subsequent scholars, to be critical, reflexive, and compassionate.

In 2005 Michael Banton wrote a retrospective on 55 years of research in sociology (Banton, 2005). In particular his work focused on ethnic and racial studies. Widely regarded as one of the leading international sociologists, his reflections on his approaches to the sociology of 'race' and ethnic relations was published in the same year that I was challenging academics in the sociology of sport and leisure to engage in a more inclusive and critical exposition of racialised phenomena (Hylton, 2005). Some of the questions that I was asking included: (1) At what point will those in the field recognise that a narrow academic focus will leave them with charges of repetition and theoretical myopia? (2) Do academics in the field recognise that even critical theories with a social justice focus can ignore 'race'? (3) Are academics in the field willing to incorporate other marginalised ideas and voices to address these imbalances? In regards to the academy my ire was focused on how sport and leisure studies, a necessarily multidisciplinary field, marginalised specific issues of 'race' and racism.

My paper written on Critical Race Theory (CRT) in *Leisure Studies* (Hylton, 2005) consisted of three sections, concluding with a call to sport and leisure theorists and policymakers to centralise 'race', racism, and race equality in their everyday considerations (p. 94). The first part of the article explored the shared racial justice agenda of CRT and other areas of ethnic and racial studies. The paper unpacked the fundamentals of CRT's precepts as a useful introductory point for readers new to the framework. As a device to emphasise how a critical 'race'-centred approach can strengthen social theorising the paper then moved on to the second section that mapped out the flawed analogous developments of critical theory in sport and leisure sociology and the North American-based critical legal studies as both were inconsistent in their treatment of 'race' in their analyses. In the final part of the paper CRT is advanced as 'a worthy theoretical framework from which to interrogate issues of "race", and to refocus the theoretical lens onto anti-oppressive theory, race equality, and related areas in sport and leisure studies' (Hylton, 2005: 82).

I haven't shifted from this position, although I wish to make the point firmly that in attempting to develop theoretically informed interventions one is bound to make mistakes (Banton, 2005). I also wish to make a few brief related points: (a) CRT is not a theory but a framework, which I outline in this chapter, and elsewhere, through the use of precepts or tenets (Hylton, 2009, 2012); (b) though 'race' and racism are central CRT has a larger anti-essentialist focus to contest other forms of subordination; (c) CRT uses the term 'race' that incorporates discourses of ethnicity and urges all to use racialised terminology politically, pragmatically, and with caution.

In many ways I have seen CRT gain a foothold and flourish at conferences, in academic journals, and in postgraduate studies across a plethora of disciplines, while BritCrit, the substantive application of CRT in the UK, has become more conspicuous (Gillborn, 2011). Yet there will still remain criticism of the place of intersecting identities/forms of oppression that are being de-centred, or worse, devalued in opposition to 'race'. Even though CRT is an anti-essentialist framework that embraces intersectionality and all forms of social justice agendas there will inevitably be complaints of topics that have not yet significantly emerged in some areas using this emerging framework.

In 2005 I summarised the precepts of CRT as: (1) the centralising of 'race' and racism at the same time as recognising their connection with other forms of subordination and oppression; (2) challenging traditional dominant ideologies around objectivity, meritocracy, colour-blindness, race-neutrality, and equal opportunity; (3) a clear commitment to social justice that incorporates elements of liberation and transformation; (4) centralising the marginalised voice; (5) necessarily transdisciplinary. These are not exhaustive precepts, though they are popular in most theorising of this framework. If sociology has taught us anything it is that 'race' has no foundation in science and remains a social construction. However, if history has taught us anything it is that 'race' is a lived reality and it is this fundamental point that forces CRT to recognise its constructed nature while pragmatically putting racialisation and racism in the sights of these activist scholars. CRT is distinctive because it centres 'race' and racism where other critical perspectives are more circumspect in their pursuits of social justice. Critical race theorists ensure that the salience of 'race' is recognised and racism is disrupted so as to ensure racial justice or even racial transformations become goals in the way we do business (Delgado and Stefancic, 2001).

CRT's starting point is that society is ridden with racisms that have been explained historically, politically, culturally, economically, and epistemologically. Seminal writers Richard Delgado and Jean Stefancic (2001: 7) are typical of critical race theorists' expositions on racism when they state that racism is ordinary, not aberrational, 'normal science', the usual way society does business, the common, everyday experience of most people of colour (Crenshaw et al., 2009; Dixson and Rousseau, 2006; Gillborn, 2009). Similarly, Lord Cluny MacPherson's conclusion at the end of his inquiry into racism in the London Metropolitan Police reinforced a CRT viewpoint when he stated that there must be an unequivocal acceptance that the problem actually exists as a prerequisite to addressing it successfully (Macpherson, 1999: 652). For social transformation to occur this must be understood.

Simple conceptions of racism as, for example, overt and covert do not fully engage the sophistication of its manifestations in society, ergo sport and leisure. These racial processes and formations (Omi and Winant,

1994; Winant, 2001) are experienced discursively, materially or affectively, ranging from 'actual' events to those that are 'felt'. Racisms can be viewed simply as perceived or more comprehensively as a cancerous social concern that affects all of us. Though this intellectual debate must be taken seriously it is important that scholarly gymnastics make us limber in a practical sense to challenge historical racialised inequalities in the everyday. Like Macpherson (1999: 6.50) it is imperative not to be stymied by these debates and to 'take the view that the important issue now is to stop arguing about definitions and do something about the racism'.

Racism in sport

Racism in sport is a serious contemporary issue and one that, on any given day, is likely to produce multiple examples of global controversies. Today it is the turn of Italy's FA President, Carlo Tavecchio, to be banned from any position within European football body UEFA as a result of making racist remarks in his campaign for the FIGC presidency. Reuters reports that his remarks were based upon a fictitious African player when he said: 'In England, they identify the players coming in and, if they are professional, they are allowed to play. [...] Here instead we get "Opti Poba", who previously ate bananas and then suddenly becomes a first-team player with Lazio' (Homewood, 2014). Other recent and sensational events that fall into this category include NBA Clippers owner Donald Sterling, fined $2.5million and banned from owning an NBA franchise because of the cynical racism he inadvertently divulged to the world via a telephone conversation with his partner (Barrabi, 2014). The presence of racism in sport and society is obvious to many; Table 6.1 shows ten of the most egregious examples still plaguing the athletic field and the boardrooms as reported in the New York Daily News (Bondy, 2014).

In relation to the New York Daily News' final point, it is overly simplistic to suggest that racism is only the vestige of the far right and/or hooligans, though we should be clear that there were periods where their presence was much more conspicuous. One thing we see less of in the professional domain internationally, but specifically where it comes to football in the UK, is the racist violence that blighted stadia in the 1970s and 1980s. However, a review of the Runnymede Trust's[1] bulletin reports reveals the intergenerational prevalence of 'race' and racism in sport, leisure, and society. One year after the European Parliament's Committee of Inquiry into the rise of fascism and racism in Europe we witnessed horrific scenes in the Heysel stadium in Brussels where 39 people died fueled by such bigotry (Runnymede Trust, 1985a). Football stadia, the recruiting grounds for neo-Nazis like the National Front (NF), found the NF distributing racist literature urging their followers to 'kill the n*****s' (Runnymede Trust, 1987). Some of the leaflets that they distributed at

Table 6.1 New York Daily News – current examples of racism in sport

1 Ice Hockey Fans on the Internet – the abuse that black players endure on social media is something relatively new, and truly disgusting. When Wayne Simmonds was creating problems for the Rangers in the first round of the playoffs, a torrent of racist tweets hit the web.

2 Lack of Translators for Spanish-Speaking Players

3 Redskins – The NFL's franchise in Washington continues to churn out public relations releases, citing surveys that indicate Native Americans don't really mind the obviously offensive nickname.

4 Graduation Rate for Black College Athletes – Top college basketball and football programs continue to recruit and then exploit black athletes without proper academic counseling. The majority who don't make it will need to find a different profession — without a college degree. At Wisconsin they reported a 100% graduation rate among its white basketball players and a 0% rate among its black players.

5 Stereotypes of Asian Players – Asians and Asian Americans are pigeonholed too often by sport. They're supposed to be good at golf, baseball, tennis, and figure skating, but not at basketball or football.

6 The Coverage of Black Players in the Media – The cultural gap remains huge between the largely white media that cover professional sport and the largely black population of players in football and basketball.

7 Owners – Until ownership of professional sports teams becomes more diverse there can never be a trickle down effect. Too many white owners employ too many white vice presidents who employ too many white general managers.

8 Upper Management in Baseball

9 Cleveland Indians Baseball Team Mascot

10 European Football Fans – Football supporters in Spain, Italy, Holland and all over Eastern Europe have demonstrated over the years they are the most ignorant bunch of all. Crowd behavior was awful at Euro 2012 in Poland and Ukraine. Then last year, players from AC Milan courageously walked off the field in Lombardy after spectators there uttered derisive chants at Ghanian-German player Kevin-Prince Boateng. Most recently, Barcelona's Dani Alves tried to defuse matters by picking up a banana thrown at him by a Villarreal fan (who was arrested), peeling it and eating it before he took a corner kick.

Source: Bondy, 2014.

Heysel were asking questions of supporters that are disturbingly being heard in 2013. 'One leaflet at Heysel entitled "Unemployment" asked, Have you been thrown on the scrapheap by foreign imports?' (Runnymede Trust, 1985a: 7). Politics of 'race' shift over time, although it may disturb some how closely aligned elements of the far-right NF discourse from the racist violence in sport from the 1980s are still with today's major political parties: Labour wish to secure borders and crack down on immigrants undercutting British workers, while the Tories wish to implement a new 'hardline' immigration strategy. The notion of 'sport as a prism on society' becomes clearer at these times.

The mingling of British neo-Nazis and Italian fascists before Liverpool vs. Juventus at Heysel in 1985 should not be lost on those in football today who feel that fascism is acceptable. It was the Tyneside and District Anti-fascist Association in 1985 that called for a total ban on the National Front at football matches as these activities had been ignored for so long, yet it was on neighbouring Wearside in 2013 when an openly fascist manager was taken on by Sunderland Football Club. The controversy following Paolo Di Canio's management contracts at both Swindon FC and Sunderland were prompted by those unwilling for history and politics to remain forgotten in the direction they pointed their moral compass. The European Union Fundamental Rights Agency (FRA, 2010) study on racism, ethnic discrimination, and exclusion of migrants and minorities in sport found that racism, anti-Semitism, and anti-gypsyism were consistent across all 27-member nations. As we go back and forwards in decades, and as the social and political climate change, we can see that racism and policy responses in and through sport tangle with recurrent issues. Integration, xenophobia, far-right politics, racist violence, and even fascism reminds us that the genealogy of these ideas and politics metamorphose into new discourses. For example, in 1985 the Runnymede Trust (1985b) reported on an article in the *Telegraph* that a Chelsea fan was fined £100 for wearing a T-shirt that read 'Chelsea's Yid-busters coming soon to rid the world'.[2] This was an obvious anti-Semitic dig at rivals Tottenham Hotspur (Spurs) whose history of attracting Jewish fans has made them a target for rivals. Twenty-nine years later in 2014 the tensions continue and are more complex, as Spurs fans express a fondness for the use of self-identifying chants such as 'Yid Army!' and 'Yiddo!' that could easily be read as anti-Semitic. Spurs are in the middle of a heated debate as to who can use the word 'Yid': is it offensive when 'reclaimed' by Spurs fans? Spurs fans in 2014, as well as rival supporters, risk being prosecuted for anti-Semitic chants just as the Chelsea fan was two decades earlier. Prime Minister David Cameron added to the debate that it was acceptable for Spurs fans to chant the word, even after the Football Association warned that fans could face criminal charges and long banning orders (Telegraph-Sport, 2013; Johnson, 2013). Here two major stakeholders in the race equality landscape of sport are at complete odds and are another example of the significance and complexities of 'race' and racism in sport. Furthermore, sport demonstrates here how contemporary racialised issues of terminology, identities, politics/policy, and racist intent in the use of language abound as ideas are constructed and reworked.

In an example where intent was unequivocal, Norman Tebbit used sport as a starting point for another famous discussion on integration in 1990 as he argued that if you don't support the national team where you are living then you couldn't be integrated into that society (Runnymede Trust, 1990). Tebbit used the sport of cricket to make this point and, in particular, targeted south Asian communities to challenge their validity as productive and integrated citizens. This Loyalty Test was not well received, yet it further demonstrates that over the years sport and leisure spaces have emphasised the broader divisions we see every day while, as with the Spurs chants, not necessarily resolving them. Racial abuse in sport is still rife and the Runnymede Trust has recorded many incidents and responses to them. For example, soon after 1993 when the Commission for Racial Equality launched its Let's Kick Racism Out of Football campaign (now Kick it Out), Derby County players, Gary Charles and Paul Williams, were substituted at Millwall after receiving racist abuse (Runnymede Trust, 1994); a BNP councillor had also just been elected in the Isle of Dogs.[3] Interestingly, Brendan Batson, spokesperson for the Professional Footballers' Association, felt that taking the players off was a backward step and that the players should have been kept on the pitch. However, two decades later in 2013 many ex-players and football governing bodies lauded as heroic the action by Kevin Prince Boateng who walked off the pitch for being racially abused by spectators as he played for AC Milan against Pro Patria. Ideas and tolerances shift and move on yet 'race' and racism remain significant.

In 1999 I wrote a paper for *The Leisure Manager* entitled 'Where are the Black Leisure Managers?' I am disappointed that over 15 years later the same questions are being asked (Hylton, 1999). As Chelsea football club manager, Jose Mourinho, is roundly condemned by FIFA for saying there is no racism in football (Ackerman, 2014) his naivety and white privilege become exposed. The discourse of 'race' in sport has retained the equivalence of Guinier and Torres' (2003) 'Miner's Canary' as it continues to be reiterated in discussions of leadership, management and coaching, the media, local government, pedagogy, science, migration, research, to name a few. A miner's canary was used in the past to detect levels of poisonous gases in mines; the death of the canary signaled the presence of this danger. The continued presence of 'race' as a starting point to focus critical 'race' scholars on such projects, as CRT's key writings develop fluidly to engage new and challenging racialised phenomena in sport, denotes the pernicious and permeating presence of racism in society. The resilience of 'race' and more specifically, racialised issues, processes, and formations to manifest themselves inter-generationally, internationally, intersectionally, culturally, politically, economically, and socially force a constant revisioning of ways to disrupt their insidious onslaught.

Leading up to and subsequent to the *Leisure Studies* paper in 2005 part of my challenge has involved balancing the development of CRT as a theoretical framework to explain and challenge more complex subjects. In the vein of Banton's (2005: 466) urgings that sociologists need to make their theories less abstract and to consider more diligently the adequacy of the explanations of problems that can be derived from theories, I have developed and applied CRT in my work through examinations of theories of education and 'race' (Hylton *et al.*, 2011; Pilkington *et al.*, 2009); 'race' and culture in tourism and events (Hylton and Chakrabarty, 2011); social capital and social integration (Hylton, 2008, 2010b), football studies (Hylton, 2013, 2014; Long *et al.*, 2000), Olympism (Hylton and Morpeth, 2012), antiracism, sport and its development (Hylton, 2010a, 2011), migration (Long *et al.*, 2014; Spracklen *et al.*, 2014), methodologies (Hylton, 2012), and whiteness (Hylton and Lawrence, 2014; Long and Hylton, 2002). At the same time it is important not to lose sight of the fact of racism and the constant need to restate the issues for new generations of policymakers, practitioners, and students that often require 'old wine in new bottles'. Hence, my policy- and practice-oriented research informed by CRT has included studies for a range of national governing bodies, government departments, and local authorities. The difficulty of continuing any sociological development is the requirement to engage intellectual pursuits while ensuring they are couched in lived realities. Critical Race Theory's movement towards social justice cannot be purely theoretical, even though theoretical debates can be had, neither can it be purely interventionist because of our need to observe thoughtful action.

Academics with an interest in ethnic and racial studies in sport and leisure would draw similar conclusions to me in the *Leisure Studies* paper that

> The resultant outcome of using a CRT perspective is likely to lead towards a resistance to a passive reproduction of the established practices, knowledge and resources, that make up the social conditions that marginalize 'race' as a core factor in the way we manage and experience our sport and leisure.
>
> (Hylton, 2005)

Research and writing informed by CRT have become widespread and more common than in the 2000s; they definitely outstrip the foundations on which I based my initial ideas in the 1980s that developed into the application of CRT in my doctoral studies in the 1990s (Hylton, 2003). For many, CRT's attraction comes from its ability to articulate and explain the lived realities of racialised and minoritised actors. Just as other theoretical standpoints enable a more accurate and honest telling of social relations from the perspective of the classed, gendered, or disempowered in other ways, CRT offers a pragmatic critical framework that facilitates different uses and approaches. This framework can be encapsulated in what I referred to as precepts, sometimes tenets, and it is to these issues that I now turn.

Critical race theory

I often describe journeys to CRT in ontological terms. CRT is a way to say 'this way ... this explains my reality ... these realities'. CRT's framework enables an articulation of issues that reflect a lived experience, a lived experience where activist scholars such as Derek Bell (1987), Patricia Williams' (1997), Gloria Ladson Billings (1997), and Charles Mills (1997) begin much of their work. From such an experiential starting point they then apply razor sharp critiques to challenge embedded racial inequalities in the law and wider society (Bell), colourblindness (Williams), racialised inequalities in education (Ladson-Billings, 'race' and white racism (Mills). Similarly, my doctoral thesis emerged out of my unease at the glass ceiling in the local authority that I was working in as an inner-city community sport development officer, and a desire for social justice and transformation. I had few black role models in my authority and felt further isolated in meetings in and out of my organisation. In conducting master's research across a number of authorities I found, scattered across other local authorities, similar stories from black officers where 'race' and racism affected their opportunities and well-being in the workplace. Yet at the same time I needed to establish what institutionalised processes framed and perhaps even caused these racial formations. At that point I began my PhD journey.

Using CRT I was able to explore issues that were being ignored or marginalised, thus enabling me to challenge orthodoxies in sport and leisure settings. The very process of asking new questions from a particular social location, identifying the power-to-knowledge dynamic, theoretical, and methodological colourblindness forced an uncomfortable framing of the academic landscape and persuasive reasons for change. Change for the academy was matched by the demystifying of ideas concerning sport for all and meritocracy in local government as equal opportunities and race equality policies failed to be implemented in practice, thus impacting minoritised participants and practitioners in terms of access, recruitment, retention, and progression (Hylton, 2003). The work had to cross exciting theoretical fields in a transdisciplinary fashion. Though not exhaustive, it included the policy sciences, sociology, community studies, ethnic and racial studies, critical whiteness studies, black feminism and gender studies, urban studies, and human resource management. Using CRT to centre 'race' meant that a transdisciplinary critique enabled a more persuasive need for research on 'race'. Here the limitations of the past were surpassed by a theoretical approach that shifted the marginalised voice of black academics and 'race' research from the margins to the centre.

My PhD and subsequent work for antiracism in the sport organisation, Kick it Out, forced me to more diligently consider the place of whiteness, white privilege, and white supremacy in sport and leisure (Hylton, 2009; Hylton and Lawrence, 2014; Long and Hylton, 2002; Long et al., 2000).

Processes privileging whiteness in local government that systematically ignore and historical inequalities and the 'snowy peaks' at senior levels became apparent in related applied research on the nature and extent of racism in grass-roots football. This ranged from the whiteness of league officials, disciplinary panels, and county officers, to racism on and off the pitch that went unpunished, often leading to the internalisation of racism by black players. For instance, some predominantly black teams would not represent themselves at disciplinary hearings because they knew that they would feel alienated: they would not see anyone who looked like themselves across the table, and therefore faced a double-jeopardy, i.e. if they defended a fine and were found guilty they would receive an additional fine. However, if they did not turn up for a disciplinary hearing the panel would deem them guilty. The perception of racial hierarchies and racialised inequalities were 'accepted' and the 'game played' accordingly to the detriment of black and minoritised players.

A concern with racism and the regular suspicion towards its nature and extent from academic, practitioner, and policy circles has led me to aim to be more specific not only about naming racism but also to recognise that it is imperative to explain the specific conditions under which particular forms of racism thrive in sport and leisure arenas. For example in *'Race' and Sport: Critical Race Theory* (Hylton, 2009: 86) I move to illustrate how racial practices are recreated while naming their specific incarnations as (1) racialisation and mediated racial identities, (2) whitecentrism, (3) the myth of difference and mimetic accuracy, and (4) the myth of assimilation and enlightened racism. Though not mutually exhaustive, my use of a CRT lens enabled an analysis able to persuasively explain how the print media reproduced racialised ideologies while naming the different techniques. Similarly a critique of the London 2012 Olympic Games through the lens of interest convergence (Hylton and Morpeth, 2012) enabled a telling of how state/white interests merged with those black and minoritised communities in East London who were overdue infrastructure improvements and employment opportunities (Gillborn, 2009; see Bell, 1980). Such observations caution against superficial approaches to sport policymaking where hubris and plain idealism alone cannot purport to address the embedded racialised inequalities in sport and wider society with a one-off event.

Conclusion

As I continue to develop ideas that use CRT and its related concepts I find it imperative to work through processes of naming, describing, and disrupting 'race', racialisation, and racism in relation to how they are experienced, for example, as microaggressions in the everyday (Burdsey, 2011; Hylton, 2010a, 2011). As a reflexive and non-dogmatic framework CRT encourages a critique of those on the political Left as much as they do on the Right. To this end I utilise microaggressions as a descriptive and explanatory technique to critique loose approaches to antiracism. The question 'Anti-What?' in the context of challenging antiracists to be clear about what they are against shores up the efficacy of their campaigns and interventions as they use thoughtful action against racism rather than the less focused knee-jerk responses we sometimes witness. Being critical of those on the Left as well as the Right strengthens our activist-scholarship, antiracist interventions, and continues the agenda to undermine racism.

I agree with Banton that in attempting to develop theoretically informed interventions one is bound to make mistakes (Banton, 2005). As we work reflexively and critically we cannot escape our subjectivities. As we make decisions to research and write we are also making inadvertent decisions to exclude subjects that could potentially be incorporated into these analyses. Yet it is this process of trying to improve explanations that 'obliges scientists to improve their conceptual armoury' (Banton, 2005: 466).

Notes

1 The UK's foremost black think-tank.
2 'Yid' is an abbreviation of the word 'Yiddish', a language used by Jews in central and Eastern Europe. The term is often used in the shortened version as a derogatory term.
3 Millwall is an area in London, in the Isle of Dogs, in the London Borough of Tower Hamlets.

References

Ackerman, N. 2014. Jose Mourinho Blasted for Racism Stance by FIFA Vice-President Jeffrey Webb. Bleacher Report. Available: http://bleacherreport.com/articles/2225671-jose-mourinho-blasted-for-racism-stance-by-fifa-vice-president-jeffrey-webb [accessed 10 October 2014].

Banton, M. 2005. Finding, and Correcting, My Mistakes. *Sociology*, 39, 463–479.

Barrabi, T. 2014. 7 Quotes From Donald Sterling's Interview with Anderson Cooper about Racism, Magic Johnson and V. Stiviano. Available: www.ibtimes.com/17-quotes-donald-sterlings-interview-anderson-cooper-about-racism-magic-johnson-v-stiviano-1583621 [accessed 8 October 2014].

Bell, D. 1980. Brown v. Board of Education and the Interest Convergence Dilemma. *Harvard Law Review*, 93, 518–533.

Bell, D. 1987. *And We Are Not Saved: The Elusive Quest for Racial Justice*. New York: Basic Books.

Birrell, S. 1989. Racial Relations Theories and Sport: Suggestions for a More Critical Analysis. *Sociology of Sport*, 6, 212–227.

Bondy, P. 2014. 10 Places where Racism is Still a Major Issue in Sports. Available: www.nydailynews.com/sports/bondy-10-places-racism-major-issue-sport-article-1.1778178 [accessed 8 October 2014].

Burdsey, D. 2011. That Joke Isn't Funny Anymore: Racial Microaggressions, Colour-Blind Ideology and the Mitigation of Racism in English Men's First-Class Cricket. *Sociology of Sport Journal*, 28, 261–283.

Crenshaw, K., Taylor, E., Gillborn, D., and Ladson-Billings, G. 2009. Foundations of Critical Race Theory in Education. London: Routledge.

Delgado, R. and Stefancic, J. 2001. *Critical Race Theory: An Introduction*. New York: New York University Press.

Dixson, A. D. and Rousseau, C. K. 2006. *Critical Race Theory in Education: All God's Children Got a Song*. New York, London: Routledge.

FRA (European Union Agency for Fundamental Rights) 2010. *Racism, Ethnic Discrimination and Exclusion of Migrants and Minorities in Sport: A Comparative Overview of the Situation in the European Union*. Vienna.

Gillborn, D. 2009. *Racism and Education: Coincidence or Conspiracy?* London: Routledge.

Gillborn, D. 2011. Once upon a Time in the UK: Race, Class, Hope and Whiteness in the Academy (Personal Reflections on the Birth of 'BritCrit'). In K. Hylton, A. Pilkington, P. Warmington, and S. Housee (eds), *Atlantic Crossings: International Dialogues on Critical Race Theory*. Birmingham: CSAP/Higher Education Academy.

Guinier, L. and Torres, G. 2003. *The Miner's Canary: Enlisting Race, Resisting Power, Transforming Democracy*. Cambridge, MA: Harvard University Press.

Homewood, B. 2014. Italian FA Chief Barred from UEFA over 'Banana' Comment. Available: http://uk.reuters.com/article/2014/10/07/uk-soccer-italy-racism-idUKK CN0HW1GM20141007 [accessed 8 October 14].

hooks, b. 1990. *Yearning: Race, Gender and Cultural Politics*. New York: South End Press.

Hylton, K. 1999. *Where are the Black Leisure Managers?* London: Institute for Leisure and Amenity Management.

Hylton, K. 2003. *Local Government, 'Race' and Sports Policy Implementation: Demystifying Equal Opportunities in Local Government*. PhD Thesis, Leeds Metropolitan University.

Hylton, K. 2005. Race, Sport and Leisure: Lessons from Critical Race Theory. *Leisure Studies*, 24, 81–98.

Hylton, K. 2008. Race Equality and Sport Networks. In M. Nicholson and R. Hoye (eds), *Sport and Social Capital*. Oxford: Elsevier.

Hylton, K. 2009. *'Race' and Sport: Critical Race Theory*. London: Routledge.

Hylton, K. 2010a. How a Turn to Critical Race Theory Can Contribute to Our Understanding of 'Race', Racism and Anti-Racism in Sport. *International Review for the Sociology of Sport*, 45, 335–334.

Hylton, K. 2010b. Social Integration through Sport. In B. Houlihan and M. Green (eds), *Routledge International Handbook of Sports Development*. London: Routledge.

Hylton, K. 2011. Too Radical? Critical Race Theory and Sport Against Racism Ireland. In J. Long and K. Spracklen (eds), *Sport and Challenges to Racism*. London: Routledge.

Hylton, K. 2012. Talk the Talk, Walk the Walk: Defining Critical Race Theory in Research. *Race, Ethnicity and Education*, 15, 23–41.

Hylton, K. 2013. 'Race', Racism and International Football. In P. Mason (ed.), *Encyclopedia of 'Race' and Racism*. Detroit: MacMillan Reference.

Hylton, K. 2014. 'Race', Racism and Football. In J. Hughson, J. MacGuire, K. Moore, and R. Spaajj (eds), *Handbook of Football Studies*. London: Routledge.

Hylton, K. 2016. This Way.... This Explains My Reality: Critical Race Theory in Sport and Leisure. In G. Cunningham, J. S. Fink, and A. Doherty (eds), *Routledge Handbook of Theory in Sport Management*. New York: Routledge.

Hylton, K. and Chakrabarty, N. 2011. Guest Editorial, Introduction: 'Race' and Culture in Tourism, Leisure and Events. *Journal of Policy Research into Tourism Leisure and Events*, 3, 105–108.

Hylton, K. and Lawrence, S. 2014. Reading Ronaldo: Contingent Whiteness in the Football Media. *Soccer and Society*, 16(5–6), 765–782.

Hylton, K. and Morpeth, N. D. 2012. London 2012: 'Race' Matters, and the East End. *International Journal of Sport Policy and Politics*, 4, 1–18.

Hylton, K., Pilkington, A., Warmington, P., and Housee, S. (eds) 2011. *Atlantic Crossings: International Dialogues on Critical Race Theory*. Birmingham: CSAP/Higher Education Academy.

Johnson, D. 2013. Tottenham Hotspur and West Ham United Supporters could be Arrested for Chanting 'Yid', Met Warns. *The Daily Telegraph*, 3 October 2013.

Ladson-Billings, G. 1997. Just What is Critical Race Theory, and What's it Doing in a Nice Field Like Education? *Qualitative Studies in Education*, 11, 7–24.

Long, J. and Hylton, K. 2002. Shades of White: An Examination of Whiteness in Sport. *Leisure Studies*, 21, 87–103.

Long, J., Hylton, K., and Spracklen, K. 2014. Whiteness, Blackness and Settlement: Leisure and the Integration of New Migrants. *Journal of Ethnic and Migration Studies*, 40(11), 1779–1797.

Long, J., Hylton, K., Welch, M., and Dart, J. 2000. *Part of the Game: An Examination of Racism in Grass Roots Football*. London: Kick it Out.

MacPherson, W. 1999. *The Stephen Lawrence Inquiry*. London: HMSO.

Mills, C. Wright 1997. *The Racial Contract*. Ithaca: Cornell University.

Omi, M. and Winant, H. 1994. *Racial Formation in the United States: From the 1960s to the 1990s*. London: Routledge.

Pilkington, A., Housee, S., and Hylton, K. (eds) 2009. *Race(ing) Forward: Transitions in Theorising 'Race' in Education*. Birmingham: CSAP/Higher Education Academy.

Runnymede Trust 1985a. *Football Violence*. Runnymede Trust Bulletin. London.

Runnymede Trust 1985b. *National Front and Football Violence*. Runnymede Trust Bulletin. London.

Runnymede Trust 1987. *Fascism and Football Violence*. Runnymede Trust Bulletin. London.

Runnymede Trust 1990. *Tebbit Cricket Loyalty Test*. Runnymede Trust Bulletin. London.

Runnymede Trust 1994. *Racism and Football*. Runnymede Trust Bulletin. London.

Scraton, S. 2001. Reconceptualising 'Race' Gender and Sport: The Contribution of Black Feminism. In B. Carrington and I. McDonald (eds), *'Race', Sport and British Society*. London: Routledge.

Spracklen, K., Long, J., and Hylton, K. 2014. Leisure Opportunities and New Migrant Communities: Challenging the Contribution of Sport. *Leisure Studies*, 40, 1779–1797.

TelegraphSport. 2013. Andre Villas-Boas Welcomes David Cameron's Support for Tottenham Fans' 'Yid' Chants. *Daily Telegraph*, 19 September 2013.

Weekes, D. and Mirza, H. S. 1997. *Black British Feminism: A Reader*. London: Routledge.

Williams, P. J. 1997. *Seeing a Colour-Blind Future: The Paradox of Race*. London: Virago Press.

Winant, H. 2001. *The World is a Ghetto: Race and Democracy since World War II*. New York: Basic Books.

Chapter 7

Sport, exercise and health

A social science perspective

Joseph Maguire

Advocating a social science perspective

The importance and relevance of a social scientific perspective on sport and physical activity becomes more pressing as a range of problems, issues and concerns merge within and impact on the sport, exercise and health worlds. This recognition was shared by Margaret Talbot throughout her career, including during her presidency of the International Council for Sport Science and Physical Education (ICSSPE), sadly cut short by her death during late 2014. For Margaret, the task was not simply to understand the relevance of social science but to use this perspective to help change the sport, exercise and health worlds. With this in mind let me outline some thoughts on this subject more generally. A social scientific perspective is needed not only as a necessary complement to natural science. In some ways this perspective is better equipped to make sense of a range of phenomena that are evident in global sport and physical cultures today. Yet, too often, a natural science explanation is used in isolation and without recourse to a social scientific analysis. This is evident in several respects: in the teaching of sport, exercise and health science students; in the views of politicians and senior official in the sports world; and in the folklore of people who seek to explain different aspects of sport, exercise and health. In contrast, social science seeks to explore what we think, how we feel, the ways we live and how we cope with the problems of interdependence with each other and the world as a whole (Maguire, 2014).

While the genesis of a social scientific perspective is a more recent development in human knowledge relative to the natural sciences, seeking to explain human behaviour, social groups and societal relations in a systematic way represents a decisive breakthrough in our understanding of ourselves. Connected, in part, to the transition to 'modern' societies, a social scientific perspective sought not only to explain this transition but also to use such knowledge to 'improve' the human condition. Such sentiments also underpin the advocacy of a human development model in sport, exercise and health sciences which is outlined below. A range of issues, problems and concerns have intensified within sport over the past three decades. Indeed, as noted, this perspective can provide a necessary corrective to mythologies, political ideologies and wishful thinking held by a range of people, politicians and practitioners. In particular, a social scientific perspective better equips us to explain:

1 the function and meaning of sport and exercise in the lives of people, the identities they form and the communities they create together;
2 the role sport and exercise does and could play in dealing with societal and global problems, issues and concerns and the resources consumed;
3 the need to address issues of local and global questions of inequality, power, governance, democracy, transparency and accountability in sport and society more broadly.

To equip us in this way involves not simply a knowledge of social science but also the development of an intellectual approach that emphasises certain qualities in the teaching and research agenda of sport, exercise and health sciences. Sadly, some of those in authority are content to pursue research income, academic rankings and 'impact' in terms of improving performance or the hosting of 'events' – mega or otherwise. In contrast, the approach taken here takes a different tack. That is, we need to re-orientate our thinking away from a model that emphasises an uncritical appreciation of performance efficiency, a bioscience understanding of health and physical activity and the promotion of the sports medical industrial complex (SMIC), and instead focuses on the potential of a model that highlights human development. Let me explain further.

Different disciplines have become established features of, or outsiders in, the development of sport, exercise and health sciences. Biomechanics and exercise physiology remain part of the established group within this sub-discipline. The social science of sport has been at the margins since the development of the subject. In one sense, this was a deliberate step by natural scientists. In the shift from physical education, the quest for respectability lay in adhering to a specific view of science and statistical accuracy. In this way, sports medicine advocates and sport and exercise scientists hoped they would be more likely to be accepted by more established scientists in the academy. One consequence of this is that the philosophy of sport and the history of physical education have been actively marginalised in the development of this subject area. Increasingly, pedagogy is under threat and thus the case for a social science of sport has to be remade anew. Yet, it too, at least in the form of critical social science, is also under threat. Those advocates of the SMIC can but see the merit of an applied sport management concerned with marketing, branding and hosting mega-events.

What counts in sport, exercise and health sciences also relates to what matters in terms of the 'sports ethic' – this reinforces the marginalisation of the social sciences. The sports ethic reflects the actual practice of sport. Also, the practices of sports science teaching and research are embedded in these assumptions. Several features of the sports ethic can be identified (Coakley, 2003). These include: a willingness to make sacrifices; a striving for distinction; an acceptance of risk and the possibility/probability of participating while enduring pain; and a tacit acceptance that there is no limit to the pursuit of the ultimate performance. The practice of this sports ethic is learnt early on and becomes normalised and taken-for-granted – it is part of the body of the performer and the agenda of the teacher and researcher.

Social scientists have documented the logical consequences of this sports ethic – cheating, drug abuse and disorderly eating. The debate on drugs and sport indicates that the binary dichotomies between what counts as natural and synthetic, diet supplementation and drug-taking, and restorative and enhancing treatments, are difficult to maintain. The next frontier in achievement sport is genetic engineering. Such features of global sport are reinforced by and reflected in the assumptions and practices of the SMIC. This complex has several dimensions – structural, institutional, ideological and cultural. It is composed of several key groups, including state agencies, transnational corporations, non-governmental agencies and sport associations. The institutional framework of this complex involves at least four main elements: sports medicine, sports science, sports science support programmes and regional/national centres of excellence. The emergence of this complex – initially in those Western/developed nations less restricted by the legacy of a play and player – orientated amateur attitude to sporting success – is not surprising. Keen to compete on a global stage, governments fund research and departments with a focus on talent identification, production and performance – with advocates of coaching science, sports science and sports medicine recruited to help deliver 'success'.

As a result of these broader processes sports and exercise scientists gear their research and teaching towards a performance efficiency model. Exercise physiologists examine the most advantageous biological conditions necessary to train and compete effectively and biomechanists trace the most rational way specific forces and angles can be utilised for the demands of competitive tasks. These natural scientists have been joined by sports medicine experts and geneticists who seek to divide the human population into specific categories, and/or contribute to the early stages of the gene transfer revolution that is unfolding. And, as sports and exercise sciences have grown in depth and range, nutrition and related sports medicine specialists sell their skills, thereby reinforcing the performance efficiency model or a bioscience interpretation of health and well-being. If, however, advocates of sport, exercise and health sciences are serious about contributing to development through sport, and not just development of sport, what must change?

Social science and a human development model in sport, exercise and health sciences

The performance efficiency and bioscience model found in the SMIC demands a mode of academic practice: the intellectual becomes a technocrat. This technocratic intellectual thinks and speaks in performance terms, and reflects the concerns of the SMIC and the bioscience health nexus. This type of logic was vividly captured by C. Wright Mills (1959) who wrote about the hierarchies of state, corporation and army (the military-industrial complex). Arguably, there are clear echoes of such themes in the development of sports, exercise and health sciences, sports science support programmes and the establishment of centres of excellence. Academic practice is guided and shaped by a technological discourse which focuses attention on talent identification, optimal training regimes, masking agents, goal-setting, attention styles and health regimes. Yet, not all natural scientists embrace this focus; the humanistic intellectual still survives in the study of physical culture. The humanist tradition was once an integral part of physical education and found expression in areas such as history, philosophy and pedagogy: at its best it was concerned with themes and issues such as morality, equity, participation, learning, cooperation and the intrinsic properties of play and games. Like folk body cultures, however, humanists, at least in the context of sport, exercise and health science departments, are in danger of becoming extinct.

A reconfiguration of sports, exercise and health sciences would not only liberate the natural scientist from this technocratic model, but would also promote the mission of the humanistic intellectual. This approach would counter the continuing drift towards a restrictive scientisation of physical education discourses and the consolidation of technocratic physical education. The alternative proposed here is underpinned by a belief that science has the potential to be a mode of enlightenment and emancipation – but that left in the hands of the power elite of the SMIC and the bioscience health nexus, this potential will be diminished. As presently configured, sport, exercise and health sciences thus takes rather than makes the problems it examines. That is, academics should exercise greater autonomy in the selection of what constitutes a problem, how this problem can be interpreted and explained and what 'solutions' can be offered. Failure to do so stems from being too closely tied to the here and now and from seeking to provide solutions to short-term performance-based problems. 'Short-termism' and pandering to vested interests lead potentially to the critical and sceptical character of sports science to be lost. Teaching is no longer a 'subversive' activity. Questions of power become neglected. Not challenging the trend towards short-termism in departments, universities and associations involves its own specific danger, namely that of a further acceleration in the decline of those aspects of physical education, sport, exercise and health promoted by the humanities and social sciences. Sports and exercise scientists risk being seen both as technicians involved in the production of high performance and becoming the mouthpiece of the SMIC and the bioscience health complex. The generation of fundamental knowledge that would potentially be of benefit to humanity is thus neglected, and the grounds on which scientists can research the sporting status quo is reduced to their contributions to performance efficiency, the medal count and activity rates.

The impact of this trend is not only evident in the allocation of research funds and academic posts, and, indeed, the orientation of university departments. Students quickly grasp whose knowledge counts, and how such knowledge is to be used. As Ingham and Lawson remarked, students 'learn that technical, market-driven science and professionalism [TMSP] ... is more advanced and esteemed than social-trustee, civic science and professionalism' (1999: np). Here, then, there are questions regarding the scale and sources of funding for teaching and research, curriculum design and development, and the status and esteem given to different forms of knowledge and modes of communication within the sport, exercise and health sciences. Reviewing global sport, exercise and health sciences it is clear that technical, market-driven science professionalism holds sway and this tendency may be increasing. Natural scientists command attention, attract the funds, claim the key academic positions and set the teaching and research agenda.

There is, however, an alternative. For Ingham and Lawson, the social-trustee, civic science and professionalism approach requires that sport, exercise and health scientists and professionals should 'integrate their formal roles with that of their own citizenship' (1999: np) We have to become sensitive to the production, dissemination, curriculum development and application of the knowledge we provide. The same issues apply whether we are providing knowledge for students, athletes, coaches, administrators, the media or governmental agencies. A series of questions have to be addressed by sport, exercise and health science practitioners including: How wasteful is the present system? Who are the winners and the losers in global sport – both on and off the field of play, at different levels of sport and in different modes of movement culture? What are the costs, as well as the health benefits to the system being constructed – for the individual, the community and the society as a whole?

The shift to a human development model would not only provide emancipatory knowledge for sport communities and societies as a whole, it would also release the sport, exercise and health sciences community from the tentacles of achievement sport. Thus, 'involved advocacy' of a human development model – with its emphasis on justice, citizenship and equity is required. Social-trustee, civic science professionals must act 'as stewards of the just society' and act to 'protect and support free spheres of action and public social spaces' (Ingham and Lawson, 1999: np) These observations need to be extended and linked to a consideration of environmental concerns, green issues and the development of notions of sustainable sport. In so doing, sport, exercise and health scientists would be engaging in forms of 'committed service' similar to those in which some physical educationists used traditionally to be involved. That would have real impact.

How best, then, to nurture such sentiments and practices? How can we build coalitions of advocates for such an approach within sport, exercise and health sciences? Ironically, perhaps, in mainstream natural science there is a tendency to recognise the complexity of the problems under investigation and to appreciate the value of a multidisciplinary approach that draws on the natural and social sciences and the humanities. In the context of sport and physical activity questions of injury, pain, violence and drugs could also benefit from such an approach. One step forward in this regard would be to ask whose body culture counts? Modern achievement sport can continue to be promoted in our universities and schools as the dominant, exclusive form of body culture. Sports education replaces physical education, coaches replace teachers, and talent identification schemes channel young people's early experiences of movement along narrow, prescribed lines. Alternatively, sport, exercise and health sciences degree programmes underpinned by a model of human development can be formulated. Diversity can be promoted and the richness of different body cultures recognized. Through the development of sustainable sport and the teaching of environmental ethics, a sense of stewardship of both habitat and habitus could be encouraged. These changes would be one part of the attempt to move global sport in the direction of being more democratic, with its decision-making more transparent and its decision-makers more accountable. Natural and social scientists of sport can, if they choose, serve a humanistic role and thus contribute to development through sport – or they can continue to serve the SMIC and bioscience health complex.

My hope is that organizations such as ICSSPE open up the intellectual space for natural and social scientists to discuss and debate and to come together in a teaching and research agenda that focuses on how the subject area can help development of and through sport and physical cultures. The world of sport, locally, nationally and globally, seems both beset by a range of problems, dilemmas and concerns, yet also contain within its subcultures people and practices that enhance our lived experiences and the communities we form. Betting scandals, the use of drugs, unethical behaviour, violence and discrimination along class, gender, ethnic and disability lines are but some of the more negative features of contemporary sports worlds. In addition, power and control of such worlds and subcultures is exercised in unaccountable, opaque and undemocratic ways. Does this state of play reflect a broader societal context or are there aspects of sporting subcultures that give rise to or exacerbate these social issues and concerns? For social scientists the answer lies in probing the specific context – the evidence suggests that sport does not just reflect society but that, in certain respects, its subcultures can compound wider dilemmas and concerns.

The benefits of a social science perspective on the challenges facing and prospects for sport worlds become clear. Several strands stand out. First, it is important to remember that things are not what they seem. Common-sense assumptions regarding the role, function, meaning and impact of sport are not a sound basis on which to assess its social worth – to individuals and the communities they form. Social scientists seek to establish how things really are rather than rely on the explanations offered by those in positions of power. Thus, they 'debunk', challenge and critique and use their knowledge to question the status quo. Second, social scientific knowledge reveals how complex, contradictory and unpredictable aspects of sport and the sport experience actually are – there is no magic bullet to explain elite performance or instant use of sport to solve social ills. There are no simple answers or solutions – yet, what we can sometimes do is to suggest what not to do as much as what we could or should do.

Third, the social scientific knowledge should enhance and empower – develop a healthy scepticism towards the claims made by such groups as politicians, sport officials and media personnel regarding the impact of sport on individuals and communities but also engage social groups in seeking social change and making sport a better place and space. Social scientists may differ in their disciplinary approach and methods adopted but they all share an assumption which can be expressed succinctly as 'show me the evidence' – rather than policy-led evidence. A sensitivity to change and continuity over time and across space, in the realms of individual perceptions, thoughts and feelings, and in cultural, economic and political activity, requires social scientists of sport to hold those who make claims about the role and meaning of sport to account. It is not sufficient, however, to debunk and critique – vital though that is. In addition, it is also necessary to map out the sort of sport worlds that are possible and desirable. Hence, reference was made to the notion of sport and human development. We have to become sensitive to the production, dissemination, curriculum development and application of the knowledge we provide. Social scientists enable us to ask crucial questions such as: How wasteful is the present system? Who are the winners and the losers in global sport – both on and off the field of play, at different levels of sport and in different modes of movement culture? What are the costs, as well as the health benefits to the system being constructed – for the individual, the community and the society as a whole? In addition, a social scientific perspective keeps open the possibility of developing the 'social-trustee, civic science and professionalism' discussed in the introduction.

Over 50 years of research indicates that social scientists have ably captured the 'known knowns' and indicated the 'unknown knowns' of their areas as they relate to sport, health and physical activity. But there are also 'unknown unknowns' about the sport, exercise and heath nexus – things we have yet to think about and where we have to think outside of the box. Social science helps us do this and the advocacy of a human development model arguably enhances this possibility. It provides us with a different way to see the use and study of sport. Social science thus equips us with the thinking tools to help us in this process. In doing so, one needs to be ever mindful of not only what knowledge we generate but for whom and what for. The adoption of a human development model of the kind previously outlined is not easy. For students it can be uncomfortable as it asks us, as noted, to recognise that things are not what they seem but also that our own beliefs and assumptions are open to scrutiny. In addition, those social scientists who teach students in departments of Physical Education, Exercise and Health Sciences know only too well that the subject area is increasingly being (re-)embedded within the SMIC. That is, governments across the globe want such departments to produce bioscientific knowledge that aids in the development of elite sport performance and 'solves' the health problems of individuals. In this scenario social scientists are considered 'useful' in the production and transference of knowledge regarding the gaining/hosting and social use of mega-events. Students quickly learn whose knowledge counts in sport in general and in such departments in particular – you have to have impact.

Yet, the problems, challenges and dilemmas facing sport worlds cannot be addressed solely from a bioscientific perspective. Indeed, in certain respects such knowledge is part of the problem not the solution. In other respects bioscience is just ill-equipped to deal with questions of ethics, perception, identity, community, politics and economics. Our challenge is to use the knowledge of social science to make a difference, to building sport, exercise and health worlds that are less wasteful of lives and resources – where a healthy habitus can be expressed and a living habitat thrive. In this way, communities and nations could utilise sport to create mutual understanding and respect – of different body cultures and traditions. Failure to do so will ensure we continue along the trajectory we are already on. Social scientific knowledge shows us that this trajectory reflects past and present actions – but it also reminds us that it does not have to be this way. And, as Margaret Talbot's words and actions embodied, the future is still to be made, that alternatives exist, and that we can use a social scientific perspective to equip ourselves to map out a better sporting future.

References

Coakley, J. (2003). *Sport in Society*, 8th edn. Boston, MA: McGraw Hill.

Ingham, A. and Lawson, H. (1999). *Prolympism and Globalization: Knowledge for Whom, by Whom?* Paper presented at 14th Conference of the German Association of Sport Science, Heidelberg, 27–29 September.

Maguire, J. (ed.) (2014). *Social Sciences in Sport*. Champaign, IL: Human Kinetics.

Mills, Wright C. (1959). *The Power Elite*. Oxford: Penguin.

Chapter 8

Walk the talk?

How the EU and the UN contribute to the development of holistic sport policies

Jonas Burgheim, Karen Petry and Ben Weinberg

Introduction

Sport has a reputation for being the stepchild of politics. Leaders and decision-makers have traditionally tended to neglect sport in their political agendas, while prioritising other economic, social and cultural goals. Apart from few exceptions sport has mostly been of governmental interest in the context of hosting events, winning medals and building national identities.

In recent years governmental actors have however come to realise that sport and physical activity carry a large potential. The political talk has changed correspondingly, more and more taking into consideration the crosscutting character of sport and physical activity. Politicians now frequently refer to societal benefits related to sport such as health enhancement, mental well-being, economic and social development as well as inclusion and integration. It is nonetheless questionable as to how far the increased mentioning of such assumed benefits can be considered a serious attempt to address and assess sport and physical activity comprehensively in their specificity as multi-layered themes that encompass various actors and policy areas.

The aim of this chapter is to explore how the European Union and the United Nations have contributed to advocating holistic policies and thereby to 'walking the talk'. This includes an analysis of objectives, recent policy initiatives and developments. It is argued that supra- and intergovernmental initiatives offer potential for instigating comprehensive sport policy approaches which relate to and are based on a (sport) governance system including all relevant stakeholders.

The chapter comprises a section portraying the relationship between sport and politics from a theoretical perspective including a description of how sport can be located within concepts concerned with international relations, European integration, regionalisation and governance. It continues with a section offering an overview of the development of the sport policy of the European Union including its legal framework, the institutional structure and in particular current themes and priorities. This is followed by an analysis of sport policy as developed within the United Nations system, including by the United Nations Educational, Scientific and Cultural Organization (UNESCO) and the UN Office on Sport for Development and Peace (UNOSDP) and the activities of the Human Rights Council (HRC) related to sport. Finally, the chapter ends with conclusions regarding the approaches of both the European Union and the United Nations and their potential implications for the evolution of sport policies in the future.

Sport and politics: a special relationship?

Actors involved in the organisation and implementation of sport often consider it to be politically neutral. Others meanwhile emphasise and utilise its potential with regard to fostering social integration, inclusion and community building. It is this spectrum in which it can be a challenge to maintain a differentiated view on the relationship between sport and politics. But such an interconnection does in fact exist and it is characterised by being multi-layered and multi-dimensional (Woyke and Delschen, 2006).

Two basic streams on how to assess sport and politics have emerged in research, each employing a different definition of politics. The first understands politics as being driven by governmental actors and thus concentrates on respective decision-making processes and policy outputs such as the regulation or prohibition of certain types of sport, sport as training for war, sport as vehicle for social integration, sport and national identity, the support of elite sport as means of enhancing national self-images, sport as economic motor or sport as diplomatic tool (Houlihan, 1997, 2003, 2006).

The second stream employs a more pluralist understanding and thus views politics as being shaped by governmental, non-governmental and economic actors alike (Hödl, 2002; Sage, 2006). In fact it assumes a decreasing significance of the role governements play and refers to the extent to which civil society has its say, considering that sport organisations are mostly non-governmental actors formally belonging to the third sector. For analytical purposes it also draws upon categories such as class, ethnicity and gender and looks at how societal discourses are produced and enforced (Fozooni, 2004; Hargreaves, 1994; Hayhurst, 2009; Hong and Mangan, 2003; Majumdar and Bandyopadhyay, 2005).

Güldenpfennig (1981: 24–25) has advocated differentiating between sport as an activity system (*Tätigkeitssystem*) and an institutional system. In this interpretation the former relates to the actual physical activity, which accords to certain rules and does regularly not have any political connotation, while the latter comprises all social providers of sport, its organisations as well as relations with other actors from politics and society. Sport in this sense can be viewed as political because these institutional activities imply aspects of power and influence and require expressing and exercising interests towards or together with governmental actors (Lösche, 2010: 13). A strong involvement of sport organisations with governmental and economic actors has pointed towards this interpretation.

In fact the international sport policy arena includes interactions between various governmental and non-governmental actors in a multi-level system, accompanied by debates on interdependence, regulation and arguments pointing to a specificity or autonomy of sport. In the context of identifying relevant research foci, Houlihan (2009) has thus emphasised studying not only the governmental dimension of sport, but also 'the role of trans-national government organisations such as the EU [...], and NGOs, such as the International Olympic Committee and the major international federations, in relation, for example, to the regulation and development of sport'.

EU integration and regionalisation theories offer useful perspectives on different kinds of political and institutional models and thus assist in theorising the complexity of local, national and international sport politics and policies. Theories of Europeanisation have been adopted and reflected upon in sport studies in relation, for instance, to football (Brown, 2000; Garcia, 2007; Martin, 2005; Niemann et al., 2011), as well as from a legal perspective with regard to the implications of the EU contracts and treaties also on football (Parrish, 2003). Mittag (2007) has elaborated on the reactions and adjustment processes of national actors. In this context Europeanisation approaches have also been applied to restructuring processes taking place in the media, communication and event sectors (Mittag and Legrand, 2010).

Recent studies and publications strongly point to notions of European, global and multi-level governance (Amara et al., 2005; Ducrey et al., 2003; Hassan and Hamil, 2010; Holt, 2009; Ronge, 2006). Being regarded less as middle-range theories but rather as theoretical concepts, both employ an actor-oriented perspective on the roles of governmental and especially non-governmental actors assuming that regulatory competences and decision-making processes have increasingly shifted towards levels of negotiation and bargaining including a relative restriction of the traditional status of governments and states (Mayntz, 2009). As has been pointed out by Hindley (2002: 3), however, 'the elasticity of the governance concept can cause confusion and make it difficult to define precisely'. Therefore its applications can remain somewhat indistinct at times and require further differentiation (Grix, 2010). However, the fact that this concept offers a wide perspective enhances the possibility to pool various theoretical streams into coherent research on sport politics and policies (Steinbach, 2006).

The European Union and sport

Before the Lisbon Treaty was agreed upon and ratified, the European Union's primary legal framework did not include a specific basis for policy activity in the field of sport. Instead other policy areas such as economic collaboration for the single market, competition rules, health or anti-doping measures affected the sport sector indirectly. In particular European jurisdiction in form of decisions made by the European Court of Justice (ECJ) left a mark on the development of sport in Europe. With the cases Walrave-Koch (1974), Bosman (1995) and Lehtonen (2000) amongst others, the ECJ established its position that EU law also covers professional sport once the latter constitutes an economic activity (Tokarski *et al.*, 2009: 137–145).

At the political level meanwhile various parliamentary initiatives such as the Larive Report (1988) and the Pack Report (1997) were put forward and addressed the specificity of sport, namely its social and organisational dimensions, including considerations on the autonomy of the sport system. Influenced by efforts of sport organisations, non-governmental organisations and some governmental actors, sport and its educational, cultural and health enhancing potentials were explicitly mentioned in a protocol note in the Treaty of Amsterdam in 1997, albeit without a binding character. The Helsinki Report complemented this development in 1999 and advised the EU Commission to acknowledge the social dimension of sport and promote the integration of all forms of physical activity into member states' education systems, while stressing that the EU does not have any direct competence with regard to sport at national level. A year later the Nice Declaration was signed which again emphasised the social and cultural dimension of sport and addressed the need for fostering these at national and European levels, while reiterating that this would not imply any EU legal authority (Mittag, 2010: 103–105).

In 2007 the European Commission published its White Paper on Sport, which contained extensive proposals for policy-making and implementation as well as references to the importance of increasing the significance of sport in EU policy in general, not least because of its crosscutting character just like its social and economic value. Divided into three sections covering, first, the social role of sports, second, the economic dimension of sport, and third, the organisation of sport, the paper was linked with the Commission's Pierre de Coubertin Action Plan, which provided a list of 53 concrete policy measures, including for instance the development of EU Physical Activity Guidelines, the fight against and prevention of racism in sport and the organisation of an annual European Sport Forum involving a broad range of stakeholders. The White Paper was perceived as and still constitutes a landmark in EU sport policy for it is the first major document including strategies and measures for the further development of policies related to sport (European Commission, 2007; Tokarski *et al.*, 2009: 66–68).

After the unsuccessful attempt had been made to pass and ratify a new EU constitutional treaty, the European Council eventually decided to modify the existing contracts governing the Communities and their policy areas. The amended version, commonly known as the Lisbon Treaty, became effective in 2009 and, for the first time in EU history, its primary law thereby included an article specifically on sport. Article 165 is based on prior sport-related EU outputs and stipulates 'the specific nature of sport, its structures based on voluntary activity and its social and educational function'. An EU obligation to contribute to the development of 'the European dimension in sport' arises from this. The article further stipulates that the EU is to foster fair competitions, the cooperation between sport organisations and the integrity of athletes. At the same time, it reinforces the authority of EU member states with regard to direct specific contents and policies, meaning that under consideration of the principle of subsidiarity the EU cannot harmonise the laws of the member states in the field of sport but shall undertake complementary, coordinative or supportive measures.

The first outputs under application of the Lisbon Treaty comprise a Commission's Communication on Developing the European Dimension in Sport and a Working Plan 2011–2014 put forward by the Council. The Communication describes how a European dimension can be implemented and thus complements the contents of the White Book and the Pierre de Coubertin Action Plan with more concrete indication of the potential EU policy ambition. The Work Plan defines the strategic and thematic priorities of the Council, including specific objectives such as promoting sustainable development in and through sport, sustainable financing of sport and integrity of sporting competitions (Council of the European Union, 2011; European Commission, 2011).

In terms of institutional structures and arrangements, the EU Commission has been a key player. Previous initiatives such as the White Paper and the fact that article 165 provides a legal basis to initiate recommendations and funding schemes as well as to prepare policy-making and to control implementation measures make explicit the Commission's status. Through application of the Lisbon Treaty the EU Council has most significantly gained in relevance, for it henceforth is to provide an intergovernmental forum for the sport ministers from EU member states to be convened twice a year. Forum results can come in form of recommendations and support mechanisms for the effective development and implementation of EU policy steps. Support schemes require approval by the European Parliament in its controlling function. The Council's work is supported by the Working Party on Sport, which consists of high-rank civil servants and meets several times a year in order to prepare the ministers' meetings (European Union, 2007; EOC EU Office, 2011: 10–22).

In May 2014, the EU Council adopted the European Union Work Plan for Sport 2014–2017, which comes in line with its previous activities.[1] It is therein reaffirmed that there is a need to continue the cooperation on sport in the EU context and to work closely with the sport movement as well as relevant organisations at national, European and international level, such as the Council of Europe or the World Anti-Doping Agency (WADA) and others. The Work Plan is inter alia built around the principles of aiming at an evidence-based sport policy, reflecting the need for mainstreaming sport into other EU policies and contributing to the Europe 2020 Strategy. A specific funding line was also established within the ERASMUS+ programme in complementarity with the other EU relevant sources of funding for education, youth and sport.

The Work Plan provides a long list of identified key topics, such as anti-doping, protection and safeguarding of minors, gender equality, economic benefits of sport, legacy of major sport events just like education, training, employment and volunteering. On the latter theme, for example, the following outputs are included:

- exchange of best practices and report on the status concerning the inclusion of sport qualifications in National Qualification Frameworks (NQFs) with a reference to the European Qualification Framework (EQF);
- preparation of recommendations on the contribution of sport to the employability of young people and the creation of jobs in the sport and sport related labour market;
- preparation of a report on the status concerning the implementation of the EU Guidelines on Dual Careers.

In light of the Work Plan, five "Expert Groups" have been launched, with members appointed by EU member states for the following areas: match fixing, good governance, economic dimension, health enhancing physical activities (HEPA) and human resources development. It is envisaged to ensure a high level of representativeness from the member states as well as to promote exchange of views within the groups. Participation is voluntary and the member states are to nominate qualified individuals as members, who take part in the meetings. Each expert group can then decide to add other participants and/or to allow other interested stakeholders to take part as observers. Meetings of the expert groups take place twice a year and each expert group nominates its chair/co-chair in the first meeting for them to prepare and coordinate the further deliberation process with support from the European Commission. By the end of 2016, EU member states should present a report about the implementation of the respective activities. This report will form the basis for the preparation of the future EU Work Plan in 2017.

Adding to this form of participation, the Council has organised a structured dialogue with important governmental and non-governmental actors, while the Commission has installed an annual EU Sport Forum as a further means of engaging with the relevant stakeholders (EOC EU Office, 2011: 10–22). During the EU Sport Forum, which took place in December 2014 in Milan, calls for proposals from the ERASMUS+ Sport programme 2014 and 2015 were discussed and information about selection criteria as well as requirements and financial aspects were disseminated. The Forum is a meeting place for all stakeholders in the area of sport and EU and it is one of the major communication events organised by the European Commission for this field. It thereby relates to the so-called structured dialogue between the EU and sport organisations.[2]

Further activities related to the structured dialogue are theme-specific conferences, the launch of different studies as well as the 'European Week of Sport', the first instance of which will take place in September 2015. The five pillars of the sport-themed week are: focus days, one major event as well as national events in the member states, the selection of a team of EU sports ambassadors and the appointment of European partner sport organisations such as the European Olympic Committees (EOC), European Non-Governmental Sports Organisation (ENGSO), Union of European Football Associations (UEFA), Special Olympics, International Sport and Culture Association (ISCA) and The Association For International Sport for All (TAFISA).

The above-mentioned developments indicate, first, that sport has been affected by other policy areas before having been explicitly addressed through article 165, which henceforth provides better grounds for funding schemes and specific policy initiatives. This has found a concrete manifestation in the specific budget line attributed to sport as part of the 2014–2020 EU financial framework. Second, they show that the European Union pursues a pluralist approach comprising diverse stakeholders and providing platforms and instruments for exchange (including memoranda of understanding), which signifies the multi-dimensionality of sport in the European political context.

The United Nations and sport

Sport has played an increasingly prominent role within the United Nations (UN) system for decades. The interrelations between the organisation's principal activities and priorities on the one hand and sport on the other seem to have become particularly close since the beginning of the new millennium and throughout recent years. Third-party stakeholders have developed to be more and more involved and relevant in this context. Some organisational structures have been established to address the sport theme specifically. In the UN system as a whole, sport, despite the worldwide popularity of its particular *Tätigkeitssystem* (Güldenpfennig, 1981: 24–25), remains a rather exotic field and niche. Nevertheless, activities in this area are not an exclusive prerogative of the entities mainly described in the following paragraphs. They are rather multi-dimensional as they extend to and are conducted by numerous UN agencies, funds and programmes in diverse ways and with varied goals.

With the International Charter on Physical Education and Sport, member states of the United Nations Educational, Scientific and Cultural Organization (UNESCO) agreed on and adopted a corner-stone of international relations and sport in 1978.[3] In its article 1, access to physical education is described as a 'fundamental right for all'. This characterisation has been a reference point for many considerations in sport and international relations throughout the years. UNESCO further provides the institutional framework in which the International Convention against Doping in Sport[4] has been established, administered and governed.

With the Intergovernmental Committee for Physical Education and Sport (CIGEPS), the organisation can rely on a formally elected subject-specific group of expert representatives from 18 of its member states. In engaging government and sports organisations' representatives, commissioning research and addressing policy themes in the field of physical education and sport, the group offers a forum for concrete subject-specific government deliberations and activities. Together with the International Conference of Ministers and Senior Officials Responsible for Physical Education and Sport (MINEPS),[5] it forms an important pillar in the implementation of government ambitions and decisions guided by MINEPS recommendations. With member state representatives at its core, the structure of CIGEPS is only complete with its Permanent Consultative Council (PCC). This PCC constitutes a standing mechanism of stakeholder involvement. Members of PCC comprise other UN agencies, funds and programmes as well as sport organisations, including the International Olympic Committee (IOC), International Paralympic Committee (IPC), International Federation of Association Football (FIFA) and International Association of Athletics Federations (IAAF), as well as experts from research, civil society, the media and the field of sport at large (WADA amongst others). It can, therefore, be considered an example in practice of the description by Mayntz of an increasingly modern negotiation-based policy development approach with a vertically open and diversified structure.

In light of a growing professionalisation, the UN eventually embarked on the pursuit of a more active general inclusion of sport in its activities. In 2001 the organisation's Secretary-General (1996 to 2006), Kofi Annan, for the first time called on and appointed a Special Adviser on Sport for Development and Peace. Wilfried Lemke, a politician and former general manager in professional football from Germany, has held the position since 2008 until today. The Special Adviser and Under-Secretary-General is supported by the UN Office on Sport for Development and Peace (UNOSDP). This office forms a part of the UN Secretariat and has come to be the exclusively specialised office in this field within UN providing content contributions for relevant processes, representatives and agencies, funds and programmes of the organisation. UNOSDP serves as a gateway between actors from the UN system and stakeholders from sport or sport-related fields. It has witnessed and been involved in an evolution of the member state-driven policy activities within the designated principle organs and bodies of the organisation. It also hosts the Secretariat of the Sport for Development and Peace International Working Group (SDP IWG), a policy deliberation forum for interested UN member states. A central role in policy development processes is that of the UN General Assembly (GA). The GA has expressed and recognised the relevance of sport as a tool for the common work of member states towards overriding organisational goals such as development and peace in international legally binding instruments, as well as in an array of its political resolutions.[6] The structural review of a string of more recent resolutions and political statements can serve as a good yardstick for the attention sport has been accorded as part of the work of the GA as well as by other UN organs and bodies.

'Sport as a means to promote education, health, development and peace' is the established title of a biennial resolution at the core of a thematic evolution in this field. The resolutions principally constitute a reinforcement of the organisation's activities, as particularly pursued by UNOSDP. They have become a regular political manifestation of the relevance that member states accord to the utilisation of sport for the attainment of UN development goals in particular and they regularly include an encouragement for continued coordinated activity in this area. In form of GA resolution 69/6 the latest one of them was adopted on 31 October 2014.

In another and complementary string of resolutions, the GA biennially calls upon all member states to observe an 'Olympic Truce' at the time of the Olympic and Paralympic Games. This type of resolution is regularly entitled 'Building a peaceful and better world through sport and the Olympic ideal'. The latest version of these specific documents was adopted by member states on 6 November 2013. Such resolutions constitute a general political yardstick outlining member state positions. Resolutions in relatively non-controversial fields are regularly adopted without a vote, as has also been the case for the recent resolutions cited above. Requests for action towards other UN organs, frequently the Secretariat, form a regular part of GA resolutions. The regular reports provided by the Secretary-General on sport for development and peace activities accordingly find their origin in the documents.[7]

A tendency for a growing inclusiveness in international government considerations has been notable in sport for development and peace and sport policy fields for a number of years. The IOC and IPC have particularly been regarded and referred to as two important stakeholders from the field of sport. For the IOC this has become manifest through another GA resolution, which accorded it a particular role: on 19 October 2009 the IOC was invited by member states 'to participate in the sessions and the work of the GA in the capacity of observer'.[8] This observer status for the IOC was granted by the GA in 'wishing to promote cooperation between the UN and the IOC'. The IOC was thereby formally recognised by UN member states, which identified a good level of coherence between the Olympic Charter and general UN goals and values.

A more recent development towards the observation of sport themes can be observed for the other UN body in which resolutions are regularly negotiated and adopted by member states, the Human Rights Council (HRC). Established and mandated by the GA in 2006, the HRC is comprised of 47 of the total of 193 UN member states at a time. Throughout recent years, there has been a noteworthy increase in HRC activities, considerations and documents related to the topic of sport and human rights. Initially focusing on specific human rights questions like adequate housing[9] or racism and xenophobia,[10] the HRC has more recently addressed sport and human rights as a theme with more general implications. This is not to say, of course, that the previously addressed specific aspects were no longer of relevance or no longer considered in the central UN human rights body.[11]

During the 27th HRC session, HRC resolution 27/8 was adopted by member states which asked for its Advisory Committee to finalise and to present a 'study on the possibilities of using sport and the Olympic ideal to promote human rights for all and to strengthen universal respect for them' at the 30th HRC session in September 2015. Member states and other relevant stakeholders have been asked to contribute to this study. A progress report about the drafting process and the contributions already received by the Advisory Committee was presented in August 2014.[12] Further sport-related documents by the HRC came in the form of a joint cross-regional statement on Sport and Human Rights and a cross-regional statement on Mega [Sport] Events delivered by member states on 23 March 2015. Both statements reaffirm and address the role and responsibility of sport and its stakeholders in a human rights context.[13]

While a pattern similar to the development of resolutions in the GA is not recognisable for the HRC (yet), sport as addressed in its framework can be looked at as an example for the structure and evolution of UN policy work: policy work is mainly (still) a government domain in international organisations' processes. Third-party and non-nation state actors are not designated decision-makers, but see an increasing inclusion in political deliberations also in international relations and sport. UN policy in the field of sport has long been in existence; a particular evolution and more specific initiatives have been noteworthy since the beginning of the new millennium, also linked to the organisation's Millennium Development Goals. A next step in this evolution can be expected for the period and structures to go along with the Sustainable Development Goals to be adopted in autumn 2015. An impact on policy developments within the organisation is to be assumed; the specific field of sport will also be affected by this.

Walk the talk: EU and UN initiatives as roadmap?

Sport in a political context is characterised by a multi-dimensionality that finds expression in a diverse array of actors and related themes. It is, by comparison, not a traditional policy area, which is clearly defined in terms of competences and contents both at national and international levels. While its crosscutting character has impeded coherent approaches, it does provide potential to employ an innovative, holistic and inclusive perspective on policy-making and developments. In this sense, the aim of this chapter was to explore how, on the one hand, a regional international organisation such as the EU, historically based on the idea of creating a common market and, on other hand, a global international organisation like the UN, originally set up to create and maintain peace, have dealt with sport and physical activity in their respective policy work and initiatives.

In order to conclude how the European Union and the United Nations have contributed to advocating holistic policies and walking the talk, it can easily be stated that both have strengthened their approach related to sport and physical activity throughout the last ten years. The analysis and descriptions of EU and UN sport policies indicate a wide range of different activities and show a strong potential for comprehensive sport policy approaches based on a sport governance system including all relevant stakeholders, with member states in the decisive role.

The Lisbon Treaty provides the EU with a legal basis to refer to and allocate funds in the area of sport, but the direct, firmly established policy options remain relatively restricted. While the latter applies also to the UN, a specific budget line for sport does not exist within its structures; the respective dedicated work is even partly conducted with funds to be raised for this purpose specifically in an extra-budgetary format. Both, however, have established themselves as active agents in terms of agenda-setting and multi-stakeholder initiatives with regard to themes such as sport and sustainable development, human rights, health-enhancing physical activity, good governance, match fixing or anti-doping, some of this even in form of firm, legally binding international instruments.

It is nonetheless important to bear in mind that the general legal frameworks of both the EU and the UN merely provide coordinating instruments and that both organisations continue to explore their own role in the context of sport. From a political perspective it is thus pertinent to recognise the importance of creating synergies in an institutionalised framework, realising own strengths and weaknesses and sharing competences for the sake of a coherent strategy. Notwithstanding the potential of employing a multi-stakeholder approach, a critical assessment of who talks, why and who shapes which discourses is important within and among the different international organisations.

UN and EU policy work is mainly governed by their member states. Relating to Houlihan's (2010: 50ff.) observation regarding the 'significance of states in the international system and the relative significance of non-state international organisations as independent variables in the policy process', it is however noteworthy that with sports organisations like IOC/IPC and FIFA/UEFA non-state actors are actively involved – or at least addressed in – a broad scope of policy decisions and statements in the sport context. The collaborations of the European Union and the United Nations with relevant actors in sport and society sometimes involve difficult coordination processes and are described as 'inter-agency coordination'. This tendency of involving or specifying and engaging third-party actors could be described as a trend to transcend traditional state-oriented perspectives.

A comparable tendency can also be observed in other more recent policy shaping processes within UN and EU policy: Member states tend to open their considerations to relevant societal interest groups and representatives. The negotiation process for the new Sustainable Development Goals (SDGs) can be cited as a prominent example of this tendency within the UN system,[14] while the integration of different societal stakeholders into the new established working groups of the EU as well as the establishment of the social dialogue support this process at European level. The greater inclusion of such actors is intended to provide a 'real' societal perspective. Compared to the EU, in the UN system an institutionalised inclusive approach may only be at an embryonic stage. With an increasing tendency towards the inclusion of this practice in diverse fora (like the GA and HRC), the selection and the representativeness of chosen actors for a specific area can always be a cause for critical consideration. An overall extended dialogue between government representatives and diverse theme-specific expert groups can contribute to increased levels of accuracy and suitability of government-driven decision.

It will be an important task to mutually develop and define the respective roles and responsibilities of stakeholders (state and non-state) for future policy shaping processes. The road to such work and the selection of the appropriate partners may be rocky at times, but an added value for policy developments is a desirable ambition. This can also be assumed for policy shaping with a relevance to the field of sport with its multi-layered and multi-dimensional interrelations to politics. Sport can be affected by, it can be observed in and it can take an activating or awareness-raising function in international policy shaping. This has also increasingly been acknowledged and taken into consideration in political decision-making processes.

From an academic perspective this implies conducting more sport policy research with a focus on actors and structures, identifying intersections and potentials for collaboration, while providing policy advice and support is a much-needed competence and contribution. Specifically in terms of theoretical assessments of the matter, governance concepts provide a useful toolkit to address the plurality of actors and diversity of processes. It can be expected that future research will concern itself increasingly with the role of particular countries, governmental and non-governmental actors and – as for the international dimension – the reciprocities between EU, UN and other international organisations' policies as well as international sport organisations will constitute a relevant point of interest to be analysed further.

Notes

1 Resolution of the Council and of the Representatives of the Governments of the Member States, meeting with the Council, of 21 May 2014 on the European Work Plan for Sport (2014–2017), (2014/C 183/03).
2 Sport Unit of the European Commission (2014). Report on EU Sport Forum.
3 Charter adopted by the UNESCO General Conference on 21 November 1978; the Charter is currently under review and is to be reconsidered by the General Conference as newly titled 'International Charter of Physical Education, Physical Activity and Sport' at its 38th session in November 2015.
4 Convention adopted by UNESCO General Conference on 19 October 2005.
5 MINEPS is considered the only official summit of ministers responsible for sport. The latest MINEPS V was hosted by the Federal Republic of Germany in Berlin in May 2013 where the policy guideline 'Declaration of Berlin' was adopted by the ministers. Previous editions of MINEPS had been fundamental for the establishment of the International Charter on Physical Education and Sport as well as the Convention against Doping in Sport (see above for both).
6 Sport has been addressed in the UN Convention on the Rights of Persons with Disabilities in a dedicated article 30 since its adoption by the GA on 13 December 2006 (see www.un.org/disabilities).
7 The latest report of the UN Secretary-General 'Sport for Development and Peace: Realizing the Potential' (document 69/330) was provided to the GA on 18 August 2014.
8 Resolution 64/3, adopted by the GA on 19 October 2009.
9 Report by Special Rapporteur on adequate housing, Raquel Rolnik, HRC/13/20 of 18 December 2009 as 'acknowledged with appreciation' in resolution HRC/13/10 of 25 March 2010.
10 Initial resolution on the theme HRC/13/27 adopted by the HRC on 26 March 2010.
11 In the 27th HRC session, an HRC Ad hoc Committee meeting with expert consultation was, for example, held on the theme of Sport and Racism on 7 October 2014.

12 Information about this process as well as the progress report can be downloaded and reviewed at www.ohchr.org/EN/HRBodies/HRC/AdvisoryCommittee/Pages/HumanRightsThroughSport.aspx.
13 The two statements can be retrieved from the official websites of the permanent missions to the UN at Geneva of China and Germany respectively.
14 Sport was already mentioned in the Millennium Development Goals context as part of the United Nations Millennium Declaration and related documents; it is currently also considered in the SDG process.

References

Amara, M., Henry, I., Liang, J. and Uchiumi, K. (2005). The governance of professional soccer: Five case studies – Algeria, China, England, France and Japan. *European Journal of Sport Science*, 5(4), 189–206.

Brown, A. (2000). European football and the European Union: governance, participation and social cohesion – towards a policy research agenda. *Soccer and Society*, 1(2), 129–151.

Council of the European Union (2011). *European Union work plan for sport 2011–2014*. Brussels.

Council of the European Union (2014). *European Union work plan for sport 2014–2017*. Brussels.

Ducrey, P., Ferreira, C., Huerta, G. and Marsto, K. (2003). *UEFA and football governance: a new model*. Final Project Work. FIFA Master.

EOC EU Office (2011). *Europäische Sportpolitik. Grundlagen, Entwicklungen, Perspektiven*. Brussels.

European Commission (2007). *White Paper on sport*. Brussels.

European Commission (2011). *Developing the European dimension in sport*. Brussels.

European Union (2007). *Lisbon Treaty*. Brussels.

Fozooni, B. (2004). Religion, politics and class: conflict and contestation in the development of football in Iran. *Soccer and Society*, 5(3), 356–370.

Garcia, B. (2007). UEFA and the European Union: from confrontation to co-operation? *Journal of Contemporary European Research*, 3, 202–223.

Grix, J. (2010). The 'governance debate' and the study of sport policy. *International Journal of Sport Policy*, 2(2), 159–171.

Güldenpfennig, S. (1981). *Internationale Sportbeziehungen zwischen Entspannung und Konfrontation*. Vol. 18 of Sport, Arbeit, Gesellschaft. Köln: Pahl-Rugenstein.

Hargreaves, J. (1994). *Sporting females: critical issues in the history and sociology of women's sport*. London: Routledge.

Hassan, D. and Hamil, S. (2010). Models of football governance and management in international sport. *Soccer and Society*, 4(11), 343–353.

Hayhurst, L. (2009). The power to shape policy: charting sport for development and peace policy discourses. *International Journal of Sport Policy*, 1(2), 203–227.

Hindley, D. (2002). *An examination of the utility of the concept of governance in relation to the sports of swimming, football and cricket*. Unpublished dissertation. Loughborough University.

Holt, M. (2009). *UEFA, governance, and the control of club competition in European football*. Report funded by the FIFA João Havelange Research Scholarship.

Hong, F. and Mangan, J. A. (eds) (2003). *Soccer, women, sexual liberation: kicking off a new era*. London: Routledge.

Houlihan, B. (1994). *Sport and international politics*. London: Harvester Wheatsheaf.

Houlihan, B. (1997). *Sport, policy and politics: a comparative analysis*. London: Routledge.

Houlihan, B. (2003). Politics, power, policy and sport. In B. Houlihan (ed.), *Sport and society: a student introduction*, 1st edition (pp. 28–48). Los Angeles: SAGE.

Houlihan, B. (2006). Politics and sport. In J. Coakley and E. Dunning (eds), *Handbook of sports studies* (pp. 213–227). London: Sage Publications.

Houlihan, B. (2009). Mechanisms of international influence on domestic elite sport policy. *International Journal of Sport Policy*, 1(1), 51–69.

Houlihan, B. (2010). International perspectives on sport structures and policy. In W. Tokarski and K. Petry (eds), *Handbuch Sportpolitik* (pp. 48–62). Schorndorf: Hofmann.

Hödl, G. (2002). Zur politischen Ökonomie des Fußballsports. In M. Fanizadeh, G. Hödl and W. Manzenreiter (eds), *Journal für Entwicklungspolitik*, Ergänzungsband: Vol. 11, Global players – Kultur, Ökonomie und Politik des Fußballs, 1st edition (pp. 13–35). Frankfurt a. M.: Brandes & Apsel.

Lösche, P. (2010). Sportpolity, Sportpolitics und Sportpolicy als theoretische Annäherung an eine Sportpolitikwissenschaft. In W. Tokarski and K. Petry (eds), *Handbuch Sportpolitik* (pp. 12–29). Schorndorf: Hofmann.

Majumdar, B. and Bandyopadhyay, K. (2005). Race, nation and performance: footballing nationalism in colonial India. *Soccer and Society*, 6(2–3), 158–170.

Martin, P. (2005). The Europeanization of elite football: scope, meaning. significance. *European Societies*, 7, 349–368.

Mayntz, R. (2009). *Über Governance: Institutionen und Prozesse politischer Regelung*. Frankfurt: Campus.

Mittag, J. (2007). Die Europäische Union und der Fußball. Die Europäisierung des Profifußballs zwischen Bosman- und Simutenkow-Urteil. In J. Mittag and J.-U. Nieland (eds), *Das Spiel mit dem Fußball. Interessen, Projektionen und Vereinnahmungen* (pp. 203–218). Essen: Klartext Verlag.

Mittag, J. (2010). Theoretische Ansätze zur Analyse europäischer und transnationaler Sportpolitik und Sportstrukturen. In W. Tokarski and K. Petry (eds), *Handbuch Sportpolitik* (pp. 98–113). Schorndorf: Hofmann.

Mittag, J. and Legrand, B. (2010). Towards a Europeanization of football? Historical phases in the evolution of the UEFA European Football Championship. *Soccer and Society*, 11(6), 709–722.

Niemann, A., Garcia, B. and Grant, W. (eds) (2011). *The transformation of European football: towards the Europeanisation of the national game*. Manchester: Manchester University Press.

Parrish, R. (2003). *Sports law and policy in the European Union*. European Policy Research Unit Series. New York: Manchester University Press; distributed exclusively in USA by Palgrave.

Ronge, V. (2006). Governance: Begriff, Konzept und Anwendungsmöglichkeiten im Sport. In W. Tokarski, K. Petry and B. Jesse (eds), *Veröffentlichungen der Deutschen Sporthochschule: Vol. 15. Sportpolitik. Theorie- und Praxisfelder von Governance im Sport* (pp. 9–20). Köln: Sportverl. Strauß.

Sage, G. (2006). Political economy and sport. In J. Coakley and E. Dunning (eds), *Handbook of sports studies* (pp. 260–276). London: SAGE Publishing.

Steinbach, D. (2006). Das Governancekonzept als innovativer Ansatz für die Sportpolitik und Sportpolitikforschung. In W. Tokarski, K. Petry and B. Jesse (eds), *Veröffentlichungen der Deutschen Sporthochschule: Vol. 15. Sportpolitik. Theorie- und Praxisfelder von Governance im Sport* (pp. 21–30). Köln: Sportverl. Strauß.

Tokarski, W., Petry, K., Groll, M. and Mittag, J. (eds) (2009). *A perfect match: sport and the Europen Union*. Aachen: Meyer & Meyer.

Woyke, W. and Delschen, A. (eds) (2006). *Sport und Politik: Eine Einführung*. Schwalbach am Taunus: Wochenschau-Verl.

Chapter 9

The Human Capital Model

Realising the benefits of sport and physical activity

Richard Bailey, Ed Cope, Dan Parnell, and Matthew J. Reeves

Introduction

There is mounting evidence of the benefits associated with participation in sport and physical activity, and this evidence has led to the development of a wide range of international and national initiatives aimed at increasing levels of physical activity and engagement in sport (Bull *et al.*, 2014; World Health Organization Regional Office for Europe, 2011). For all of this action, however, there continues to be a general under-appreciation of the scope of the role sport and physical activity can play – both for individuals and the wider society. When the value of sport and/or physical activity are discussed, there is a strong and somewhat exclusive tendency to focus on a narrow range of issues related to physical ill-health, such as obesity, diabetes, and coronary heart disease (WHO, 2013). There is no disagreement that physical (ill-)health is important, but it is argued in this chapter that it represents only a fraction of what empirical studies suggest are the full range of benefits available to those participating in sport and physical activity. Moreover, there may be a danger of prioritising negative consequences of inactivity at the expense of positive outcomes, both in terms of representing a complete picture, and of offering a sustainable vision for the future. In other words, a narrowly focused, negatively framed agenda for sport and physical activity can be useful in the short term, primarily through scaring policymakers and politicians into action, but its potency will be inversely related to its success. This is not just a rhetorical or political device: as will be seen below, the positive outcomes of sport and physical activity are interconnected in nature and reinforcing in their interaction. The true value of sport and physical activity can only be fully appreciated from a broad, holistic perspective.

In this chapter, we offer a summary and extension of a relatively new framework for discussing the outcomes of sport and physical activity. The Human Capital Model (HCM) is a framework that assumes a wider and more inclusive perspective of sport and physical activity, and offers a holistic consideration of human development (Bailey *et al.*, 2012, 2013).[1]

Underlying the HCM is an assertion that the stock of competencies, knowledge, and personal attributes are embodied in the ability to take part in activity-related activities. Such activities produce value(s) that can be realised through increased well-being, educational attainment, and, ultimately, economic value. There is a compelling and growing evidence-base related to the broader benefits of sport and physical activity and there is increasing acceptance that participation in regular sport and/or physical activity forms an important and necessary feature of healthy living and development, precisely because of the consequences of inactivity (UNESCO, 2013; WHO, 2013).

The physical inactivity pandemic

Globally, the major cause of death and disability are non-communicable diseases (NCDs), such as obesity, heart disease and stroke, cancer, chronic respiratory disease, and diabetes (Lozano et al., 2010; WHO, 2011). The World Health Organization (WHO) estimated 35 million people per year die from these types of chronic disease. That number is double the number dying from infectious diseases (HIV/AIDS and malaria) combined (WHO, 2005). Indeed, for the first time in history, children are expected to have a shorter lifespan than their parents due to non-communicable diseases (Wang and Veugelers, 2008). Physical inactivity is the fourth leading risk factor for mortality (WHO, 2011). People who are insufficiently active have a 30 per cent increased risk of all-cause mortality, and physical inactivity is 'conservatively' estimated to cause 6–10 per cent of deaths from NCDs (Lee et al., 2012; Lim et al., 2012). Such figures serve to highlight the need for a global response in tackling non-communicable diseases.

The value of sport and physical activity for most policymakers and politicians lies in their effectiveness and economic value as among the most effective preventative measures for prevent and alleviating chronic diseases (Bonow et al., 2002). Therefore, it is not surprising that they have increasingly become associated with the equation that 'Exercise is Medicine' (American College of Sports Medicine, 2011). While it is important to acknowledge that activity is one of a number of factors associated with health, its distinctive appeal should also be recognised – it is a palatable 'medicine'. For these reasons, increasing participation in sport and physical activity forms a core objective across a range of government policies in most developed countries (Breuer and Pawlowski, 2011).

The political and policy case for sport and physical activity has traditionally been framed in the context of the future physical health status of the individual and its consequences for local communities. However, this is a limited perspective for a number of reasons. First, it is important to consider sport and physical activity as they relate to the many biological demands of childhood and adolescence (Bailey *et al.*, 2009; Collins *et al.*, 2012). These processes vary considerably among individuals, yet they occur simultaneously and interact, and provide the backdrop against which children and young people evaluate their own status among peers, especially during adolescence. This backdrop has implications for many decisions children and young people make, including those about sport and physical activity. Second, outcomes of involvement in sport and physical activity extend far beyond physical health, including psychological and social well-being, cognitive and academic performance, and even future career trajectory (Bailey and Reeves, 2013). Third, the view of 'exercise is medicine' leaves little room for the self-determined motivations and significance of activity in the lives of children and young people (Standage *et al.*, 2003). A review of research has shown that the primary reasons children and young people participate in sport is because of the extended opportunity to be with friends and to learn new skills, rather than the health benefits associated with regular participation in sport and physical activity (Bailey *et al.*, 2013).

The serious dangers associated with inactive lifestyles are clear (Tremblay *et al.*, 2011); it is therefore not surprising that serious concerns have been expressed that the current levels of sport and physical activity among children and young people are inadequate, and that most children and young people around the world fail to meet recommended daily levels of activity (Sisson and Katzmarzyk, 2008; UNESCO, 2013; WHO, 2013). Evidence suggests that the pattern of childhood and adolescent activity in the developed world and, at an increasing rate, in the developing world, is turning downwards (Beets *et al.*, 2011). In the language of one recent consensus statement, there is a 'pandemic' of inactivity (Craig *et al.*, 2012). According to many international consensus statements, children and young people should build up at least 60 minutes of moderate intensity physical activity every day (Department of Health and Human Services, 2008; Department of Health, Physical Activity, Health Improvement and Protection, 2011; World Health Organization Regional Office for Europe, 2011).

Unfortunately, there is ample evidence that not all children and young people spend enough time being physically active. For example, a recent study of Australian children and young people found that physical activity levels remain considerably low despite 'moderately supportive social environmental and regulatory environments' (Schranz *et al.*, 2014, p. 21). Indeed, the pattern of evidence suggests a gradual reduction in levels of sport and physical activity from childhood through adolescence (Telama *et al.*, 2005; van Mechelen *et al.*, 2000). The drop off is particularly striking amongst girls (Bailey *et al.*, 2004). For example, barely one in ten 14-year-old girls in the United States meet the activity recommendations (Evans *et al.*, 2009). A pan-European study by Verloigne and colleagues (2012) found that girls spend significantly more time sedentary than boys, and also undertake less vigorous physical activity than boys. Similarly, a UK-based study found that boys are consistently more physically active than girls, and that girls should be the primary targets of interventions aimed at increasing physical activity engagement (Collings *et al.*, 2014).

The Human Capital Model

The HCM seeks to take a positive, broad and inclusive view of sport and physical activity, one that acknowledges the urgent health agenda, but locates that agenda in a holistic view of human development. In doing so it could be said to build on the foundation offered by the World Health Organisation's (1946) working definition of health: 'a complete state of physical, mental and social well-being, and not merely the absence of disease or infirmity'. The HCM positions sport and physical activity as a fundamental part of human nature, and as essential for healthy human development. It considers development in terms of different forms of 'capital' – physical, emotional, social, individual, intellectual, financial – resources that can be built on and drawn on throughout life (see Figure 9.1). The use of the language of 'capitals' is deliberate and suggests that sport and physical activity are investments capable of delivering valuable individual and social returns (Becker, 1964). The model suggests not only that sport and physical activity are key drivers of different types of capital formation, but that the capitals in turn influence both physical activity and each other, thus forming a synergistic feedback network whose whole is greater than the sum of its parts.

As Figure 9.1 illustrates, the HCM offers a synthesis, analysis, and reconceptualization of the available scientific evidence related to the outcomes of engagement in sport and physical activity. The claims made for each capital are based on judgments of quality (e.g. range of institutional settings, international applicability, etc.), for which differential weightings were given. These judgments significantly influenced both the scientific review (Bailey *et al.*, 2013), and its translation into policy-related messages (e.g. www.designedtomove.org/en_us). The evidence related to the relationship between sport, physical activity, and human development was then modelled according to six different domains of capital:

1   *physical capital:* the direct benefits of sport and physical activity to physical health and human function, including the prevention and mitigation of non-communicable diseases and conditions, such as heart disease, diabetes, cancer, and obesity.
2   *emotional capital:* the psychological and mental health benefits associated with sport and physical activity, including increased levels of self esteem and self efficacy, reduced depression and anxiety, reduced social isolation, and a greater ability to process stressful events.

The Human Capital Model

The comprehensive benefits of physical activity, sports and physical education are underestimated today. This model shows the spectrum of benefits to an individual and economy. Each "capital" refers to a set of outcomes that underpin our well-being and success.

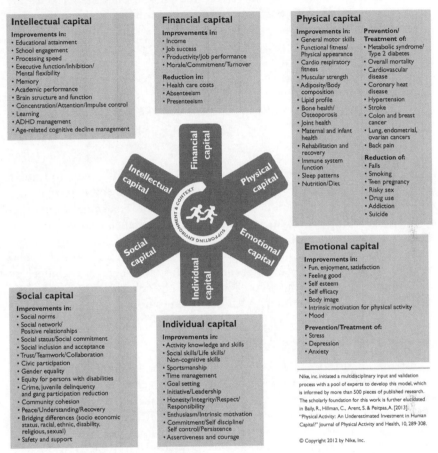

Intellectual capital

Improvements in:
- Educational attainment
- School engagement
- Processing speed
- Executive function/Inhibition/ Mental flexibility
- Memory
- Academic performance
- Brain structure and function
- Concentration/Attention/Impulse control
- Learning
- ADHD management
- Age-related cognitive decline management

Financial capital

Improvements in:
- Income
- Job success
- Productivity/Job performance
- Morale/Commitment/Turnover

Reduction in:
- Health care costs
- Absenteeism
- Presenteeism

Physical capital

Improvements in:
- General motor skills
- Functional fitness/ Physical appearance
- Cardio respiratory fitness
- Muscular strength
- Adiposity/Body composition
- Lipid profile
- Bone health/ Osteoporosis
- Joint health
- Maternal and infant health
- Rehabilitation and recovery
- Immune system function
- Sleep patterns
- Nutrition/Diet

Prevention/ Treatment of:
- Metabolic syndrome/ Type 2 diabetes
- Overall mortality
- Cardiovascular disease
- Coronary heat disease
- Hypertension
- Stroke
- Colon and breast cancer
- Lung, endometrial, ovarian cancers
- Back pain

Reduction of:
- Falls
- Smoking
- Teen pregnancy
- Risky sex
- Drug use
- Addiction
- Suicide

Emotional capital

Improvements in:
- Fun, enjoyment, satisfaction
- Feeling good
- Self esteem
- Self efficacy
- Body image
- Intrinsic motivation for physical activity
- Mood

Prevention/Treatment of:
- Stress
- Depression
- Anxiety

Social capital

Improvements in:
- Social norms
- Social network/ Positive relationships
- Social status/Social commitment
- Social inclusion and acceptance
- Trust/Teamwork/Collaboration
- Civic participation
- Gender equality
- Equity for persons with disabilities
- Crime, juvenile delinquency and gang participation reduction
- Community cohesion
- Peace/Understanding/Recovery
- Bridging differences (socio economic status, racial, ethnic, disability, religious, sexual)
- Safety and support

Individual capital

Improvements in:
- Activity knowledge and skills
- Social skills/Life skills/ Non-cognitive skills
- Sportsmanship
- Time management
- Goal setting
- Initiative/Leadership
- Honesty/Integrity/Respect/ Responsibility
- Enthusiasm/Intrinsic motivation
- Commitment/Self discipline/ Self control/Persistence
- Assertiveness and courage

Nike, inc. initiated a multidisciplinary input and validation process with a pool of experts to develop this model, which is informed by more than 500 pieces of published research. The scholarly foundation for this work is further elucidated in Baily, R., Hillman, C., Arent, S. & Peitpas, A. [2013]. "Physical Activity: An Underestimated Investment in Human Capital?" Journal of Physical Activity and Health, 10, 289-308.

© Copyright 2012 by Nike, Inc.

Figure 9.1 The human capitals.

Source: Bailey *et al.*, 2013; reproduced with permission.

3 *individual capital:* the elements of a person's character, e.g. life skills, interpersonal skills, values, that accrue via participation in play, sport and other forms of sport and physical activity. Reported benefits in this area include teamwork, co-operation, moral and social responsibility, and resilience.

4 *social capital:* the outcomes that arise when networks between people, groups, organisations, and civil society are strengthened because of

participation in group-based physical activity, play, or competitive sport. This domain of capital includes the development of both pro-social behaviours and social inclusion through participation in physical activity.

5   *intellectual capital:* the cognitive and educational gains that are increasingly linked to participation in sport and physical activity. This feature of capital focuses particularly on the effects of regular exercise on cognitive functioning, on subject-specific performance at school, and on general academic achievement.

6   *financial capital:* gains in terms of earning power, job performance, productivity and job attainment, along with reduced costs of health care and absenteeism/presenteeism (i.e. lower productivity among those who are 'present') that are linked to regular sport and physical activity participation.

Each of these capitals represents a set of important investments to human health and well-being. However, it also needs to be remembered that they act synergistically. For example, the development of intellectual capital has been shown to have significant positive effects on financial capital, and the effects of increased social capital are felt in each of the other capitals. So, while it might seem sensible to focus on specific types of outcomes (such as combatting obesity, or reducing social exclusion), there is a danger of missing a much more compelling story about the role that sport and physical activity can make to human well-being as a whole.

Early positive experiences

Whilst the empirical base of theories of sport and physical activity outcomes, like the HCM, is growing rapidly, it is also clear that the realisation of these outcomes is not simple and unproblematic. On the contrary, engagement in sport and physical activity is mediated by a range of factors that 'nudge' children and young people towards or away from sport and physical activity. Some of these factors have the status of determinants, since their presence are necessary criteria for participation. These include accessible and safe facilities, equipment, and coaching. Many other factors have a less direct influence, but nonetheless can prove extremely potent, especially when they occur together. Sallis and Owen (1999) usefully classify the correlates of physical activity as intrapersonal, social, and environmental variables. According to the HCM, the host of determinants, correlates, causal variables, mediators, moderators, and confounders either stimulate or inhibit the value of the different capitals (see Figures 9.2 and 9.3).

As the levels of childhood and adolescent physical activity continue to fall, the need to rethink the ways in which activity is presented to children

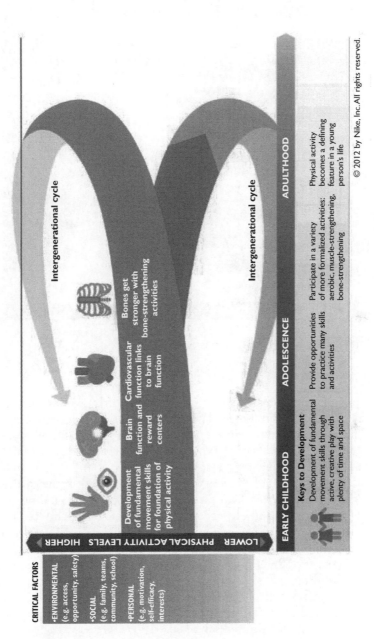

Figure 9.2 Human development and the human capitals.

Source: Bailey *et al.*, 2013; reproduced with permission.

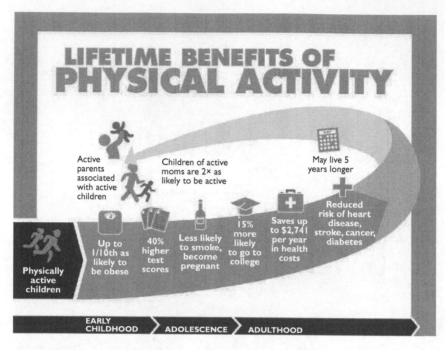

Figure 9.3 The human capitals act synergistically.

Source: Bailey *et al.*, 2013; reproduced with permission.

and young people takes on increasing importance. Early experiences are important as they encourage longer lasting participation, whilst negative experiences are more likely to cause permanent dropout (Wall and Côté, 2007). Put simply, positive early experiences encourage longer lasting participation, whilst negative experiences are more likely to cause permanent dropout (Smoll and Smith, 1996; Wall and Côté, 2007). If the earliest experiences of sport and/or physical activity are uninspiring, young people are less likely to continue, and evidence suggests that inactive children are more likely to become inactive adolescents, and, subsequently, inactive adults (Craigie *et al.*, 2011; Janz *et al*, 2005).

An implicit goal for adults responsible for children and young people's engagement in sport and physical activity is to ensure that they continue to participate and remain active beyond their childhood years (Siedentop, 2002), and affect a lifestyle choice that retains sport and physical activity as part of a daily routine (Kjønniksen *et al.*, 2009). Generally speaking, early positive experiences incline children and young people towards sustained engagement with an activity, whilst negative experiences turn them off (Wall and Côté, 2007), although the relative potency of these two forces are not equally weighted. Just as a singular inspiring experience can inspire a lifelong commitment to a domain (Pickard and Bailey, 2009), one negative encounter can undermine years of enjoyable sporting and physical activities (Smoll and Smith, 1996).

Social factors are particularly significant in relation to engagement in sport and physical activity. Researchers have traced positive and negative responses to sport and physical activity, primarily, to social factors. In fact, children, adolescents, and adults tend to define the quality of their sporting experiences in terms of socially oriented perspectives (Allen, 2003), and it has been suggested that social bonds are important elements of healthy functioning. The need for these social bonds explains the tendency to seek out social interactions and build relationships. As a consequence, young people derive positive feelings from forming and sustaining social bonds, and negative emotions when relationships are broken, threatened, or refused (Baumeister and Leary, 1995), and define positive and negative experiences through socially oriented perspectives, such as contributing to the team, social support and approval, pleasing others, and affiliation (Schilling and Hayashi, 2001). In a review of literature, Bailey et al. (2013) found that children's participation in sport is mediated by five primary factors: perception of competence; fun and enjoyment; parents; learning new skills; and friends and peers. Supporting that sport and physical activity settings are among the most common through which children and young people can develop social relationships and feel that they are part of a group. The presence of significant others (e.g. parents, friends, siblings, coaches, teachers, and teammates) may have a considerable influence on the experience (Partridge et al., 2008), whilst also directly supporting children's participation in sport (Light and Lemonie, 2010). Given the option, relatively few people choose to engage with activities on their own and, once they have started, social climate and affiliation can be powerful motivators for remaining involved.

Motivation to participate in sport and physical activity has also been linked to social cognition (e.g., Gandhi, 2010; Humpel et al., 2002). Premised on the work of Bandura (2001), it is posited that social factors serve as important influences on behaviour, as they provide feedback for behaviours, opportunities, and consequences of actions. The degree of this influence varies according to different contextual factors, such as social support, family and peer influences, and access to resources (Booth et al., 2000). According to Bandura's theory, human behaviour is understood as a triadic, dynamic, and reciprocal interaction of personal factors, behaviour, and the environment. Satisfying experiences occur when an individual has positive, personal characteristics, exhibits appropriate behaviours, and stays in a supportive environment. For example, a coach who structures practice and employ behaviours in a way that reinforces a child's motives for participating will lead to a positive experience.

The final area to consider is social development, linked to the work of Bronfenbrenner (1993). It is suggested that behaviour needs to be considered as a function of developmental status as it interacts with the environment. From this perspective, the developing individual is engaged in a dynamic process of development and change. Therefore, social influencers on behaviour need to be understood in relation to an individual's stage of development.

There are evident differences between these different theoretical frameworks, which should not be ignored. However, it is also possible to identify a core of shared presumptions about social influencers on human activities, like sport and physical activity. For example, such influencers need to be understood as parts of a complex and dynamic whole that are inherently connected, so that change in one part of this web of interconnectedness will result in changes elsewhere, too (Bailey *et al.*, 2009). These influencers are not unilinear – there is always a reciprocal relationship with the family influencing the behaviour and actions of its children, who influence their family, which influences the wider community, which influences the family, and so on (Côté, 1999).

Parents

Parents are uniquely important social influencers for sport and physical activity engagement (Brustad, 1992). They are the first and most enduring presenters of activity to children and young people, and have been found to influence their children's experiences of exercise in a number of ways (Hohepa *et al.*, 2007). For example, parents have been found to have the greatest influence on children's perceptions of sport competence, particularly during childhood (Horn and Weiss, 1991), and these perceptions can have powerful effects on children's willingness to enter the sport and physical activity environments. Parents also provide practical support, including paying for lessons and equipment, providing transportation, and providing emotional support; they also give their children a sense of their and the community's perceptions of which activities are most suitable, valuable and acceptable (Babkes Stellino *et al.*, 2012; Miller, 2011).

A useful model for conceptualising the relationships between parental influence and children's views of their own competence is the 'expectancy-value model' (Eccles and Harold, 1991). According to this model, socialisation behaviours are influenced jointly by parental expectation for the child's success in a given area, and the value parents place on this success. Parents who expect that their children can be successful in sport and physical activity, and who value success in this area, will be more likely to influence their children to pursue this behaviour. Adults' beliefs often express cultural norms and prejudices, and the model predicts that these norms will significantly influence the messages they portray to their children. For example, the common acceptance by parents of gender-role stereotypes translates into values and expectations that boys ought to be more physically active than girls, and that activities should be strictly delineated according to gender. This can establish a self-fulfilling prophecy whereby the idea that girls and boys are essentially different becomes validated by progressively differing experiences and rewards (Welk, 1999a). It ought to be noted at this point that many of the constructs that have been developed from research with parents also transfer to other social influencers. The expectancy-value model, for example, could easily be adapted to relate to the effects of peers' beliefs on young people's behaviours, or on teachers' and coaches' social control over children.

There are various ways that parents (and other social influencers) can socialise their children to be physically active. Five different parental socialisation variables are shown to considerably influence physical activity behaviours:

- initiation;
- encouragement
- involvement;
- facilitation;
- role modelling.

Children's first involvement in sport and physical activity is usually as a consequence of their parents who are, therefore, initiators of their children's participation. For example, in studies by Light and colleagues (Light and Lemonie, 2010; Light *et al.*, 2013) a common finding was that children originally joined sports clubs because their parents had, in some way, influenced their decision, enrolled them at a sports club, or had been the main reason why they first started participating. A further study revealed that talented children's early involvement was heavily dependent upon their parents introducing them to sport, particularly in the case of swimming, with 70 per cent of children sampled citing this as their reason for initially taking part in this sport (Baxter-Jones and Maffulli, 2003). Children and young people rely heavily on their parents and, to a lesser extent, other adults as sources of information regarding their physical abilities, and this perceived physical competence is strongly associated with involvement with sport and physical activity (Welk, 1999b; Edwardson and Gorely, 2010). This suggests that parents wishing to promote their children's sport and physical activity involvement would be well-advised to focus on building their physical competence and sense of confidence in movement domains.

Parents become involved in their children's sport and physical activity in many ways, including teaching new skills, helping them practice, observing sessions, and introducing new activities (Walters, 2011). It seems that the most efficacious level of parental involvement is something of a balancing act between under- and over-involvement (Gould et al., 2008). The former implies that parents do not value sport and physical activity, the latter that they have attached an inappropriate degree of seriousness to their child's involvement. Both of these forms are associated with children's reduced motivation to continue to participate (Grolnick et al., 1997). Thus, parents need to be supportive of their children, but not overly directive. In particular, being overly directive is a cause for concern, as it can become a source of excessive pressure on children which is associated with drop-out once the child has the opportunity to do so (Fraser-Thomas and Côté, 2006).

Some forms of sport and physical activity are free and almost universally available, but sport participation is often mediated by parents' ability and willingness to financially support their child (Fredricks and Eccles, 2006). Given the increasing cost of participating in sport and physical activity, there is some evidence to suggest that children and young people from middle to high socio-economic statuses are afforded more opportunities than those from low socio-economical statuses (Brockman et al., 2009). However, the financial strain placed on parents to support their children is high regardless of socio-economic status. For example, Harwood and Knight (2009a, 2009b) found funding their children to play tennis was financially costly and emotionally stressful. These increase if a child turns out to be talented (Kirk et al., 1997), as this not only costs more, but places greater pressure on being able to balance time between siblings (Kay, 2000). In fact, such are the financial and time costs of participation in certain sports that some parents refuse to fund them (Hardy et al., 2010).

There is little doubt that parents are significant role models for children. Indeed, the importance parents place on sport and physical activity through their own involvement has been found to significantly influence the involvement of their child (Anderssen and Wold, 1992). Parents are the most sustained providers of social messages, compensating for their children's immature social skills. At the same time, children rely on their parents for feedback on their own competencies (Brustad, 1996). Whilst there are many ways that other people can influence the sport and physical activity participation of children and young people, studies tend to suggest that the relationship between parental engagement and childhood activity is also particularly strong. For example, 11- and 12-year-old children with one or two active parents are much more likely to be physically active themselves, and that relationship seems to be linear (i.e. the more active the parents, the more active the children) (Mattocks et al., 2008). Indeed, children with active mothers have been found to be twice as likely to be active; similarly, children with active fathers are three and a half times more likely to be physically active; and children with two active parents are nearly six times more likely to be active (Moore et al., 1991).

Many other studies around the world suggest that parental engagement is the strongest predictor of sport and physical activity levels in both boys and girls (McMinn *et al.*, 2008). Indeed, parents hold the monopoly of social influence on their child's activity until the beginning of school, after which children are exposed to a wider range of people (Payne *et al.*, 2003). During their early years, sport and physical activity tends to be play-based, rather than structured and formalised (Pellegrini and Smith, 1998), but as children move to school-age, they are introduced to a variety of sports, most often by their father. The playful attitude towards movement remains, driven by a sense of fun and enjoyment derived from the activities themselves. As children move through their elementary school, parents often relinquish primary responsibility for instruction to a coach, and focus their efforts more on providing logistical support for participation. Later childhood and the teenage years are often characterised by a shift in motivation from fun and play towards skill learning and development, and specialisation in a small number of sports (Côté and Hay, 2002). By the time a person has reached their twenties, their parents' role is mainly one of emotional support (Partridge *et al.*, 2008).

Siblings

Brothers and sisters represent a significant form of social influence throughout life, partly because of its endurance, and partly because of the distinctive nature of sibling's interactions (Cicirelli, 1995; Keresztes *et al.*, 2008). Social influence is ever-changing and overlapping, as the extent of the influence depends, in part, on the location, time of day, and the context of the activity being examined (Spence and Lee, 2003). Siblings usually spend more time together than they do with their parents throughout childhood, and the intensity of this interaction is greatest during the early years and impacts across a range of the capitals. As is the case with parents, siblings' role as social influencers are likely to be strongest during the early years and progressively weaken as they move into adolescence. However, as part of the dynamic family support system that effects people's participation in sport and physical activity at every stage of life (Davison, 2004). Siblings who play sport and engage in physical activity together are more likely to be co-operative and have supportive relationships (Davis and Meyer, 2008), which can impact across the capitals, especially when the children or young people are each able to express their uniqueness and establish their own niche within the family.

Such is the dynamic complexity of sibling roles within the family that research has generated somewhat contradictory findings. For example, some have suggested that brothers can exert a strong influence over sisters' sporting participation, while others have found no effect (Greendorfer *et al.*, 2002). Nonetheless, there is compelling evidence that older siblings play a central role in guiding and reinforcing their sibling's sports participation (Anderssen and Wold, 1992). Case studies of talented athletes and dancers reveal that older siblings are among the most common role-models, inspiring and encouraging their younger family members to begin their sport in the first place, and guiding them towards norms of behaviour and approach (Côté, 1999; Pickard and Bailey, 2009). It has also been found that inactive older siblings have a more detrimental effect on the child's likelihood to be active than having no sibling at all (Partridge et al., 2008). As such, siblings can play a major influential role of a child's sport and physical activity participation and any subsequent progress towards the capitals.

Peers

Most theories of social influence on child development assume the central role of parents. However, some researchers have claimed that parents matter much less than is typically assumed, at least when it comes to determining the behaviour of their children, and that peer groups are far more important (Harris, 2011). Within sport and physical activity, this position appears to be somewhat implausible, at least when considering the whole phase from childhood to early adulthood. Nevertheless, an increasing body of literature has demonstrated that peers do have a significant effect on the sport and physical activity of children and young people (Salvy et al., 2008).

Peer influence can be both positive and negative – as is the case for all forms of social influence. For example, children and young people tend to be more physically active in the presence of friends in unstructured settings (outside of school) than when they are alone. However, some children and young people, especially those overweight, become less active in more formal settings (i.e. school physical education lessons) in the presence of peers (Rittenhouse et al., 2011). This pattern seems to be caused by the rejection of peers who are less physically fit or competent (Gray et al., 2008). As such, peer rejection can be damaging to self-esteem and social engagement, which can result in further rejection of sport and physical activity, and the establishment of sedentary behaviours instead. More positively, sporting and physical activity experiences can provide children and young people with opportunities to be with friends, developing close relationships, and gaining recognition and social status (Rubin et al., 2006). In fact, friendship and social acceptance seem to be motivations in themselves, associated with fun and enjoyment, and sport and physical activity often follow the pursuit of these experiences. This relationship becomes reciprocal as young people view physical competence and appearance as key social status determinants (Chase and Dummer, 1992).

The most significant impact of peer social influence can be seen during adolescence. With adolescence comes an increase in the time spent with peers. Teenagers report that they spend more time with their friends than with family members or on their own, which represents a significant developmental change compared to childhood (Savin-Williams and Berndt, 1990). As well as influencing time, peers also impact others' decisions about the seriousness of their involvement in activities. Indeed, this is a time when young people turn towards their friends, and away from family and school, for social support. So, perhaps, it is not surprising that the onset of adolescence coincides with dramatic changes of sport and physical activity participation, especially for girls (Bailey *et al.*, 2004). For many girls impressing other peers, particularly males, is seen as more important than sport and physical activity participation, and while many of them would like to be physically active, a tension presents itself: to appear feminine and attractive, or sweaty and muscular (Krane, 2001). These changes do not necessarily result in a rejection of sport and physical activity, as the peer group can strengthen young people's perceptions of themselves as sporting people, so that sports become closely linked to their sense of identity.

School

School represents the main institution for the development of physical skills and the provision of sport and physical activity for children and young people (Bailey, 2006). For many, school is the main environment for being physically active, whether through physical education lessons, during recess, or after-school activities (Telama *et al.*, 1997). There is evidence that, for a growing number of children and young people, school provides the main opportunity for regular, structured sport and physical activity participation, as a combination of economic pressures and parental concerns for safety mean that fewer children are able to play games in non-school settings. Physical education, physical activity, and sport in schools all are associated with students having better physical fitness. Longitudinal data have shown that for each weekday that a normal weight adolescent participated in physical education, the odds of becoming an overweight adult decreased by 5 per cent (Menschik *et al.*, 2008). Clearly physical education presents an obvious social influencer for sport and physical activity. Most curricula around the world aim to promote a combination of regular physical activity and movement skill development and understanding (Bailey and Dismore, 2005). It seems to be the case that the outcomes are most positive when the school as a whole works to encourage participation (Sallis *et al.*, 2001). This is probably because the messages from the different aspects of the school day can – if appropriately planned and managed – operate synergistically to exert a positive influence on children and young people. Instead, another consequence of schools' reach into children and people's lives is that negative experiences are likely to have especially harmful effects. For example, teenage girls report that inappropriate physical education experiences are the strongest factor discouraging participation in sport in any setting (Kirk et al., 2000).

There are numerous contexts linked to schools for encouraging and reinforcing sport and other physical activity (Jago and Baranowski, 2004). Taken as a whole, the school becomes a very compelling influencer, not least because it works with a captive audience for approximately 40–45 per cent of children and young people's waking hours, during a period when they are most receptive for health messages/attitudinal/behaviour change (Harris and Elbourn, 1997). As with all social influencers, however, the intensity of its influence changes over time. Research suggests that attitudes towards physical education, and school in general, are most positive during elementary school. While boys tend to maintain enthusiasm towards sports into their teenage years, girls often experience a marked decline in positive attitudes from around 13/14 years of age (Dismore, 2006).

Table 9.1 summarizes the ways in which different social factors influence the physical activity behaviours of children and young people.

Table 9.1 Influences of social factors on physical activity behaviours of children and young people

		0–6 years	6–12 years	12–18 years
Parents	Intensity of influence	High	High–moderate	Moderate–low
	Form of influence	Encouragement Role-modelling	Role-modelling Facilitation Involvement	Facilitation
Siblings	Intensity of influence	High–moderate	Moderate	Moderate
	Form of influence	Encouragement Role-modelling	Encouragement Role-modelling Involvement	Role-modelling Involvement
Friends	Intensity of influence	Moderate	High–moderate	High
	Form of influence	Involvement	Role-modelling Involvement	Role-modelling Facilitation Involvement
School	Intensity of influence	–	High	Moderate
	Form of influence	–	Encouragement Role-modelling Facilitation	Encouragement Role-modelling Facilitation Involvement

Conclusions

It is now clearly recognised that sport and other forms of physical activity have the potential to make contributions to people's lives beyond their physical health. Referring back to WHO's definition of health, sport and physical activity is also able to impact on people's mental and social well-being. However, we would argue, based on recent empirical evidence that sport and physical activity can make an even greater contribution to people's lives than WHO's definition suggests. The concept of human capitals is a useful framework to consider the potentially universal benefits of regular participation in sport and physical activity. The attractiveness of this conceptualization lies in that the six of these, which have been defined in this chapter and elsewhere, are inextricably linked in that high levels of one capital will often result in having high levels of another capital.

Unfortunately, while there is evidence to support these as benefits from consistently engaging in sport and physical activity, given the current participation figures it is clear that for many, these benefits are not capable of being realised. WHO reported that globally, 31 per cent of adults aged over 15 did not meet the sufficient levels of physical activity, with this being higher for women than men (WHO, 2010). The economic costs of such high levels of physical inactivity are, unsurprisingly, great. Most recent data has indicated that lack of physical activity contributes to diseases that cost Europe more than €80 billion a year. On the basis of this evidence, it is difficult to support current government policies towards sport and physical activity. However, as we have articulated throughout this chapter, the cost of physical inactivity has wider implications beyond that of physical and mental health. With this in mind, we argue that the overall cost of physical inactivity is much higher than the estimated €80 billion if the other capitals are taken into account.

Nonetheless, if we were to only consider the economic cost of physical inactivity towards disease (given there are estimates of what this costs), it is fairly reasonable to argue that current government initiatives concerning sport and physical activity are not working. Indeed, high-profile events such as the Olympic Games or the football World Cup are campaigned for as a mechanism to increasing participation for all by providing sustainable and accessible opportunities. Yet, current figures suggest that such events are not having the impact they set out to achieve despite the significant investment in these. The consequence of such expenditure is that it redirects money away from initiatives that would potentially have a much greater impact on ensuring an increase in participation levels.

We suggest that any government initiative that has the purpose of increasing participation levels needs to better consider the roles of social influencers. Parents, siblings, coaches, and friends are examples of prime social influencers, who through their actions and behaviours are able to determine whether sport is experienced positively or negatively. So, although it is true that regular sport and physical activity can lead to improvements in, for example, cognitive functioning, self-esteem, school grades, and economic achievement, it is absolutely not the case that these outcomes will necessarily follow. Put simply, it is primarily social factors that decide whether sport is experienced as positively nurturing and joyous activities, or negative, damaging ones. Because of this, social influencers need to become much more aware of how to ensure that they are helping to create learning environments that foster participation, rather than hinder it. However, the roles that social influencers play in a person's development changes as they move through different stages of their life. The whole period of childhood, from infancy to puberty, can be considered the critical life phase in the development of predispositions to act or behave in certain ways. This has enormous implications for sport and physical activity as it suggests that parents lay foundations of participation during the first decade of life. The propensity to be physically active and to engage in sports is set during childhood. Of course, human behaviour is too complex to be 'determined' from an early age, in a restricted sense, as different social factors leave their marks throughout the lifecourse. However, it seems reasonable to suggest that those wishing to promote an active lifestyle among children will need to recognise the effect of social influences, and plan their strategies accordingly.

Note

1 The Human Capital Model is an element in a wider, international programme of research and advocacy entitled 'Designed to Move', co-authored by Nike, Inc., the American College of Sports Medicine, and the International Council of Sport Science and Physical Education. Further information is available from www. designedtomove.org.

References

Allen, J. (2003). Social motivation in youth sport. *Journal of Sport and Exercise Psychology*, 25, 551–567.

American College of Sports Medicine (2011). 'Exercise is medicine', an initiative led by the American College of Sports Medicine. Retrieved from www.exerciseis-medicine.org/public.htm.

Anderssen, N. and Wold, B. (1992). Parental and peer influences on leisure-time physical activity in young adolescents. *Research Quarterly for Exercise and Sport*, 63(4), 341–348.

Babkes Stellino, M., Partridge, J. A., and Moore, K. (2012). Social influence on emotion and coping. In J. Thatcher, M. Jones, and D. Lavallee (eds), *Coping and emotion in sport*, 2nd edition (pp. 145–166). New York: Nova Science Publishers.

Bailey, R. P. (2006). Physical education and sport in schools: a review of benefits and outcomes. *Journal of School Health*, 76(8), 397–401.

Bailey, R. P. and Dismore, H. (2005). *Sport in education: the place of physical education and sport in schools* (SpinEd world-wide study). Berlin: International Council for Sport Science and Physical Education.

Bailey, R. P. and Reeves, M. J. (2013). *Research into sport and economic benefits of sport and physical activity*. Paris: UNESCO.

Bailey, R. P., Collins, D., Ford, P., MacNamara, A., Toms, M., and Pearce, G. (2009). *Participant development in sport: an academic review*. Leeds: Sports Coach UK.

Bailey, R., Cope, E. J., and Pearce, G. (2013). Why do children take part in, and remain involved in sport? A literature review and discussion of implications for sports coaches. *International Journal of Coaching Science*, 7(1), 56–75.

Bailey, R. P, Hillman, C., Arent, S., and Petitpas, A. (2012). Physical activity as an investment in personal and social change: the Human Capital Model. *Journal of Physical Activity and Health*, 9, 1053–1055.

Bailey, R. P, Hillman, C., Arent, S., and Petitpas, A. (2013). Physical activity: an underestimated investment in human capital? *Journal of Physical Activity and Health*, 10, 289–308.

Bailey, R. P., Wellard, I., and Dismore, H. (2004). *Girls' participation in physical activities and sports: benefits, patterns, influences and ways forward*. Technical Report. Geneva: WHO.

Bandura, A. (2001). Social cognitive theory: an agentive perspective. *Annual Review of Psychology*, 52, 1–26.

Baumeister, R. F. and Leary, M. R. (1995). The need to belong: desire for interpersonal attachments as a fundamental human motivation. *Psychological Bulletin*, 117(3), 497–529.

Baxter-Jones, A. D. G. and Maffulli, N. (2003). Parental influence on sport participation in elite young athletes. *Journal of Sports Medicine and Physical Fitness*, 43(2), 250–255.

Becker, G. S. (1964). *Human capital*. Chicago: University of Chicago Press.

Beets, M., Bornstein, D., Dowda, M., and Pate, R. (2011). Compliance with national guidelines for physical activity in US preschoolers: measurement and interpretation. *Pediatrics*, 127, 658–664.

Bonow, R. O., Smaha, L. A., Smith, S. C., Mensah, G. A., and Lenfant, C. (2002). World Heart Day: the international burden of cardiovascular disease. Responding to the emerging global epidemic. *Circulation*, 106(13), 1602–1605.

Booth, M. L., Owen, N., Bauman, A., Clavisi, O., and Leslie, E. (2000). Social-cognitive and perceived environmental influences associated with physical activity in older Australians. *Preventive Medicine*, 31(1), 15–22.

Breuer, C. and Pawlowski, T. (2011). Socioeconomic perspectives on physical activity and aging. *European Review of Aging and Physical Activity*, 8(2), 53–56.

Britain, G. and Donaldson, L. J. (2004). *At least five a week: evidence on the impact of physical activity and its relationship to health*. London: Department of Health.

Brockman, R., Jago, R., Fox, K. R., Thompson, J. L., Cartwright, K., and Page, A. S. (2009). 'Get off the sofa and go and play': Family and socioeconomic influences on the physical activity of 10–11 year old children. *BMC Public Health*, 9, 253–259.

Bronfenbrenner, U. (1993). The ecology of cognitive development: research models and fugitive findings. In R. H. Wozniak and K. W. Fischer (eds), *Development in context: acting and thinking in specific environments* (pp. 3–44). Hillsdale, NJ: Erlbaum.

Brustad, R. J. (1992). Integrating socialisation influences into the study of children's motivation in sport. *Journal of Sport and Exercise Psychology*, 14(1), 59–77.

Brustad, R. J. (1996). Attraction to physical activity in urban schoolchildren: parental socialization and gender influences. *Research Quarterly for Exercise and Sport*, 67(3), 316–323.

Bull, F., Milton, K. Kahlmeier, S. *et al.* (2014) Turning the tide: national policy approaches to increasing physical activity in seven European countries. *British Journal of Sports Medicine*, published online 28 March 2014. doi:10.1136/bjsports-2013-093200.

Ceccarelli, A. (2011). Review of policies adopted in 34 countries to improve diet and physical activity. *Italian Journal of Public Health*, 9(8), 156–171.

Chase, M. and Dummer, G. (1992). The role of sport as a social status determinant for children. *Research Quarterly for Exercise and Sport*, 63(4), 418–424.

Cicirelli, V. G. (1995). *Sibling relationships across the lifespan.* New York: Plenum Press.

Collings, P. J., Wijndaele, K., Corder, K., Westgate, K., Ridgway, C. L., Dunn, V., Goodyer, I., Ekelund, U., and Brage, S. (2014). Levels and patterns of objectively-measured physical activity volume and intensity distribution in UK adolescents: the ROOTS study. *International Journal of Behaviour Nutrition and Physical Activity*, 11, 23.

Collins, D., Bailey, R. P., Ford, P., MacNamara, Á., Toms, M., and Pearce, G. (2012). Three worlds: new directions in participant development in sport and physical activity. *Sport, Education and Society*, 17(2), 225–243.

Côté, J. (1999). The influence of the family in the development of talent in sport. *The Sport Psychologist*, 13(4), 395–417.

Côté, J. and Hay, J. (2002). Children's involvement in sport: a developmental perspective. In J. M. Silva and D. Stevens (eds), *Psychological foundations of sport* (pp. 484–502). Boston, MA: Allyn and Bacon.

Craig, C. L., Lambert, E. V., Inoue, S., Alkandari, J. R., Leetongin, G., and Kahlmeier, S. (2012). The pandemic of physical inactivity: global action for public health. *The Lancet*, 380(9838), 294–305.

Craig, R., Mindell, J., and Hirani, V. (2009). *Health Survey for England 2008. Volume 1: Physical Activity and Fitness.* Leeds: NHS Information Centre.

Craigie, A. M., Lake, A. A., Kelly, S. A., Adamson, A. J., and Mathers, J. C. (2011). Tracking of obesity-related behaviours from childhood to adulthood: a systematic review. *Maturitas*, 70(3), 266–284.

Davis, N. W. and Meyer, B. B. (2008). When siblings become competitors: a qualitative investigation of same-sibling competition in elite sport. *Journal of Applied Sport Psychology*, 20, 342–347.

Davison, K. K. (2004). Activity-related support from parents, peers, siblings and adolescents' physical activity: are there gender differences? *Journal of Physical Activity and Health*, 1, 363–376.

Department of Health and Human Services (2008). *2008 physical activity guidelines for Americans*. Rockville, MD: Office of Disease Prevention and Health Promotion.

Department of Health, Physical Activity, Health Improvement and Protection (2011). *Start active, stay active*: a report on physical activity from the Four Home Countries' Chief Medical Officers. London: Department of Health.

Dismore, H. (2006). *Primary/secondary school transitions in physical education*. Unpublished Doctoral Thesis. University of Kent.

Eccles, J. S. and Harold, R. D. (1991). Gender differences in sport involvement: applying the expectancy-value model. *Journal of Applied Sport Psychology*, 3(1), 7–35.

Edwardson, C. L. and Gorely, T. (2010). Parental influences on different types and intensities of physical activity in youth: a systematic review. *Psychology of Sport and Exercise*, 11(6), 522–535.

Evans, J. M. M., Shelia, C. M., Kirk, A., and Crombie, I. K. (2009). Tracking of physical activity behaviours during childhood, adolescence and young adulthood: a systematic review. *Journal of Epidemiology and Community Health*, 63 (Suppl. 2), 9.

Fraser-Thomas, J. and Côté, J. (2006). Youth sports: implementing findings and moving forward with research. *Athletic Insight*, 8(3), 12–27.

Fredricks, J. A. and Eccles, J. S. (2006). Is extracurricular participation associated with beneficial outcomes? Concurrent and longitudinal relations. *Developmental Psychology*, 42(4), 698–713.

Gandhi, S. (2010). *Parent-youth associations of physical activity and the influence of family and neighbourhood social factors*. Unpublished Dissertation. University of Montréal.

Gould, D., Lauer, L., Rolo, C., Jannes, C., and Pennisi, N. (2008). The role of parents in tennis success: focus group interviews with junior coaches. *The Sport Psychologist*, 22, 18–37.

Gray, W. N., Janicke, D. M., Ingerski, L. M., and Silverstein, J. H. (2008). The impact of peer victimization, parent distress and child depression on barrier formation and physical activity in overweight youth. *Journal of Developmental and Behavioral Pediatrics*, 29(1), 26–33.

Green, M. and Houlihan, B. (2005). *Elite sport development: policy learning and political priorities*. London: Routledge.

Greendorfer, S., Lewko, J., and Rosengren, K. (2002). Family and gender-based influences in sport socialization of children and adolescents. In F. Smoll and R. Smith (eds), *Children and youth in sport: a biopsychosocial perspective*, 2nd Edition (pp. 153–186). Dubuque, IA: Kendal/Hunt.

Grolnick, W. S., Deci, E. L., and Ryan, R. M. (1997). Internalization within the family: the Self-Determination Theory perspective. In J. E. Grusec and L. Kuczynski (eds), *Parenting and children's internalization of values: a handbook of contemporary theory* (pp. 135–161). Hoboken, NJ: John Wiley & Sons.

Hardy, L. L., Kelly, B., Chapman, K., King, L., and Farrell, L. (2010). Parental perceptions of barriers to children's participation in organised sport in Australia. *Journal of Paediatrics and Child Health*, 46(4), 197–203.

Harris, J. and Elbourn, J. (1997). *Teaching health-related exercise at Key Stages 1 and 2*. Champaign, IL: Human Kinetics.

Harris, J. R. (2011). *The nurture assumption: why children turn out the way they do*. New York: Free Press.

Harwood, C. and Knight, C. (2009a). Stress in youth sport: a developmental investigation of tennis parents. *Psychology of Sport and Exercise*, 10, 447–456.

Harwood, C. and Knight, C. (2009b). Understanding parental stressors: an investigation of British tennis-parents. *Journal of Sport Sciences*, 27, 339–351.

Hohepa, M., Scragg, R., Schofield, G., Kolt, G. S., and Schaaf, D. (2007). Social support for youth physical activity: importance of siblings, parents, friends and school support across a segmented school day. *International Journal of Behavioral Nutrition and Physical Activity*, 4(1), 54.

Horn, T. S. and Weiss, M. R. (1991). A developmental analysis of children's self-ability judgments in the physical domain. *Pediatric Exercise Science*, 3(4), 310–326.

Humpel, N., Owen, N., and Leslie, E. (2002). Environmental factors associated with adults' participation in physical activity: a review. *American Journal of Preventive Medicine*, 22(3), 188–199.

IWG (2008). *Harnessing the power of sport for development and peace: recommendations to governments*. Toronto: Sport for Development and Peace International Working Group.

Jago, R. and Baranowski, T. (2004). Non-curricular approaches for increasing physical activity in youth: a review. *Preventive Medicine*, 39(1), 157–163.

Janz, K. F., Burns, T. L., and Levy, S. M. (2005). Tracking of activity and sedentary behaviors in childhood: the Iowa Bone Development Study. *American Journal of Preventive Medicine*, 29(3), 171–178.

Kay, T. (2000). Sporting excellence: A family affair? *European Physical Education Review*, 6(2), 151–169.

Keresztes, N., Piko, B. F., Pluhar, Z. F., and Page, R. M. (2008). Social influences in sports activity among adolescents. *The Journal of the Royal Society for the Promotion of Health*, 128(1), 21–25.

Kirk, D., Carlson, T., O'Connor, T., Burke, P., Davis, K., and Glover, S. (1997). The economic impact on families of children's participation in junior sport. *Australian Journal of Science and Medicine in Sport*, 29(2), 27–33.

Kirk, D., Fitzgerald, H., Wang, J., and Biddle, S. (2000). *Towards girl-friendly physical education: the Nike/YST Girls in Sport Partnership Project – Final Report*. Loughborough: Institute for Youth Sport.

Kjønniksen, L., Anderssen, N., and Wold, B. (2009). Organized youth sport as a predictor of physical activity in adulthood. *Scandinavian Journal of Medicine and Science in Sports*, 19(1), 646–654.

Krane, V. (2001). We can be athletic and feminine, but do we want to? Challenging hegemonic femininity in women's sport. *Quest*, 53(1), 115–133.

Lee, I. M., Shiroma, E. J., Lobelo, F., Puska, P., Blair, S. N., Katzmarzyk, P. T., and Lancet Physical Activity Series Working Group. (2012). Effect of physical inactivity on major non-communicable diseases worldwide: an analysis of burden of disease and life expectancy. *The Lancet*, 380(9838), 219–229.

Light, R. and Lemonie, Y. (2010). A case study on children's reasons for joining and remaining in a French swimming club. *Asian Journal of Exercise and Sports Science*, 7(1), 27–33.

Light, R., Harvey, S., and Memmert, D. (2013). Why children join and stay in sports clubs: case studies in Australian, French and German swimming clubs. *Sport, Education and Society*, 18(4), 550–566.

Lim, S. S., Vos, T., Flaxman A. D. *et al.* (2012) A comparative risk assessment of burden of disease and injury attributable to 67 risk factors and risk factor clusters in 21 regions, 1990–2010: a systematic analysis for the Global Burden of Disease Study. *The Lancet*, 380, 2224–2260.

Lozano, R., Naghavi, M., Foreman, K. *et al.* (2010) Global and regional mortality from 235 causes of death for 20 age groups in 1990 and 2010: a systematic analysis for the Global Burden of Disease Study 2010. *The Lancet*, 380: 2095–2128.

Mattocks, C., Ness, A., Deere, K., Tilling, K., Leary, S., Blair, S. N., and Riddoch, C. (2008). Early life determinants of physical activity in 11 to 12 year olds: cohort study. *British Medical Journal*, 336(7634), 26–29.

McMinn, A. M., van Sluijs, E. M. F., Wedderkopp, N., Frobers, K., and Griffin, S. J. (2008). Sociocultural correlates of physical activity and adolescents: findings from the Danish Arm of the European Youth Heart Study. *Pediatric Exercise Science*, 20(3), 319–332.

Menschik, D., Ahmed, S., Alexander, M. H., and Blum, R. W. (2008). Adolescent physical activities as predictors of young adult weight. *Archives of Pediatrics and Adolescent Medicine*, 162(1), 29–33.

Miller, S. C. (2011). *Families moving together: increasing physical activity by targeting parents exclusively versus parents together with children.* Unpublished Doctoral Thesis. Texas State University-San Marcos.

Moore, L. L., Lombardi, D. A., White, M. J., Campbell, J. L., Oliveria, S. A., and Ellison, R. C. (1991). Influence of parents' physical activity levels on activity levels of young children. *Journal of Pediatrics*, 118(2), 215–219.

Nike (2012). Designed to move: a physical activity action agenda. Retrieved from www.designedtomove.org/en_us.

Partridge, J. A., Brustad, R. J., and Babkes Stellino, M. (2008). Social influence in sport. In T. S. Horn (ed.), *Advances in Sport Psychology*, 3rd edition (pp. 269–291). Champaign, IL: Human Kinetics.

Pate, R. R., Heath, G. W., Dowda, M., and Trost, S. G. (1996). Associations between physical activity and other health behaviors in a representative sample of US adolescents. *American Journal of Public Health*, 86(11), 1577–1581.

Payne, W., Reynolds, M., Brown, S., and Fleming, A. (2003). *Sports role models and their impact on participation in physical activity: a literature review.* Carlton South, Victoria, Australia: VicHealth.

Pellegrini, A. D. and Smith, P. K. (1998). Physical activity play: the nature and function of a neglected aspect of play. *Child Development*, 69(3), 577–598.

Pickard, A. and Bailey, R. P. (2009). Crystallising experiences among young elite dancers. *Sport, Education and Society*, 14(2), 165–181.

Rittenhouse, M., Salvy, S. J., and Barkley, J. E. (2011). The effect of peer influence on the amount of physical activity performed in 8- to 12-year-old boys. *Pediatric Exercise Science*, 23(1), 49–60.

Rubin, K. H., Bukowski, W., and Parker, J. G. (2006). Peer interactions, relationships, and groups. In W. Damon, R. M. Lerner and N. Eisenberg (eds), *Handbook of child psychology: Volume 3. Social, emotional, and personality development*, 6th edition (pp. 571–645). New York: Wiley.

Sallis, J. and Owen, N. (1999). *Physical activity and behavioral medicine*. Thousand Oaks, CA: Sage.

Sallis, J. F., Conway, T. L., Prochaska, J. J., McKenzie, T. L., Marshall, S. J., and Brown, M. (2001). The association of school environments with youth physical activity. *American Journal of Public Health*, 91(1), 618–620.

Salvy, S. J., Roemmich, J. N., Bowker, J. C., Romero, N. D., Stadler, P. J., and Epstein, L. H. (2008). Effect of peers and friends on youth physical activity and motivation to be physically active. *Journal of Pediatric Psychology*, 34(2), 217–225.

Savin-Williams, R. C. and Berndt, T. J. (1990). Friendship and peer relations. In S. S. Feldman and G. R. Elliott (eds), *At the threshold: the developing adolescent* (pp. 277–307). Cambridge, MA: Harvard University Press.

Schilling, T. A. and Hayashi, C. T. (2001). Achievement motivation among high school basketball and cross-country athletes: a personal investment perspective. *Journal of Applied Sport Psychology*, 13(1), 103–128.

Schranz, N., Olds, T., Cliff, D. *et al.* (2014). Results from Australia's 2014 Report Card on Physical Activity for Children and Youth. *Journal of Physical Activity and Health*, 11 (Supp. 1), S21–S25.

Siedentop, D. (2002). Junior sport and the evolution of sport cultures. *Journal of Teaching in Physical Education*, 21(4), 392–401.

Sisson, S. B. and Katzmarzyk, P. T. (2008). International prevalence of physical activity in youth and adults. *Obesity Reviews*, 9(6), 606–614.

Smoll, F. L. and Smith, R. E. (1996). Competitive anxiety: sources, consequences, and intervention strategies. In F. L. Smoll and R. E. Smith (eds), *Children and youth in sport: a biophysosocial perspective* (pp. 359–380). Brown & Benchmark: McGraw-Hill.

Spence, J. C. and Lee, R. E. (2003). Toward a comprehensive model of physical activity. *Psychology of Sport Exercise*, 4(1), 7–24.

Standage, M., Duda, J. L., and Ntoumanis, N. (2003). A model of contextual motivation in physical education: using constructs from self-determination and achievement goal theories to predict physical activity intentions. *Journal of Educational Psychology*, 95(1), 97.

Sulloway, F. (1996). *Born to rebel*. New York: Pantheon Books.

Telama, R., Yang, X., Laakso, L., and Viikari, J. (1997). Physical activity in childhood and adolescence as predictor of physical activity in adulthood. *American Journal of Preventive Medicine*, 13(1), 317–323.

Telama, R., Yang, X., Viikari, J., Välimäki, I., Wanne, O., and Raitakari, O. (2005). Physical activity from childhood to adulthood: a 21-year tracking study. *American Journal of Preventive Medicine*, 28(3), 267–273.

Tremblay, M. S., LeBlanc, A. G., Kho, M. E., Saunders, T. J., Larouche, R., Colley, R. C., Goldfield, G., and Gorber, S. C. (2011). Systematic review of sedentary behaviour and health indicators in school-aged children and youth. *International Journal of Behaviour Nutrition and Physical Activity*, 8(1), 98.

UNESCO (2013). Berlin Declaration. MINEPS V, Berlin, Germany, 28–30 May.

van Mechelen, W., Twisk, J. W., Post, G. B., Snel, J., and Kemper, H. (2000). Physical activity of young people: the Amsterdam Longitudinal Growth and Health Study. *Medicine and Science in Sports and Exercise*, 32(9), 1610–1616.

Verloigne, M., Van Lippevelde, W., Maes, L., Yildirim, M., Chinapaw, M., Manios, Y., Androutsos, O., Kovács, E., Bringolf-Isler, B., Brug, B., and De Bourdeaudhuij, I. (2012). Levels of physical activity and sedentary time among 10- to 12-year-old boys and girls across 5 European countries using accelerometers: an observational study within the ENERGY-project. *International Journal of Behavioural Nutrition and Physical Activity*, 9(1), 34–41.

Wall, M. and Côté, J. (2007). Developmental activities that lead to drop out and investment in sport. *Physical Education and Sport Pedagogy*, 12, 77–87.

Walters, S. (2011). The effects of adult involvement on children participating in organised team sports. Unpublished Doctoral Thesis. Auckland University of Technology.

Wang, F. and Veugelers, P. J. (2008). Self-esteem and cognitive development in the era of the childhood obesity epidemic. *Obesity Reviews*, 9(6), 615–623.

Welk, G. J. (1999a). *Promoting physical activity in children: parental influences*. New York: Educational Resources Information Center (ERIC) – Clearinghouse on Teaching and Teacher Education.

Welk, G. J. (1999b). The youth physical activity promotion model: a conceptual bridge between theory and practice. *Quest*, 51(1), 5–23.

Wheeler, S. (2012). The significance of family culture for sports participation. *International Review for the Sociology of Sport*, 47(2), 235–252.

WHO (World Health Organisation) (1946) Preamble to the Constitution of the World Health Organization as adopted by the International Health Conference, New York, 19–22 June 1946; signed on 22 July 1946 by the representatives of 61 States. Official Records of the World Health Organization, 2, 100.

WHO (World Health Organisation) (2005). *Facing the facts #1: chronic diseases and their common risk factors*. Geneva.

WHO (World Health Organisation) (2010). *Global recommendations on physical activity for health*. Geneva

WHO (World Health Organisation) (2011) *Global status report on non-communicable disease*. Geneva.

WHO (World Health Organisation) (2013). *Global action plan: for the prevention and control of noncommunicable diseases (2013–2020)*. Geneva.

World Health Organization Regional Office for Europe (2011) *Promoting sport and enhancing health in European Union countries: a policy content analysis to support action*. Copenhagen.

Chapter 10

From the creation of a concept to the globalisation of physical literacy

Margaret Whitehead and Patricia Maude

Introduction

The growth of 'physical literacy' from the insights gained from a PhD study to an internationally recognised concept is a remarkable journey. Advocacy developed from a small group of UK-based professionals, mainly in the field of physical education, to a larger group of colleagues in Europe, Canada and Australia. Physical literacy is now known in very many countries and is generating a re-examination of the goal of physical activity throughout the lifecourse. Interest has also spread to other professionals in related fields such as those in coaching and the leisure industry. That physical literacy has blossomed into a world-wide topic of interest would seem to indicate that the concept is making a timely contribution to the thinking in this area. Throughout this process Margaret Talbot has been unerringly supportive and her national and international advocacy has been highly significant throughout the course of this development.

The chapter is divided into three Parts. Part one, 'The beginnings', will outline briefly the research which formed the foundation of physical literacy and this will be put into context by setting out what was perceived as the general attitude to physical education and physical activity at the turn of the century. Also included will be mention of some of the projects and programmes that were created at this time, in many ways mirroring the developments concerning physical literacy. Part two is entitled 'Developmental milestones since 2009'. In the main this will be presented in a series of sections showing the range of activity that developed from the initial interest in the work, namely publications, conferences and the establishment of the International Physical Literacy Association (IPLA). An example of research into an aspect of physical literacy is also outlined here, as well as a diagram setting out examples of Margaret Talbot's advocacy in her various positions of responsibility. The final Part, 'Current challenges and future plans', looks at the challenges facing the International Physical Literacy Association and a sample of future plans.

Part one: the beginnings

The concept of physical literacy

In one sense it would be true to say that 'physical literacy' is not a completely new concept. A comprehensive search of the literature from the developed world would reveal a number of writers who have referred to this concept from the start of the twentieth century, if not before. However, the notion of physical literacy was never seriously discussed, analysed or explored; it was mentioned in passing and never became part of the physical activity lexicon.

When the concept was introduced at the beginning of the twenty-first century it was clearly in line with respected philosophical thinking and thus carried with it scholarly credibility. This credibility has generated significant interest and a real re-assessment of the value of physical activity in human life as we know it.

The concept of physical literacy was first presented as a serious consideration within the field of physical activity and physical education in 1993 at the International Association for Physical Education and Sport for Girls and Women Congress in Melbourne Australia. This chapter was based on a PhD thesis completed in 1987. Work on the thesis opened the door to an appreciation of three schools of philosophical thought: monism, existentialism and phenomenology. Each in their related but distinctive ways signaled the fallacy of dualism and the significance of our embodied dimension in human existence as we know it. These views had far-reaching ramifications in relation to the value and justification of physical activity throughout life and consequently sent out a challenge to current views of physical activity that tended to see it as purely therapeutic or recreational.

Briefly, monism denies that we, as humans, are comprised of two separate aspects of human nature – the mind and the body. This philosophy, known as dualism, spells out a dichotomy with the mind/intelligence/cognition seen as separate from, and superior to, the body, with the body being viewed as playing only a subsidiary role in human functioning. Monism, on the contrary, sets out a case for the human as a whole, endowed with a range of capabilities that work in concert, being intricately interdependent and mutually enriching (Gibbs 2006). In fact, current neuro-scientific study now reveals that our embodied capability is not subservient to the intellect but indeed provides the ground for all intellectual development, conceptual appreciation and understanding (Lakoff and Johnson 1999). Existentialism and phenomenology both adopt a monist perspective and explain in more detail how humans function as a whole.

Existentialism is concerned to argue that we create ourselves as we interact with the world. Our existence precedes our essence and we become who we are as we live in and interact with our surroundings (Burkitt

1999). All those aspects of our human nature that afford us the opportunity of relating to the world are, therefore, significant and should be nurtured. Our embodied dimension is one such medium of interaction and should be respected. Phenomenology builds on the views of existentialists and explains how every interaction is unique to the individual, with perception always being coloured by previous experiences. The corollary of this is that we each come to understand the world from our own perspective and each create our own world. Following this through, phenomenologists explain how we each perceive the world from the perspective of an embodied being (Leder 1990). The world and therefore existence is defined by our embodied nature. The outcome of these philosophical insights is that attention to our embodied dimension is as worthy of serious consideration as that of our other dimensions.

The notion of 'literacy' used in relation to our physical dimension has been questioned; however, this is justified with reference to the existentialist position that we, as humans, create ourselves in interaction with the world. Literacy in this context should be understood more liberally than just relating to facility with language and, instead, be seen as describing interaction between a human dimension and a corresponding aspect of the world. Literacy develops in any field where interaction is enriched through meaningful experience – that is, experience characteristically supported by appropriate knowledge, understanding, recognition, appreciation, understanding, assimilation and accommodation. UNESCO (2004) sets out a definition of literacy that describes an ability in the area of language understanding and use. This definition can be readily translated into the area of physical activity and would read as follows: physical literacy can be understood as a human capability that affords us the ability to identify, understand, interpret, create, respond effectively and communicate, using the embodied human dimension, within a wide range of situations and contexts. Physical literacy involves a continuum of learning in enabling individuals to achieve their goals, to develop their knowledge and potential, and to participate fully in their community and wider society.

While the use of the term 'literacy' in relation to the 'physical' in 1993 attracted scepticism, this is no longer such an issue as the it is now used widely in conjunction in numerous disciplines and areas or work such as music literacy, computer literacy, nutrition literacy, political literacy, media literacy, maths literacy, science literacy, geographic literacy, arts literacy, health literacy and leisure literacy – to name but a few.

Clearly there has been a major shift in the understanding of the term 'literacy'. Developing different literacies enables an individual to capitalise on what is on offer in the world that has the potential to enhance the quality of life. Considered in these terms it is not hard to see a common thread of understanding among all those who are now adopting 'literacy' as an element of their lexicon.

Any definition of literacy should look ahead with the goal of enhancing the quality of life on account of enriching experience. The above considerations have been the background to developing the concept of physical literacy. The definition has been modified slightly since it was first introduced and now reads:

> In short, physical literacy can be described as a disposition to capitalize on the human, embodied capability, wherein the individual has: the motivation, confidence, physical competence, knowledge and understanding to value and take responsibility for engagement in physical activities for life.
>
> (IPLA 2015)

Prevailing attitudes to physical activity at the start of the twenty-first century

That considerable interest was shown in this concept with its focus on life-long physical activity is likely to have been stimulated by a growing concern about the lack of physical activity in adulthood, obesity and poor physical and mental health in some sections of the community. The overriding goal of physical education and perhaps all physical activity at the start of the century was the development of physical skills as the forerunner of the production of highly skilled individuals. For many participants of all ages this was not an aspiration with which they could identify. With an end goal that they felt they would never reach, many lost motivation and, viewing that physical activity was not for them, turned their back on any sort of involvement on leaving compulsory education.

That this situation had developed can be seen as the outcome of a number of features that were prevalent at that time, particularly in schools but also at governmental level. The Physical Education National Curriculum was very concerned with the delivery of the subject content of activities and seemed to overlook the importance of the learning experience. Activities that were to be worked on tended to be predominantly competitive and there was a general view that as many as possible of these competitive activities should be introduced. The outcome of these recommendations was that schools tended to create curricula that comprised numerous short blocks of work. As a result learners had little opportunity to develop the necessary competence in any activity to the best of their ability to make it satisfying and meaningful. Moreover the weighting towards competitive games was not a context in which every learner found achievement and satisfaction. The National Curriculum also set out Levels of competence which learners were expected to reach at designated Stages of their education. As a result reports on learners often stated that the learner had not reached the expected Level, in other words was 'failing' in the subject area. Such norm referencing tended to disregard the fact that learners were differentially endowed in physical ability and thereby the physical education programme itself was not able to provide for these differences.

At governmental level not only was there stress on competition – within school work and in extra-curricular situations – but among the overall goals set out for physical education was that every learner should excel in the physical domain. This excessively challenging goal resulted in more weight being given in many schools to the most able and those who played in school teams. Finally, throughout the late twentieth and early twenty-first centuries there was a prevailing focus on physical education to be a means to other ends, such as fitness, cognitive development or social skills. No mention was made that physical development and physical activity might be of value in their own right.

Physical literacy addresses all these issues. It is strongly advocated that in school curricula equal weight should be allocated to a range of contrasting movement forms including adventure, aesthetic, athletic, and competitive (Murdoch and Whitehead, 2013).

Throughout the school curriculum learners should experience examples from each movement form in substantial blocks of time that enable participants to develop the physical competence, understanding and confidence to engage in that activity, such that it becomes a rewarding and positive experience. Additional experience of other activities should be accommodated in extra-curricular and community-based provision and be available for all learners.

In the teaching situation all learners are respected as having potential to develop their physical competence and their ability to engage meaningfully in a range of activities.

Differentiation in teaching enables every learner to make progress to the best of their ability and to have their efforts acknowledged. Practices in relation to assessment in the context of physical literacy are seen as making judgements on individual progress. This form of making judgements can be described as ipsative assessment – that is, judgement of progress as against previous individual performance. In this way there is no spurious comparison with others and there are no losers, all can be winners in their own right. Each individual is appreciated as being on their own physical literacy journey.

Curriculum planning and appropriately managed judgement on progress has the potential to enhance interest, commitment, motivation and confidence, all of which can encourage life-long participation in physical activities for all, not only the most able.

The underlying philosophy of physical literacy strongly supports the value of physical activity as being a basic human capability which has value in its own right. All learners are entitled to have worthwhile opportunities to develop their embodied or physical potential alongside their other capabilities. Physical activity has educational validity in its own right and should not be seen merely as a means to other ends such as cognitive or social development. That these areas of development can, in some instances, be enhanced in physical education settings is entirely dependent on the nature of the interaction between the learner and the teacher.

In short the concept of physical literacy has provided an opportunity for practitioners to re-assess their long-term goals, the material that it is appropriate to use and the methods of teaching that are most likely to enhance motivation and life-long participation.

Project and programme developments

Margaret Talbot was far-sighted and generous in the ways in which she instigated, implemented and supported projects which furthered children's movement development, physical education, active healthy lifestyles and physical literacy, through encouraging others and by facilitating the education of parents, carers and teachers, and associations, organisations and government agencies whose remit included providing for children's welfare.

In this section of Part one, three such projects and two other developments which related directly to, or have underpinned the development of, the concept of physical literacy, are presented. The three projects are the movement observation programme entitled 'Observing Children Moving', the '2Move' programme for parents and young children and a cutting-edge physical education curriculum for an overseas area. The two developments are work by the British Heart Foundation towards developing physical literacy and explorations of the concept of creativity in enhancing physical literacy.

At the turn of the century, many practitioners working with young children in Early Years settings and Key Stage 1 were eager for knowledge and resources to help them to understand better the development of young children's movement abilities. In 2002 the Physical Education Association of the United Kingdom (now the Association for Physical Education) commissioned the development of a distance-learning package to support effective movement observation and analysis techniques. This was based on the premise that interactive multimedia (a combination of different communication tools such as text, visual graphics, animation, still images and motion video through which the user can navigate) constitute a powerful tool from which to learn. This was the birth of 'Observing Children Moving', an interactive software package, made up of videos of children's typical movement abilities, analysis grids describing the movement abilities shown in the videos, hotspots to identify key teaching points in performance, observation tasks for practitioners and suggested activities for practitioners to try with children.

Observing Children Moving seeks to enhance knowledge and under-standing of movement development, to raise standards by promoting effective movement education and to assist those working with children aged 3–7 years to provide movement-learning experiences that match pupil needs. In achieving this, the resource also helps practitioners to provide play opportunities and learning experiences in movement education and physical education that are based on knowledge and understanding of pupils' capabilities at different stages of motor development. It has been found that Observing Children Moving successfully promotes the provision of greater knowledge to enable Early Years practitioners to become confident in their ability to observe children's movement, to describe and analyse what they see and then to make a difference to the quality of per-formance of every child with whom they work, thereby also enhancing physical literacy.

'2Move', initially published through the Central Council for Physical Recreation (CCPR) and the Child Growth Foundation in 2005 under Mar-garet Talbot's aegis, was a clearly presented and attractively illustrated activity programme booklet, for parent and pre-school child to participate together, every day, in active play in the home and outdoors, such as in the garden, local park or play area. The key messages were, first, to be physic-ally active together and, second, to be physically active indoors and when-ever possible outdoors, on a daily basis, thereby ensuring frequent opportunities for children's physical, movement vocabulary and health-promoting development. The minimum resource and equipment require-ments, beyond those readily available in and around the home, enabled parents and carers to access a wide range of physical activities. The overall message is the importance of providing for and ensuring the provision of young children's physical, movement and social development through interactive, physically active play, getting out of breath and having fun together and building physical literacy.

Proposing a physical development and physical education curriculum promoting physical literacy for an overseas area, offered a group of researchers a unique opportunity to create a cutting-edge curriculum for the twenty-first century. Released from the constraints of the UK physical education curriculum, normally based on activities such as gymnastics, games, dance, athletics, swimming and outdoor and adventurous activities, the researchers were free to work from the starting point of needs and out-comes for learners and to explore and establish the constituent compon-ents and lifelong educational benefits of the proposed physical education curriculum. The starting points were therefore to establish a framework and criteria for pupils' learning and to apply these across the age range from four to 18 years. The resulting proposal was made up of seven Learn-ing Strands and five Progressive Developmental Learning Stages:

Seven Learning Strands

1   Movement competence
2   Knowledge and understanding of movement forms
3   Creativity and innovation in addressing movement challenges
4   Exploration of a wide range of environments and resources
5   Participation and performance as individuals and group members
6   Principles and practices of embodied health
7   Respectful and responsible participation and performance.

Five Progressive Developmental Learning Stages

Stage 1: Establish movement vocabulary
Stage 2: Build on movement vocabulary, extend movement competence and quality
Stage 3: Refine, deploy and apply movement competences appropriately in a variety of situations and environment
Stage 4: Develop control and capacity to engage in age-appropriate movement forms
Stage 5: Demonstrate physical literacy through engagement in a range of formally structured physical activities.

This outline and structure provided for rich progress in physical literacy and for a far-reaching, wide range of activities to be explored and developed according to the experience, interests and maturation of the learners and to their cultural and social environment. Such a curriculum framework could be adapted to form the basis of the physical development and physical education curriculum for children in any society.

In 2012 the British Heart Foundation published 'Early Movers', a seven-booklet guide for early years settings providing for children from birth to the age of five. The guide is intended to help in the planning, organising and maximising of environments for physical activity, for providing and enabling appropriate physically active play experiences and for nurturing physical literacy for every child. The guidance is directed to both carers and parents. The sequel to 'Early Movers' is a national Charter for Physical Activity in the Early Years.

Curriculum development is about extending the boundaries of existing knowledge and understanding, seeking opportunities for exploration, trial and error and creating challenges in order to arrive at new avenues of experience. This is no exception in the context of creativity in physical literacy. As the concept of physical literacy has grown and become increasingly established, so it has become possible to explore more widely, to revisit past experience and to consider further the role of creativity within the parameters of the individual's lifelong physical literacy journey. Figure 10.1 is a

Contributions of creativity to enhancing physical literacy	Attributes of physical literacy	Contributions of physical literacy to enhancing creativity
Through tackling self-set as well as teacher-promoted creative challenges, learners can explore alternative aspects of movement vocabulary, enrich and evaluate creative experiences and thereby also gain further knowledge and understanding of physical competence	**Movement attributes** Physical competence Knowledge Understanding	Expanding physical competence by increasing movement vocabulary and enhancing skilful performance initiates further access to creative activity Gaining increased knowledge and understanding of movement content and performance by analysing personal performance, through observation and analysis of others and through studying movement
Enable learners to enhance their confidence, motivation and self-esteem through encouraging and supporting their playfulness, inquisitiveness, enquiry, experimentation, searching, ability to overcome failure and to recognise and value success through their creative activity	**Affective attributes** Confidence Motivation Self-esteem	Building increasing confidence engendered through skilful performance and familiarity with wide applications of movement, and enhancing intrinsic motivation and self-esteem generated through achievement and success can free learners to explore 'outside the box' of current experience
	Environmental attributes	
Creative exploration of movement spaces, the texture of the environment, work surfaces and access to various levels, pathways, and directions of movement, enhances learners' ability to read their environments	Environments - indoor and outdoor	Skilful 'reading' of a wide range of environments enables learners to apply related experience from one environment to another, thereby extending opportunities for the flowering of creativity
Working creatively alongside younger learners and peers as well as with older children and adults strengthens the ability to engage in social and interactive aspects of physical literacy, such as cooperation and competition	People	Interacting comfortably in movement with younger learners and peers as well as with older children and adults can strengthen the sense of self and stimulate creative experience
Free, creative exploration of natural resources, man-made and manufactured equipment promotes extensive variety, proficiency and enrichment in maximising uses of resources	Resources	Having the ability to interact with a wide range of natural, man-made and manufactured resources, increases the potential for exploratory and creative opportunities

Figure 10.1 Relationships between creativity and physical literacy.

Source: Maude and Pickard, 2014: 26.

summary of some ways in which aspects of creativity can enhance an individual's physical literacy and some ways in which elements of physical literacy facilitate the growth of an individual's creative development.

Physical literacy 1999–2009

Throughout the early period between 1999 and 2009, alongside the above initiatives, there was a growth in the number of publications of journal articles and a book, as well as an increasing number of presentations at conferences, all of which enabled the philosophy and practice of physical literacy to be promoted and disseminated more extensively. For example, Margaret Whitehead published in the *Journal of Philosophy of Education*, the *European Journal of Physical Education* and *Sport Ethics and Philosophy*, and Patricia Maude published *Physical Children Active Teaching: Investigating Physical Literacy* in the UK, subsequently translated into Chinese. The *British Journal of Teaching Physical Education* (Physical Education Association of the United Kingdom, PEAUK), *The Bulletin* (British Association of Advisers and Lecturers in Physical Education, BAALPE) and the *Early Years Educator* also featured articles expounding the concept of physical literacy. Several universities, local authorities and sports bodies invited presentations, and world-wide interest was launched as a result of presentations in Egypt, Greece, Canada and South Africa.

Acceptance of the concept in this early period in the UK was significantly influenced by Margaret Talbot in her role as formulating the 'Position Statement on Physical Education' at the 2005 National Summit on Physical Education and the Association for Physical Education (UK) Manifesto in 2008 (see Figure 10.2).

Part two: developmental milestones since 2009

Part one has outlined the early days of the introduction of the concept of physical literacy, the philosophical basis of the concept and the way that new thinking was being disseminated and was influencing projects and programmes. The next phase of growth, building on this increasing interest, can be seen as taking place between 2010 and 2015. Developments included the publication of the seminal text entitled *Physical Literacy throughout the Lifecourse* (Whitehead 2010), the publication of the International Council of Sport Science and Physical Education (ISCSSPE) *Bulletin on Physical Literacy* (2013) and the creation of the International Physical Literacy Association. In addition, those supporting physical literacy have been gaining knowledge and understanding about the role of this capability throughout life. There is clear evidence that acceptance of the concept is spreading across the world. This globalisation can in no small part be attributed to Margaret Talbot's endorsement of the concept

> **2005 National Summit on Physical Education** (CCPR, BAALPE, HEI Network, PEAUK (Margaret Talbot was CEO CCPR 2001–2005) **Position statement on Physical Education**
>
> Physical education aims systematically to develop physical competence so that children are able to move efficiently, effectively and safely and understand what they are doing. The outcome – physical literacy – is as important to children's education as numeracy and literacy.

> **2008 afPE Manifesto** (Margaret Talbot was CEO afPE 2006–2009)
>
> The aim of physical education is to develop physical competence so that all children are able to move efficiently, effectively and safely and understand what they are doing. The outcome, physical literacy, along with numeracy and literacy, is the essential basis for learners to access the whole range of competences and experiences.

> **2011 ICSSPE International Position statement on Physical Education** (Margaret Talbot was President of ICSSPE 2009–2014)
>
> Physical education develops physical competence so that children can move efficiently, effectively and safely and understand what they are doing. The outcome – physical literacy – is an essential basis for their full development and achievement.

> **2014 UNESCO. Statement on Physical Education** (Margaret Talbot served on a variety of UNESCO Committees, representing IAPESGW and ICSSPE)
>
> The outcome of **physical** education is a **physically literate** young person, who has the skills, confidence and understanding to continue participation in **physical** activity throughout the life span.

Figure 10.2 Endorsements of physical literacy.

on the world stage. Throughout this phase Margaret Talbot was actively promoting physical literacy through her leadership roles in ICSSPE and UNESCO. In 2011 she identified physical literacy in the ICSSPE International Position Statement on Physical Education and in 2014 she ensured that physical literacy was mentioned in the UNESCO 'Statement on Physical Education' (see Figure 10.1)

Seminars and conferences

Key milestones in the ongoing growth of the concept of physical literacy have been the ever widening participation in conferences and workshops ranging from the Bedford Seminar for 100 delegates in 2009, with follow-up seminars in Canterbury, Loughborough and Derbyshire in 2010 and the first International Physical Literacy Conference at the University of Bedfordshire in 2011. Next were the International Conference in Banff, Canada in 2013 and the third International Conference at the University of Bedfordshire in 2013. The International IPLA Seminar and workshop in the UK in 2014 focused on Charting Progress and on Continuing Professional Development. Finally, to date, the fourth International Physical Literacy Conference was held in Vancouver, Canada in 2015 with over 300 delegates.

Creation of the International Physical Literacy Association

The seeds of the Association were sown in 2013 when three colleagues gave presentations on physical literacy at an International Association of Physical Education and Sport for Girls and Women Congress. It was agreed to explore with others in UK the possibility of establishing an International Physical Literacy Association and this was subsequently proposed at the International Physical Literacy Conference later that year in England. There was unanimous agreement that an organisation of this nature was needed if the concept was to be promoted worldwide. Such was the enthusiasm that a Steering Group was set up immediately with colleagues from England, Wales, Northern Ireland, Australia and Canada giving freely of their time and expertise. Over the next year the group proceeded to establish the Association and to gain charitable status. The Association was officially launched in June 2014 with the mission to create a global community committed to physical literacy. This is both exciting and challenging, especially as IPLA has pledged to be international, multi-disciplinary and inclusive, and to work to foster physical literacy across the whole lifespan.

Widening the context of physical literacy: the early years

In 2014 IPLA established specialist teams to undertake a watching and supporting brief of all aspects of activity, research and other developments in relation to their specialism. Maintaining and developing physical literacy through the ongoing stages of life from birth and early years into childhood, the teenage years, young and mature adulthood and into older age are all encompassed within the brief for the 'Across-All-Ages' team.

This section of the chapter concerns the first of these stages of life, namely the Early Years, when all aspects of physical literacy should be introduced, established, nurtured and experienced by infants and young children. This is the stage in which the intervention of others can stimulate, promote, scaffold and ensure a sound start on the young child's lifelong physical literacy journey, enabling the maturing child to move towards the independent learning and the commitment needed to progress successfully as they proceed through that journey. Of particular significance in the early years is the development of physical competence, including the achievement of upright posture and locomotion, and the mastery of a myriad of gross and fine motor skills that provide access to independence in movement and control in daily life, inside and outside the home and, later, in school-related activities.

The first three years of life are responsible for 80 per cent of brain development (Urban Child Institute, 2015). Daniel Wolpert (2012) asserts that, although we may claim that the function of the brain is to enable us to perceive the world, the reason we have a brain is to produce adaptable and complex movements. For this movement to take place the child is dependent on neuromotor development, which is the relationship between the developing brain, the nervous and the muscular systems. Ratey and Hagerman (2008) state that 'exercise cues the building blocks of learning in the brain' and exercise is 'the single most powerful tool to optimise brain function'. They also remind us that 'to keep our brains at peak performance, our bodies need to work hard'. Frequent active play, indoors and outdoors, is therefore key to achieving optimum development of the brain and physical competence. The British Heart Foundation (2012) states: 'Children of pre-school age, capable of walking unaided, should be physically active for at least 180 minutes spread throughout the day.'

Goddard-Blythe (2012) states that, currently, many young children are deprived in neuromotor development and this seriously affects their progress once they start school. Failure to achieve optimum physical competence in the early years can also negatively affect children's motivation, self-confidence and self-esteem. This seems to arise as they become increasingly aware of the apparently greater abilities of some of their peers and can result in unwillingness to participate in physical activity and physical education sessions.

The teaching of Fundamental Movement Skills (FMS) can be a cause of this on account of the teaching method often adopted and the curriculum content presented. First, when the FMS teaching method is presented as directed teaching, requiring learners to 'match a model', to conform in their performance to an ideal model, those with differing abilities and individual learning needs may fail to achieve the prescribed and specific movement patterns and thereby come to realise their lesser ability to be successful. This can undermine feelings of well-being, unless the teacher acknowledges that 'There is no normative experience against which everything should be measured' (Winkett 2010). Enabling learners to progress to the best of their ability and at their own rate, towards achieving their full potential in physical competence, without requiring measurement against performance norms and other participants, is an excellent goal. Such a goal particularly contributes to the successful progress of learners with reduced self-confidence, motivation and self-esteem. Winkett (2010) goes on to state in relation to norm referencing, that 'when we recognise this ... our understanding as human beings will be only expanded and enriched'.

Second, the curriculum content of FMS often focuses on selected skills related mainly to competitive team sports, such as, for example, specific types of throw, catch, strike and kick. Whilst such skills may foster specific sport participation for some learners, they may limit rather than enhance the entitlement of every learner to the development of an extensive, general movement vocabulary, especially for those learners not attracted to activities involving those skills. A curriculum in the early years and primary school that enables learners to experience a broad general movement vocabulary provides them both with the foundation for learning relevant specific skills and with potential access to many physical activity horizons in the future.

Against the twentieth century backdrop of the 'couch potato' generation and the spiralling obesity epidemic in young children, much is to be gained in the twenty-first century from focused commitment to the nurturing of all aspects of physical literacy for all children in their early years, and to ensuring that young children attain their full potential in physical competence, confidence, motivation to participate, knowledge and understanding of physical activity, before they proceed into their later childhood, teenage years, adulthood and older age.

These are some of the considerations that fall within the remit of the IPLA Across-All-Ages Team, when supporting the enhancement of physical literacy in the early years.

Part three: current challenges and future plans

As Part two has shown, there has been a great deal of progress between 2010 and 2015 in respect of publications and conferences concerned with physical literacy, in addition to the creation of the International Physical Literacy Association and the growth in knowledge and understanding of the value of promoting physical literacy throughout the lifecourse. Physical literacy has now moved well beyond being a UK, physical education-based concept and is building on global interest to become established and respected across the world. In Part three consideration will be given to the outcomes of these developments and includes some of the plans that the Association has for the future.

Current challenges to the concept of physical literacy

While it is very good to report that the concept has been adopted across the world and has initiated a serious evaluation of work in physical education and physical activity, a challenge that presents itself now is the way that, in numerous settings, the interpretation of the concept has diverged from the original formulation.

IPLA is working to clarify a number of issues. These are the importance of embracing the breadth of the concept, appreciating that physical literacy is relevant to every individual throughout life, understanding physical literacy as a journey, realising the importance of using appropriate methods of charting progress and, finally, appreciating the relationship between physical literacy and physical education. Each of these issues will now be considered briefly.

Embracing the breadth of the concept

Physical literacy is best understood as a capability (Nussbaum 2000) that embraces three elements of human capacity being the affective, the physical and the cognitive. These are of equal significance. The affective element covers motivation, confidence and valuing physical activity. This is referred to first as it is felt that without motivation and confidence there is little likelihood of physical activity being pursued throughout life. There is some truth in the notion that, generally, teachers and coaches put more focus on improving the physical aspects of physical literacy. Fostering motivation and confidence are also essential foundation stones of nurturing physical literacy.

The physical element of physical literacy is, of course, the medium of embodied interaction between the individual and the world. As such it is at the heart of any experience of physical activity and thus warrants serious attention. The goal of any physical activity is to enable all individuals to have engaging, rewarding and meaningful experiences in a wide variety of physical and inter-personal settings (Capel and Whitehead 2013; Whitehead 2010). This engagement in the physical domain goes well beyond the mastery of general and specific movement patterns (Whitehead 2010). These movement patterns are not ends in themselves. While they are necessary constituents of the physical element of physical literacy they are far from sufficient to make a significant impact on physical literacy. They may be the keys to open the door to meaningful experiences, however their contribution is not realised until they are drawn on, challenged, and applied in different situations and environments. In these contexts physical competence moves from resembling a series of drills to an exciting, stimulating and enriching experience. This experience can be a powerful motivator. It is important to underline the value of, and need for, experience of a range of physical activity contexts. The nature of physical activities varies widely and it is essential that individuals experience a range of different activities to cater for the preferences of different people.

The cognitive element is embedded in involvement in physical activity and covers an understanding of the nature of movement, the diagnosis of where improvements can be made and the ability to set personal goals. The cognitive also involves the ability to use movement patterns imaginatively, as well as an understanding of the value of physical activity to holistic life-long health. This not only covers the physical health aspect but also the enrichment of the quality of life across a broad front. As indicated above the three elements of physical literacy are intricately related.

- Without motivation there would be no incentive to take part in physical activity or to appreciate the value of this activity.
- Without the development of physical competence there would be no grounds for individuals to value the experience as satisfying and rewarding, one through which they develop self-worth and self-confidence.
- Without knowledge and understanding in respect both of the nature of movement and the holistic benefits of exercise there would be little grounds for individuals to take responsibility for their participation throughout life.

To focus just on one element, such as the physical, is to overlook the holistic nature of the individual. All elements are equally important. Each is essential to realise progress on an individual physical literacy journey.

Appreciating that physical literacy is relevant to every individual throughout life

Physical literacy is relevant to all individuals whatever their age and endowments. The early years and the time in primary education cover significant stages in development during which the fostering of physical literacy is critical. The foundation of physical abilities and attitudes to physical activity are laid down and established in the early years (Maude in Whitehead 2010). The adolescent years are, indeed, equally important if young people are to develop their physical literacy so that this capability can be drawn on and further developed in later life. The significance of developing physical literacy from birth to young adulthood is as important for the able bodied and those with disability as it is for those who may have exceptional potential in respect of physical competence. The value of maintaining and developing physical literacy throughout life is multi-faceted, providing opportunities for taking part in activities that promote health and well-being in the widest sense as well as nurturing the physical and mental resources to help individuals to remain active and independent.

Understanding physical literacy as a journey

Another challenge faced by IPLA is to make clear that physical literacy is best viewed as a life-long journey. Individuals do not reach an end state of achieving physical literacy that, once achieved, is automatically maintained throughout life. As with any journey there will always be both opportunities and challenges on the way (Taplin, 2013). And this journey will be subject to the influences of others, particularly significant others, at every stage in life. Prior to schooling, outside schooling and after schooling is completed, numerous people and very many opportunities can make a huge impact on encouraging the development of motivation, confidence, physical competence and knowledge and understanding in relation to physical literacy. While teachers of physical education are not the only people responsible for nurturing physical literacy, they have an important role to play in that the school affords the one and only opportunity for all children and young people to be assured of access to the physical education curriculum. Teachers of physical education have it within their grasp to lay a sound foundation to the physical literacy journey of all learners such that when leaving school they will have developed the commitment to maintain physical activity for life.

Realising the importance of using appropriate methods of charting progress

An issue arising from the notion of a journey is the challenge for IPLA to consider and formulate how to keep a record of developing physical literacy: a record that accommodates all elements – affective, physical and cognitive – and that is personal to the individual. This is an exciting initiative that aims to find a way to chart progress or map a journey. The fundamental principle is to make judgments that are apposite to the individual and not norm- or level-related. It is argued that comparison with others is irrelevant and that any scheme must adopt ipsative assessment – that is, making judgments against previous performance (Whitehead, 2010).

Appreciating the relationship between physical literacy and physical education

The final challenge that IPLA faces is clarifying the relationship between physical literacy and physical education. Far from there being any competition between these two concepts they are, in fact, in partnership during the years of schooling. Physical literacy provides physical education with a well articulated goal that can be explained and justified within education, while physical education provides a unique opportunity for physical literacy to be nurtured. The two concepts of physical literacy and physical education, though interdependent, are of different orders. First, physical education is the name of a programme of physical activity within the school curriculum whereas physical literacy is a goal for or intended outcome of this subject area. Second, there is some truth in saying that one can teach physical education but that one can only provide the best possible opportunities to enable individuals to develop their physical literacy. This last statement highlights that there are significant implications of working towards promoting physical literacy. These have been discussed in detail in numerous publications (Almond and Whitehead, 2012a, 2012b, 2012c; Whitehead with Almond, 2013a) and include (1) maintaining an encouraging ambience in all lessons, (2) employing appropriate, differentiated teaching approaches, (3) providing learners with a worthwhile experience of a wide variety of Forms of Movement (Capel and Whitehead, 2013; Whitehead, 2010) and (4) adopting criterion referenced, ipsative assessment of progress. It is important to stress that if the development of physical literacy is the goal of physical activity these implications need to be seriously considered. In fact one could go so far as to say that such is the importance of these implications it is essential they are addressed in teaching and coaching. Work in physical education embraces a wide variety of strategies, some with particular intentions such as promoting health or developing independence. These strategies can make a valuable contribution to the physical education experience; however, whichever teaching approach is used or indeed whatever activity is being taught the underlying focus should be on promoting those attitudes and abilities that will encourage and empower learners to maintain physical activity through life. Developing physical literacy is the fundamental goal of and value of all physical activity.

Future plans

There is no doubt that the concept of physical literacy is well respected and seriously considered by many countries across the world. The International Physical Literacy Association can now look forward to an exciting future, and there is no shortage of further initiatives that the Association plans to take forward.

Three such initiatives relate to the establishment of satellite groups, to continuing professional development (CPD) and to the promotion of research.

Establishment of satellite groups in geographic locations across the world

IPLA has already established working communications with colleagues in Thailand, Brazil and Czechoslovakia, as well as in a number of provinces in Canada. Communities in these locations have each appointed a coordinator to foster physical literacy and develop supporting programmes. These programmes are thereby sensitive to the cultural/socio-political nature of each specific geographic location.

Continuing professional development

IPLA is planning a series of CPD courses to cater for practitioners across all phases of life and across a wide range of professions. These courses will be progressively demanding and will build from the Foundation Course through the Development Course to the Advanced Course. Assessment will be by submitted written work and through reports of small-scale investigations in activity settings. Completion of the course at advanced level will involve a piece of research into an aspect of physical literacy. It is planned to set up partnerships with universities to accredit the Advanced Course.

Promotion of research

IPLA is establishing a forum, which will be initiated via the IPLA website. This will have a section dedicated to research papers and will include opportunities for discussion groups. It is seen as important that all research across the world is shared and that future research builds from existing knowledge. IPLA will also support small-scale projects in schools as well as master's and PhD study in institutes of higher education. Ultimately IPLA hopes to launch an International Physical Literacy Journal. A bursary has been set up by the Association in Margaret's name to support small-scale research projects.

Conclusion

This chapter has charted the formulation and development of the concept of physical literacy. From the modest beginnings of a doctoral thesis, the concept has blossomed into a globally recognised and respected phenomenon. At all stages Margaret Talbot was highly supportive and endorsed the concept world-wide in her numerous positions of responsibility. The underlying intention of the advocacy of physical literacy is to foster the commitment to life-long physical activity. Physical literacy as a concept has already realised a remarkable journey and is effecting significant change in countries from Canada to Australia and from Brazil to Thailand. However there is still a long way to go. The more people who support the aspirations of physical literacy, the further and wider will be its growth and, as a consequence, the greater the number of lives that will be enriched by life-long participation in physical activity.

References

Almond, L. and Whitehead, M. E. (2012a) Physical Literacy. Clarifying the Nature of the Concept. *Physical Education Matters*, Spring, 68–71.

Almond, L. and Whitehead, M. E. (2012b) The Value of Physical Literacy. *Physical Education Matters*, Summer, 61–63.

Almond, L. with Whitehead, M. E. (2012c) Translating Physical Literacy into Practice for All Teachers. *Physical Education Matters*, Autumn, 67–70.

British Heart Foundation (2012) *Physical Activity Guidelines*. Loughborough: British Heart Foundation.

Burkitt, I. (1999) *Bodies of Thought. Embodiment, Identity and Modernity*. London: Sage.

Capel, S. and Whitehead, M. E. (eds) (2013) *Debates in Physical Education*. London: Routledge.

Gibbs, R. G. Jr, (2006) *Embodiment and Cognitive Science*. Cambridge: Cambridge University Press.

Goddard Blythe, S. (2012) *Assessing Neuromotor Readiness for Learning*. Chichester: Wiley-Blackwell.

International Physical Literacy Association, www.physical-literacy.org.uk.

Lakoff, G. and Jonhson, M. (1999) *Philosophy and the Flesh. The Embodied Mind and Its Challenge to Western Thought*. New York: Perseus Books Group. Basic Books.

Leder, D. (1990) *The Absent Body*. Chicago and London: University of Chicago Press.

Maude, P. M. (2000) *Observing Children Moving*. Reading: Physical Education Association.

Maude, P. M. (2001) *Physical Children, Active Teaching: Investigating Physical Literacy*. Berkshire: Open University Press.

Maude, P. M. (2005) *Physical Children, Active Teaching: Investigating Physical Literacy*. Complex Chinese Character Edition. Taipei: Hung Yeh Publishing.

Maude, P. M. (2008) From Movement Development into Physical Literacy. In D. Whitebread (ed.), *Teaching and Learning in the Early Years*, 3rd edition (Chapter 11). London: Routledge .

Maude, P. M. (2010) Physical Literacy and the Young Child. In M. E. Whitehead (ed.), *Physical Literacy throughout the Lifecourse* (Chapter 9). London: Routledge.

Maude, P. M. (2013) Growing Physical Literacy in the Young Child. *ICSSPE Bulletin – Journal of Sport Science and Physical Education*, 65. Retrieved from www.icsspe.org/content/no-65-cd-rom.

Maude, P. M. (2015) From Movement Development into Physical Literacy. In D. Whitebread (ed.), *Teaching and Learning in the Early Years*, 4th edition (Chapter 11). London: Routledge.

Maude, P. M. and Pickard, A. (2014) *Teaching Physical Education Creatively*. London: Routledge.

Maude, P. M. with Wetton, P. and Whitehead, M. E. (2005) *2Move*. London: The Central Council for Physical Recreation and the Child Growth Trust.

Murdoch, L. and Whitehead, M. (2010) Physical Literacy, Fostering the Attributes and Curriculum Planning. In M. Whitehead (ed.), *Physical Literacy: Throughout the Lifecourse* (pp. 175–188). London: Routledge.

Nussbaum, M. C. (2000) *Women and Human Development. The Capabilities Approach*. Cambridge: Cambridge University Press.

Ratey, J. and Hagerman, E. (2008) *SPARK: The Revolutionary New Science of Exercise and the Brain*. New York: Little Brown & Company.

Taplin, E. (2013) Physical Literacy as a Journey. *ICCSPE Bulletin – Journal of Sport Science and Physical Education*, 65. Retrieved from www.icsspe.org/content/no-65-cd-rom.

UNESCO (United Nations Educational, Scientific and Cultural Organization) (2004) *Education Sector Position Paper 13. 'The Plurality of Literacy and its implications for Policies and Programs'*. Retrieved from http://unesdoc.unesco.org/images/0013/001362/136246e.pdf.

Urban Child Institute (2015) www.urbanchildinstitute.org/why-0-3/baby-and-brain.

Whitehead, M. E. (1990) Meaningful Existence, Embodiment and Physical Education. *Journal of Philosophy of Education*, 24(1), 3–13.

Whitehead, M. E. (2001) The Concept of Physical Literacy. *European Journal of Physical Education*, 6(2), 127–138.

Whitehead, M. E. (2007) Physical Literacy: Philosophical Considerations in Relation to Developing a Sense of Self, Universality and Propositional Knowledge. *Sport Ethics and Philosophy*, 1(3), December, 281–298.

Whitehead, M. E. (ed.) (2010) *Physical Literacy throughout the Lifecourse*. London: Routledge.

Whitehead, M. E. with Almond, L. (2013a) Creating Learning Experiences to Foster Physical Literacy. *Physical Education Matters*, Spring, 24–27.

Whitehead, M. E. (2013b) The History and Development of Physical Literacy. *ICSSPE Bulletin – Journal of Sport Science and Physical Education*, 65. Retrieved from https://www.icsspe.org/content/no-65-cd-rom.

Whitehead, M. E. (2013c) Creating Learning Experiences to Foster Physical Literacy. *ICSSPE Bulletin – Journal of Sport Science and Physical Education*, 65. Retrieved from www.icsspe.org/content/no-65-cd-rom.

Whitehead, M. E. (2013d) Content implications of working to promote physical literacy. *ICSSPE Bulletin – Journal of Sport Science and Physical Education*, 65. Retrieved from www.icsspe.org/content/no-65-cd-rom.

Whitehead, M. E. (2014) Physical Literacy. In I. M. Vingdal (ed.), *Fysisk Akti Laering* (pp. 81–95). Glynendal.

Winkett, L. (2010) *Our Sound is our Wound*. London: Continuum.

Wolpert, D. (2012) A Moving Story. *Cambridge Alumni Magazine*, 66, Easter.

Chapter 11

Valuing leisure practices
Towards a theoretical framework[1]

Michael McNamee

Introduction

There is much confusion surrounding the notion of leisure; not merely as
to what it is but also as to the nature of its worth or value. Not only are
there terminological confusions which arise from inconsistent usage of
notions like 'intrinsic', 'inherent', 'extrinsic', 'instrumental' and 'external'
but there is a general tension in philosophical discussions surrounding the
objectivity of value. It is in no way claimed that this chapter establishes
anything especially fundamental vis à vis the objectivity or subjectivity of
values. What is attempted is a consideration of value arguments and the
language in which they are often couched. A position, termed 'relational
value and valuing', is articulated which attempts to reconcile the subjective
processes of intrinsic and instrumental valuing, and the non-subjective
status of the value of leisure practices.[2] The more modest aim is, therefore,
to provide a framework in which objectivist and subjectivist accounts of
the value of leisure practices may be contested.

Values and valuing

The notion of value is bound up with the idea of a person's capacity to
apprehend significance. Persons are intentional or purposive beings; they
do things for reasons. If a person interprets something to be of value then
this interpretation will be made in the light of an object or activity[3] which
has the capacity to confer a benefit or good to that person or group to
which he or she belongs. Conversely, something will be of no value or dis-
value if it does not have the capacity to produce a benefit or good or if its
effects are negative. To evaluate something is to be able to give relevant
reasons when contrasting some thing or activity against another. It is to
bring our capacity for reason to bear upon an issue. The subject/object distinction is often used to capture the nature of the problem here.

A distinction is commonly drawn between something which is valued
(by a subject) and saying that something is of value (objectively, or

independent of any particular subject). For philosophers of education such as R. S. Peters, value arguments ought to derive from the character of what is valued (object) and not merely from the valuing (subject).[4] But if the notion of value is tied up with a benefit which is correlative with ideas of human needs, wants and interests (let us call them 'desiderata') then it would appear that the value of an activity could not be specified in the absence of the desiderata. This will bear witness not only to the character of the activity but also to the relations that hold between the valuer and that which is valued (i.e. natural talents, dispositions etc.). Only persons could enter such a relation in a strong sense since only they could come to evaluate and contrast different desiderata.[5] This reasoning is not a purely rational affair but goes hand in hand with the agent's feelings and emotions. Where, however, there is no possibility of giving reasons to value something this should be considered mere taste or preference. The positive argument will focus on the public nature of valuing in contrast to the entirely subject-dependent notion of preference or taste.

The account developed here does not take the object–subject distinction to represent two distinct categories. Rather, it will be argued that it is less conducive to error to conceive of them as extremes of a continuum. On the one hand, then, there is someone's taste for ice cream, while on the other there is the value of a fully functioning human heart. The value of the former may be seen as a highly subjective-psychological phenomenon while the latter is objective irrespective of what any particular individual thinks about it. More needs to be said of this latter notion lest the notion of value espoused will appear timeless and asocial.

To characterise value as objective in this sense is not to say that the value resides outside of any and all human interests. The reason why a fully functioning human heart is so valuable is that human beings rely upon its functioning for just about everything else; it is a precondition of existence. Of course, there may be someone who does not wish to carry his or her life forward. They wish that, and may even try to bring about a situation, where their heart ceases to function. But sense cannot be made of a whole society wanting and valuing the same. As Hart notes, human society is not a suicide club.[6] The suicidal person is to be seen against the backcloth of persons within ways of life who project themselves forward.

Being rooted socially and historically, persons are inevitably inculcated into particular ways of life. The manner in which they participate in and/or evaluate a given activity, practice or object will be governed by the resources open to them. What constitutes a good life changes according to the ideals, hopes and aspirations which belong to that way of life. To some extent this will be an open-ended project though it has not always been so. Crudely put, traditional societies are characterised partly by the tightness of their ideals; there is little space for critical reflection. Modern societies, by contrast, cannot turn their back on this feature, especially as it relates to making sense of the meaning and value of a good life. Just as it is unlikely that these questions could be understood in earlier epochs, they cannot be escaped in modernity.

What, however, is relatively ongoing and is brought out by the discussion of the value of a human heart is the idea that there are candidates for value which are relatively resistant to social change. The heart example works well since it is tied inextricably to human survival. Unlike many other animals, human beings have to be taught survival and remain in a dependent relationship for the early years. This form of social existence (or something very like it) is necessary for beings such as ourselves. These simple ideas are embryonic to the notion that we must learn to become persons, for not only are we concerned with learning survival skills but also a vast array of other dispositions and abilities. Ways of life are the aggregate of these learnings and are the material out of which the life plans of persons are lived, formed and reformed.[7] They are open to continual revision and elaboration in order that good and full lives can be sought and lived.

If there are reasons which can be given for the consideration of the value of certain activities then these are reasons why a person, in relevantly similar circumstances, ought to value them. But these reasons only produce a hypothetical ought since they presume the presence of certain conditions which may or may not be present for the individual valuers, their dispositions and ways of life. The account of value developed here attempts to cater for the relationship of the public features of activities and the subjective process of valuing. There are others, notably R. S. Peters in his influential account of education as the development of rational mind, who argue for an objectivist account of the value of intrinsically worthwhile activities. Such arguments rest upon the value which is somehow intrinsic to the activity independently of whether it was valued by any particular persons. It is not merely the fact that persons value X which makes it valuable. Crudely put, the value of an X rests in the object (activity) and not the subject; in what is wanted and not merely the wanting. The account developed here will resist such an asocial, ahistorical and timeless vantage point. Before, however, setting out a relational account of valuing in terms of internal goods, external goods and their relationships, it will be useful to examine critically some traditional value arguments, which are either subjective or hedonistic.

Subjective value and hedonism

This section will explore briefly the possible weaknesses of arguing for the value of an activity conceived of in either subjective or hedonistic terms.

According to objectivist arguments, any attempt to give an account of value in terms of desiderata is anathema. To show that some thing or activity is wanted by an individual or group and that they were committed to it was insufficient to establish that it was objectively valuable or worth-while. In contrast, there are writers such as Thompson[8] who appear to hold the position that, if the value of an activity that is brought into question then the onus of proof is on the sceptic:

> I hold that the search for clinching criteria justifying intrinsic worth-whileness is a total waste of time. If something is for me intrinsically worthwhile there is no way at all in which I can prove its worthwhile-ness. I can only assert it.[9]

This is a particular example of a general position that will be called either subjective or object-independent, the choice of which is deliberate even though it is conceded that the general position is something of a caricature. It resembles, in philosophical terms, an intuitionist account in that it holds that value cannot be objectively proven for it is not amenable to proof. Thompson's view is not intuitionist yet it bears a strong resemblance to it, namely the presupposition that because verification or falsification do not operate in the arena of evaluative debates then the assertion of subjective value is the extent to which the value of some activity may be justified.

But assertions are not arguments. They are logically weak. If someone asserts the contrary then there is no way, for example, of assessing different positions since there is no criterion against which they may be contrasted. It must be borne in mind that setting out different positions as 'objective' on the one hand and 'subjective' on the other is rather crude. However, the point which is being laboured here is the contrast not between different sorts of reasons but of an account of value where some reasons can be given against one which makes no attempt to give justifying reasons. How would one get others to agree with one's point of view other than by argument? And how could one proceed unless evaluation was carried out in relation to public features of an object or activity? The general point is that evaluation may proceed only under certain descriptions.[10] And this accords with the account of value above. If a value is linked to some conception of benefit or satisfaction of certain desiderata then in principle one ought to be able to specify just what it is that is of value. If one could articulate the bases of this value in and through the engagement of leisure practices this would be prima facie evidence against Thompson's claim that one can only assert and not give good reasons for the intrinsic worthwhileness of activities. To fall back to the position that one may only assert intrinsic value is to assent to the sleep of reason. The position advanced here does not entail that everyone will perceive the same values in activities such as hill-walking, games and sport. Interpretation in evaluation does not necessitate this. What it does demand, however, is that the basis of such value is at least partially articulable and ipso facto on the agenda for conjecture and refutation.

Subjectivism for the purposes of this argument is, therefore, taken to mean that position whereby no reasons can be given to establish the inherent value of an activity. Our criticism of Thompson's remarks, and the general position, above is that reasons must be given though they need not be sufficient. The central reason why the subjectivist thesis, as it has been outlined here, is to be shunned by academics and other professionals concerned with leisure is that it offers no criteria (and hence no logical basis over and above mere preference) against which to evaluate such practices or make subsequent policy decisions. If, for instance, we are concerned with the question 'what leisure practices are worth pursuing/providing/ offering in preference to/commiting ourselves to?' the subjectivist thesis offers us no clues or direction. In Wittgensteinian language 'we do not know how to follow the rule'[11] since no rule can be discerned from mere preference other than the preference itself. And that is no logical guide even though it may be the basis of a market-driven justification. Thus, the beginning and ending of the subjectivist value thesis is 'I simply (dis)like it'. This response has, in another context, been termed a 'stopper'. That is to say it fails to provide any sort of logical answer to a questioner but stops the questioner from continuing. This point is pregnant for academics and professionals in leisure. In spite of the emotivist and subjectivist temper of the age, the question 'what sort of life is worth pursuing?' is a pressing, if largely ignored (the two positions are not contradictory), question that is as appropriate to us now as it was in Socrates' time. And yet it is ignored largely in favour of a fleeting engagement with unmediated consumptivism. It is presupposed, though rarely argued for, that what people value is merely that which they desire reflected in consumptive trends. The move is further made that what is valued is therefore of value independent of their consumption. The broader issues that inform this debate are inextricably linked with notions of economic rationality and ideologies of freedom, choice and power that are beyond the scope of this limited essay.

In defence of Thompson's subjectivist position it might be said that our remarks gain purchase in talk of value generally but lose their grip in reference to intrinsic value. Part of the problem here is that the language of the debate gets in the way of our understanding. A discussion of the logical and terminological problems associated with the issue will be entered into in section 4 below. For the moment, critical attention will be paid to a type of value argument along hedonistic lines whereby the value of activities resides exclusively in their capacity to induce pleasurable feelings in the experiencing agent.

Many sportsmen and sportswomen, for example, find the exercise of skilful acts deeply satisfying, fulfilling or pleasurable and attribute their value to nothing other than the experience or engagement in the activity. The language in which their accounts of the value of these experiences are often couched is hedonistic in the sense that it relates exclusively to the subjective value of pleasurable feelings. It is argued by such people that one should perform these sorts of activities simply for the pleasures they bring. In order to show that this type of argument is inadequate, or better, insufficient, five points of weakness in them will be presented before moving on to discuss various types of value and their relation to leisure practices.

First, let us consider the case that the value of these activities is their resultant pleasure, fun or enjoyment. It should be noted that many of these pursuits such as football, hockey or hill walking, though enjoyed by the skilful and somatotypically[12] suited individuals, are experienced as dissatisfying, embarrassing, frustrating, unrewarding or downright painful by others. There may be many qualities, goods or values associated with, for instance, cross-country running in the winter time. It may be assumed, however, that fun, pleasure and enjoyment are commonly not among them. These activities may come to be enjoyable but only after some considerable time and effort, and this may only be afforded to a limited number of people who are genetically predisposed to the activity or who through training have come to like them. Second, it should be noted that pleasures differ in quality. The pleasures of a child may be considered inappropriate for a mature adult. Consider the great joy that a child experiences when simply spinning around in ever-quickening circles. No-one would want to deny that these were pleasurable or that children ought to be deprived of them but one would not expect them to be suitably valuable or pleasurable pursuits for adults. Third, the pursuit of pleasure itself does not demarcate any special class of activities except those logically thus defined. The corollary of the hedonistic view would entail the justification of whatsoever people found pleasurable simply because they found it pleasurable. And the contents list of such an account could render some fairly unthinkable items; eating constantly at vomitaria, indulging in orgies, (when not engaged in the former), watching videos or combing one's hair ad infinitum, and so forth. Such a view is clearly untenable. One of the important points raised by the foregoing examples is that every account of the value of, say leisure practices (and very probably leisure itself), presupposes a particular Weltanschauung and, moreover, a particular philosophical anthropology. That is to say, conversely, that any particular and substantive account of the value of leisure practices will be related conceptually to an account of a person that is thought desirable for one to become. Leisure practices thus become seen as one of a family of engineering processes (less deterministically, practices and traditions) that are constitutive of a person's becoming just that – a person. Each culture, indeed each epoch, has more or less tightly defined horizons that inform and are informed symbiotically by the natures of both.[13]

In addition to these criticisms two related observations expose important weaknesses characteristic of our hypothetical hedonistic justification. It seems to be the case that one cannot pursue pleasure in isolation. Pleasure is derived through actions and activities. A similar point is made by Nozick in one of his thought experiments, the 'experience machine'.[14] What else matters to us, asks Nozick, other than how life is on the inside? He presents a scenario where high-powered neuropsychologists have made a machine which simulates the feelings experienced when having any and all the wonderful experiences one desired. What would it feel like to score the winning goal of a World Cup, or to receive a Nobel Prize for designing a wonder cure for cancer? These feelings are open to us through the experience machine. All that is required is to decide which experiences one desires and then, floating in a special tank wired up to electrodes, one would undergo them. There would be time, periodically, to unplug oneself and re-programme new experiences. But ought one plug oneself in? If one accepts an account of persons who are active rather than passive (i.e. not merely the subject of experiences) one ought not. In the experience machine, despite the fact that the subject has chosen the experiences, he or she is essentially passive thereafter. On a more active account of agency, persons want to do certain things: achieve the attendant satisfactions of being a successful father or mother, scientist, cook, quarterback, captain of the cricket team. To be such things is to be committed to various activities, roles and relationships that define the sort of person that one is. Plugging into the machine is a form of suicide. One would cease to be the person who one previously was since the relationship between one's experiences and one's acts no longer held. These experiences would not be related to us in the strong way that a person's plans and projects ought to be. On the contrary their status would be contingent rather than definitive. The experience machine lives our lives for us. This is not the life of a person.[15] It is clear that Nozick's proposed scenario looms ever larger with the coming of virtual reality games as a species of twenty-first century leisure practice. It is harrowing to think in such terms, yet Arnold Schwarzenegger, in his blockbuster 'Total Recall', lives out precisely such a life. Trapped in a quasi-militaristic future 'our' hero cannot adequately distinguish fact from fantasy. Imagine, too, the scenario of a child watching a video of Arnold living out either a video or real life (it is not automatically clear here how one would draw the distinction). Does this have any parallels in recent revelations of the relationship between observer behaviour, self-delusion and acts of fantasy that can be less than fantastic.[16] On the other side of that coin are the troublesome aspects of the passivity of many forms of leisure practices. Much has been made of the changing patterns of leisure commitments in more mundane situations regarding new 'choices' towards the massive increase in television and video watching of young and not so young children and the potentially dangerous biological consequences. Again, the character of this debate is necessarily philosophical; what sort of persons shall we become?

Although the point is not made by Nozick, our final criticism may be drawn from the 'experience machine'. This is the idea that means and ends cannot always be separated unproblematically. Even if our ends were hedonistically conceived, this does not imply that any or all activities might properly be conceived of as pleasurable. The point may be traced back to Aristotle:

> one might argue that pleasures are desirable in themselves, but not when they are achieved in a certain way; as, e.g., wealth is desirable, but not at the price of treason, and health is desirable, but not if it involves indiscriminate eating.[17]

The notion that the valued ends cannot be brought about by any or all means is pregnant with possibilities for a more positive value argument. Let us first, however, encapsulate what is of significance thus far. First, the value of pleasure as an action guiding reason has not been denigrated per se. It is in need of some focus if it is to be used in offering a sound account of the value of an activity or practice. Moreover, a value argument ought not be built in terms of the pursuit of pleasure alone. Pleasure can only be pursued through particular acts or activities. Second, the manner in which our satisfactions, enjoyment and pleasure are related to these activities is important. The precise nature of this relationship must now be explored.

Means, ends and instrumentality

The means–ends distinction is one that pervades the literature on educational value. It manifests itself in discussions on the nature of intrinsic and extrinsic value. The idea of intrinsic value is often couched in terms of 'doing something for its own sake'. Commonly, such claims are taken to be so obviously true that they are never given serious attention. This may be because the claims are often related to objects that are written indelibly into our cultural heritages to the extent that they appear to be above suspicion. Duty, science, truth and the contemplation of beauty are only the most obvious of such examples. And yet there is the hint of a paradox here; the idea of doing something for the sake of something else is easily understood, but how is one to understand the idea doing something for its own sake where the 'something' refers to itself?

One of the major problems encountered in setting out a positive justificatory argument is the inheritance of a vocabulary that is already predisposed to a certain way of approaching the problem. The notions of 'intrinsic' and 'extrinsic' value are already commonplace and though their meaning is contested (if not simply confused), our interpretation of both the linguistic and logical aspects of the problem runs into difficulty by using that same terminology. It is hoped that our interpretation of these notions does not muddy the waters further but will enable us to capture the problem more adequately.

Instrumental value and extrinsic valuing

Let us begin our probing by contrasting the commonplace language of intrinsic and extrinsic value and justification. First, the logical form of valuing extrinsically is instrumental: 'Do something (X) in order to achieve a purpose (Y).' One wants to achieve an end, goal or purpose or fulfil a desire (Y), which it is believed will be brought about by certain means (X). The relation between means and ends is an external one since the two are separable. Where there can be shown a logical divide between means and ends there is always the possibility of a variety of means (X_1, X_2, X_3 etc.) which can similarly bring about Y and from which they derive their value.[18]

For example, I may buy a new pair of running shoes in order to make me run faster but doing more training might bring about the same end, as might losing some weight. Or one may buy a painting for an investment, but purchasing shares or stocks and bonds might equally well achieve the purpose. One could put on a sweater to warm up but going for a jog or turning the central heating up could secure the same end. It would be easy to write out a table of such relations under the column headings of 'means' and 'ends'. The somewhat extreme position is taken that instrumental value refers to that benefit(s) which is external to the activity. By this is meant that the benefit may be identified and expressed without recourse to the activity which secures it contingently. The term 'extrinsic' will be reserved for the attitudinal relationship between the agent and the activity.

Inherent value and intrinsic valuing

Intrinsic valuing, however, is non-derivative. That is to say, unlike extrinsic valuing, it does not derive from anything beyond the activity. There are some things or activities which are judged to be good because they are directly what is enjoyed for whatever qualities they have in themselves. Here the value is realised by an agent when a quality of experience is felt to be satisfying or rewarding in itself. The value appertains to the person who experiences and evaluates those qualities.[19] But intrinsic valuing, in this sense, does not cover the same range of meaning as Peters' usage. Peters uses 'intrinsic value' to refer to the values which were inherent in the activities themselves. But there is a clear difference between these two senses. In accordance with the above the term 'intrinsic valuing' will be used in the subjective psychological sense where it binds the person to reasons for action, which are non-derivative. The problem of identifying inherently valuable characteristics is the subject of discussion on internality and externality in section 5 below.

Means, ends and relational value and valuing

If the notion of inherent value is approached from an instrumental direction,[20] the idea of something pursued for its own sake might raise difficulties. If, for instance, virtue is its own reward is it to be put in the column of means as well as the column of ends? The problem is to ascertain how something can be a means to itself.[21] What needs discovering, if this is indeed the most appropriate way of proceeding, is how means and ends relate. Consider the following example. Imagine that I play a lot of tennis and a non-sporting friend of mine wants to know why I spend so much time playing it and what value I find in it. She says to me: 'Why, exactly, do you play tennis?' and I reply: 'Oh, I just love playing the game; the enjoyment of skilful co-ordination and execution of strokes.' To this she replies: 'Ah, so what you really play tennis for is enjoyment or specifically to enjoy producing skilful actions.' If she were operating with our means–ends column approach she would characterise the situation thus:

Ends	Means
Enjoying skilful actions	Playing tennis

or maybe more reductively:

Enjoyment	Playing tennis

On this account, the means are presumed neutral to valued ends which are arrived at by reducing the ends to a single elemental or atomistic unit: what is left after all inessentials have been stripped away. But is this an adequate characterisation of the state of affairs? Can, or ought, the features of the activity be isolated thus? And is it true that the means always stand entirely distinct from ends such that they are entirely neutral or indifferent to them? This is precisely what our questioner has presumed. In attempting to cleave the enjoyment from its attendant satisfactions (and, doubtless, frustrations too) she has isolated that which was needed in order to make sense of choosing the activity for its own sake. This will be referred to pejoratively as 'isolationism'.[22] Given that pleasure, satisfaction or enjoyment cannot be pursued in isolation, it should be noted that these subjective psychological conditions flow from the exercise of skills and dispositions in a variety of circumstances. Where our questioner above has attempted to prune off enjoyment from the activity she has done so by regarding the value of the activity as merely instrumental to the real value of the end: pleasure. In contrast to the isolationist point of view, the argument developed here holds that, for complex activities at least, the means–end distinction interpreted thus is too crude an explanatory tool. It will be argued that setting out the value of such activities in terms of means and ends so often involves focusing upon certain aspects of an activity atomistically while losing the broader picture which gives it sense. These activities are better conceived of as complex wholes connected in such a way that they cannot be dissected unproblematically. The satisfactions involved in activities like personal relationships, philosophy, hill-walking or chess commonly spread over the course of a life-time and often involve dedication, commitment, imagination, tolerance, self-sacrifice, the endurance of hardship and so forth; they are not merely to be seen as neutral routes to the securing of pleasure.

For the many activities where there are a multitude of aims and sub-aims it is inadvisable to proceed to locate simple single ends and colourless means. This is to rob them of the web of interconnectedness that is charctcristic of (or at least contributes to) their significant value. Let us explore an example from the activity of running. Consider someone who is running to catch her bus to work. Clearly this is an example of an extrinsically valued activity; she values running because it is going to secure the aim of catching the bus that will get her to work on time. Getting a lift from a friend would do just as well. Her end would similarly be achieved if the bus driver stopped beside her before the designated pick-up point. But this is entirely different from the running she might undertake at lunchtime. She runs then because of the sheer joy of running freely; of enjoying the fact that she is fit and can run easily and can work herself hard, but also (again partly) because she knows it will burn off some calories; it will raise her metabolism such that when she does eat lunch she will burn it off more quickly due to her raised metabolism; because she enjoys getting out into the fresh air up in the fields and around campus; because she enjoys the company of colleagues who run with her and so on.[23]

If these values or goods were isolated then one would be tempted to say that they could be achieved by a variety of alternative means. But this would be to miss the point. First, at an empirical level, it may be the case that one can nowhere gain such a variety of goods or values in any other single activity. Maybe this is the case, maybe not. If it is, then this would represent a justification of some use yet the logical weakness would still have to be recognised. Maybe some other activity might produce the same variety of ends more effectively. But running may be valued for its inherent features and instrumental capacities becomes an instantiation of those values or goods that one seeks and not simply a means of achieving them. There is a relation of complementary interdependence. This will be referred to as relational valuing. Running thus becomes a specification of the various goods that are sought. The general point being made here is that means and ends cannot always be isolated into distinct categories where the former are neutral in respect of the latter.

It may be said, then, that both intrinsic value and extrinsic value appertain where a quality of experience is felt to be satisfying or rewarding by the person or subject. They represent, however, extremes of the continuum. The exclusive separation of the subjective valuing of an activity and its objective value is seen to be unhelpful to the overall justificatory task. An account of value has been set out, therefore, which is objective in the sense that the inherent features of the activity are seen as potential reasons for the subject's valuing of that activity which are necessary though not sufficient. Finally, the complexity of some activities, as has been indicated above and will be explored below, is such that the means and ends distinction fails to capture their nature and potential significance. This account of value and valuing must be developed in the context of a specific characterisation of valuable activities. Those inherent features that are the basis of an activities' value will be referred to as internal goods as opposed to those contingent relations which will be referred to as external goods.

Practices, internality and externality

Our attention now turns to MacIntyre,[24] who attempts to provide a modern interpretation of an Aristotelian account of the good life. He develops an account of human well-being or flourishing which consists partly in embracing the idea of 'practices' which are sustained by certain dispositions or virtues. Within these practices, though not exclusively so, the virtues are exhibited, sustained and combined in order to pursue and live the good life. An attempt will be made to make clear the value of sporting practices broadly from within this perspective.

MacIntyre presents his account of the virtues on three successive levels: (1) social practices; (2) individual lives; and (3) traditions. Whilst the first and second levels define two sets of virtues, the third level attempts to locate the virtues in historical perspective and must necessarily be apprehended in order to complete our understanding of the virtues. Although sympathetic to the idea that activities generally need to be located historically if they are to be understood and evaluated properly this aspect of the account is not of specific concern. Similarly it would be inappropriate to discuss in detail the intricacies of MacIntyre's moral theory in relation to the second layer of his analysis. Instead, concern lies in his account of practices, and therefore of virtues, as a way of opening up an argument for the value of leisure pursuits.

MacIntyre sets out his account of practices and their internal goods in the following way. A practice is thus defined as:

any coherent and complex socially established cooperative human activity through which goods internal to that form of activity are realized in the course of trying to achieve those standards of excellence which are appropriate to, and partially definitive of, that form of activity, with the result that human powers to achieve excellence and human conceptions of the ends and goods involved are systematically extended.[25]

In his examples of what are and are not practices, MacIntyre distinguishes between technical skills and the institutions that give them their context and allow us to make sense of them. Tic-tac-toe is not a practice in this sense nor is throwing a football, but the game of football is. Similarly bricklaying is not a practice but architecture is. Other examples of practices are arts, games, sciences, and the making and sustaining of family life. These practices cannot be reduced to the various skills which are required to exemplify and sustain them without remainder. Nor can they simply be thought of as the institutions that give rise to them. Soccer cannot be reduced to its technical skills or the various clubs and administrative structures, though these are important in our understanding of soccer as a practice.

The notion of goods internal to a practice can be exemplified by distinguishing them from those that are external. MacIntyre considers the example of teaching an intelligent young child how to play chess. The child is motivated to learn the game only in so far as he or she is offered a given amount of candy to play, and even more upon winning, a game. Where the candy is the primary motivation the child has every reason to cheat and no reason not to cheat since the game is irrelevant (or at the very least secondary) in his or her motivational hierarchy. Over time, however, the child may come to recognise and value the achievement of a certain kind of analytical skill, strategic imagination, competitive intensity and so forth. These are internal goods and are specific to the practice of chess. MacIntyre then holds that if the child now cheats this will not constitute defeating the tutor but his or herself.[26] This example is supposed to show that there are goods that are externally or contingently related to the practice of chess and, alternatively, that there are those which are internal to that practice. It is fairly clear here that the candy is an external good in MacIntyre's example. In other areas of life, power, prestige, status or wealth are external goods. These goods can, by definition, be isolated and achieved by alternative means that are not exclusively tied to engagement in a particular practice. This is precisely the instrumental relation noted earlier. The ends are the locus of value and these may be brought about by a variety of means that are more or less successful in that task. On the other hand there are goods internal to (or inherent in) a practice which cannot be had except by engagement in that practice.[27] MacIntyre argues that this internality is two-fold. First, such goods can only be specified in the language of such practices and through examples of them. Second, these goods can only be gained by first-hand experience of them in the relevant practice and that those who lack this experience are not competent to judge those practices.

Let us explore these ideas a little in order to see whether they can shed light on our problems of value and valuing. If the internal goods of chess such as analytical imagination, strategic skill and so forth are only to be achieved through participation in that particular practice, then their value, it might appear, is to be expressed in terms of the experience of satisfaction derived from that participation. Such an account would cohere with our earlier view that intrinsic value was entailed by the subjective psychological value gained by the participant. But such a subjective account of value will not suffice for MacIntyre and so he stresses the public nature of internal goods, not as pleasurable feelings, but as excellence in both product and performance.[28] Thus:

> A practice involves standards of excellence and obedience to rules as well as the achievement of goods. To enter into a practice is to accept the authority of those standards and the inadequacy of my own performance as judged by them. It is to subject my own attitudes, choices, preferences and tastes to the standards which currently and partially define the practice. [...] Thus the standards are not themselves immune from criticism, but nonetheless we cannot be initiated into a practice without accepting the authority of the best standards realized so far.[29]

MacIntyre's account of practices is a persuasive one. It acknowledges the depth of their social and historical situatedness. This is to be expected from MacIntyre's overall evaluative commitment to communitarianism and his zealous anti-individualism. Moreover, MacIntyre is sensitive to the authoritarian tendencies in the transmission of practices and instead posits their openness to the possibility of critical initiation. Some of the detail of his accounts of virtue and of practices will be explored before moving on to a characterisation that is more suitable to the purposes of this argument.

It was noted earlier that MacIntyre sought to avoid the reduction of virtue to the technical skills of the practice. He writes:

> What is distinctive in a practice is in part the way in which conceptions of the relevant goods and ends which the technical skills serve – and every practice does require the exercise of technical skills – are transformed and enriched by these extensions of human powers and by that regard for its own internal goods which are partially definitive of each particular practice or type of practice.[30]

The account is then layered historically:

> To enter into a practice is to enter into a relationship not only with its contemporary practitioners, but also with those who have preceded us in the practice, particularly those whose achievements extended the reach of the practice.[31]

This social emphasis is carried into the account of the relationship between persons, practices and virtues thus:

> Every practice requires a certain relationship between those who participate in it. Now the virtues are those goods by reference to which, whether we like it or not, we define our relationships to those other people with whom we share the kinds of purposes and standards which inform practices.[32]

MacIntyre argues that there are just three virtues that are required to secure internal goods in practices and by which persons define themselves and their relationships with other practitioners. These are the virtues of justice, courage and honesty.

Moving closer to the relationship between virtues and practices one might ask why MacIntyre sets out just those three virtues, justice, courage and honesty (or truth), to be central. Seung[33] suggests that the answer to this question lies in the essentially social nature of these virtues. Again, this coheres with MacIntyre's moral, social and political polemic against liberal individualism. By locating the virtues in practices in which social co-operation is essential, the virtues become irreducibly social. Seung argues that, by restricting his conception of a practice to the domain of social co-operation, MacIntyre excludes from consideration those activities which do not require social co-operation. It would follow, then, that mountain-climbing would be a practice if performed co-operatively but not if performed individually. This interpretation miscontrues MacIntyre's position. He is nowhere so exclusive about practices. Indeed, his historical aspect of practices allows precisely for such cases. Here individuals toil only in apparent isolation. Alternatively, they may be viewed as participants who co-operate over time in a tradition according to the canons developed over time between other participants. This would apply just as much to Van Gogh developing post-impressionism in seeming isolation at Arles as it would to a mountain climber attempting some new technique whilst on an ascent of Mount Everest. Their activities may only be understood in the light of the ongoing practice. To label them 'individual activities' as Seung does[34] is to ignore the purpose of MacIntyre's third tier of practices, which requires that the actions of participants ought not be wrenched from their social and historical context.

What is important in Seung's critique is his interpretation that MacIntyre's stress on the social aspects of virtues and practices obscures the notion of personal achievement. Whilst it is true that rules and standards structure the public nature of the achievements and set goals for future practitioners they also attach to the individual in a strong and important way. MacIntyre argues that external goods are characteristically someone's property or possession such that, for example, your having X denies my having it. Now although internal goods may be the object of competition, it is characteristic of their achievement that the good of the whole community of practitioners is advanced. He cites as an exemplar W. G. Grace who advanced the art of batting in cricket. However, as with the examples above, the achievement attaches to the individual in a strong and original way and though other practitioners are indebted to these individuals and may copy their achievements, they are not esteemed in the same way. Those who have broken new ground are thereby rewarded.

There is a real danger of losing sight of the personal dimension in MacIntyre's conception of practices. From the perspective of his thesis it may well be inconsequential that the standards of a practice are advanced by any particular person. But from the personal viewpoint it is not. Remember that MacIntyre is talking here of performances at the outer edges of practices. Most persons engage in practices at the humdrum level of mediocrity against this absolute standard. Few will ever become a Beethoven or a Pelé; 'ordinary mortals' very often do not possess the potential in terms of natural capacities, tendencies or capabilities to justify the pursuit of a single calling to such absolute excellence.[35] Nonetheless, anyone can pursue excellence in various activities where this is interpreted in relation to their own particular circumstances: their own previous best performances, or comparisons among standards of contemporaries in terms of age, body composition, years of training or education and so on. Most individuals who make it to the local leisure centre, or swimming pool or recreation park may make advances which are utterly insignificant to the practice as a whole but which are of enormous importance personally. Nowhere is this more the case than with beginners whose abilities may, at the initial stages, increase rapidly in range and sophistication. It is less than clear how relevant the vocabulary of excellence actually is to the leisure providing and consuming world.

It is important, however, to our account that it successfully brings the personal and public viewpoints together under the rubric of values and valuing. It is a noteworthy failure of MacIntyre's account of practices that he neglects the significance of personal achievement of internal goods, the satisfaction of which very often facilitates ongoing participation in those practices. It is the relation between the public characteristics of practices and a person's valuing and evaluation that will be prominent in the account of the values of leisure practices.

This is not the place to examine MacIntyre's thesis in its entirety. It is sufficient for present purposes to note that his theory of the virtues and the nature of their relationship to practices is deeply problematic. Notwithstanding the difficulty of restricting the value of practices to the exercise of the virtues, MacIntyre's general account may be reconstructed more profitably by arguing for the value of such practices without tying this value exclusively to a moral theory. Their value might, for instance, be justified on cultural and ethical grounds rather than exclusively moral ones. That is to say, a reconstructed account of practices as educational activities could be thought of in terms of initiation into valuable cultural activities, which can make a significant contribution to worthwhile living which is conceived of solely in the language of either duty or virtue. Although the good life may be conceived of with respect to a moral one, recognition must be made of a range of concerns that persons have about the fullness of their lives and it is this notion that supports our conception of education and justification of the activities therein. The justificatory argument presented below, therefore, will be premised on the idea that some activities matter to people in a deep and significant way such that they are what makes life full, valuable, worth living. In order to explore this idea, an examination is required of what is central to the notion of value in MacIntyre's account.

Much of MacIntyre's thesis, by his own admission, trades upon the idea of internal and external goods. And this distinction is not without its problems. By contrast, internality has here been to related to the personal achievement or satisfaction derived from various performances. This accords with the idea that intrinsic value is subject dependent. The distinction has been made in section 3 above. MacIntyre, however, wants the notion of internality to have objective status, in the sense that the internal goods existed independently of any particular person. His chess-playing example is supposed to secure this by the objective or public demarcation of goods that are internal and external to the practice. His selective example, however, wins the point without requiring vigorous defence. To be sure, his candy-seeking child exemplifies an instance where the subject is motivated by something external to the practice; her reasons for playing are derived from the candy and not the chess. At pains of labouring the point, she is extrinsically motivated. Here the means are neutral to securing the valued ends. It was argued in section 5, however, that not all relationships between goods are so straightforward. One can imagine the child playing chess for enjoyment, not because it is simply one means among many of being entertained, but because it is the exercise of her capabilities in that discipline which she desires. Furthermore, chess may well be the activity in which she is known by others to excel and is so esteemed. It is not only for the internal goods she seeks to play the game but also the external goods that she may, otherwise, be unable to secure. The playing of chess is, then, not merely instrumental to her securing entertainment, it is itself a specification of the desiderata sought.[36] Relying on the traditional vocabulary of intrinsic and extrinsic valuing is unhelpful here and to convey more clearly the attitudinal stance of the person the term 'relational valuing' was introduced.

Part of the reason why some activities are called complex is that the range of desiderata those activities encapsulate is so great. This is one aspect of those activities which prevents their explanation in simple means–ends terms. Certain activities may fulfil several aims for the participant at one and the same time. The individual aims may be sought through other activities if they are isolated in the way noted in section 4. For instance, MacIntyre argues that strategic imagination and competitive intensity are goods internal to the practice of chess and that internal goods can be sought only within their respective practices. He writes: 'There are goods internal to the practice of chess which cannot be had in any way but by playing chess or some other game of that specific kind.'[37] It could be argued, however, that strategic imagination might be developed in activities such as war, and competitive intensity might be promoted at least as well through sales marketing. Neither of these are what might be described reasonably as 'games of that specific kind'. Moreover, the desire to develop strategic imagination and competitive intensity may be no part of my motivation to play chess but may be the consequence of my playing. How are these aims to be reconciled? Which refer to internal and which to external goods? And if no-one actually valued such things as competitive intensity and strategic imagination would this make them internal goods? Before setting out an account of the value of such practices it would be helpful to articulate further what commonality such activities have, what problems they address, what needs they meet, in short, what capacity they have to be valued. A more complex account of the interdependent aims of sporting practices and their internal and external goods would be required. This task is not attempted here. Instead, what is offered is a framework within which such an account can be formed.

It is a commonplace in philosophy to argue[38] that some goods are valued in their own right, irrespective of consequences, and that others are valued exclusively for their consequences. As a matter of intuition it seems difficult to cash out these two extremes. What would an activity look like which was valued for its internal goods but which produced no valuable consequences? What sort of activity could yield valuable consequences but was, of itself, of no value? Where the value of an activity is situated between these polar extremes it is often overlooked. These goods are called, after Plato, 'mixed goods'[39] which he conceives to be the highest category of good. The motivation for considering mixed goods as higher can be seen to lie in the fact that all actions have consequences even if those consequences are not the prime feature in the motivational hierarchy of the agent. To conceive of an activity in its wholeness is to include both its internal features and the direct consequences it produces.

Chess is an example, like all sophisticated games, which belongs to the category of mixed goods; it is of relational value and may be valued thus. It can be valued for its own sake due to its internal features as one project among many to which persons become committed, while it may, at the same time, bring about external goods such as prestige, esteem among contemporaries or wealth. Further, these external goods (if this is indeed what they are) also contribute significantly towards the living of valuable lives. Finally, there are those activities that have been called relationally valuable since they have internal goods and are at the same time specifically valuable ways of achieving (what have otherwise been called) external goods. For instance, health may be valued not only for its own sake but because of the many and varied activities and actions it enables us to carry out. One ought not ignore the consequences health may bring just because those goods might be brought about alternatively. Using the notion of value as benefit avoids the 'isolationism' of considering activities apart from consequences and consequences apart from the activity. This enables us to see that if a good is valuable for its internal features and for the consequences it secures then it may be seen to confer greater benefit than that which is 'simply' valued for its own sake and that which is valued merely for its consequences. Sporting practices can be offered as exemplars of activities that may be valued relationally, which are mixed goods. Below is an account of what can be said in a general way about valuable activities.

Valuing practices

It has been the central purpose of the argument thus far to chart the issue of what is valued and what is valuable by exploring the terminology in which the problem is often couched and some of the conceptual confusions which attach to it.

The term 'intrinsic value' has been taken to mean those subjective psychological satisfactions which are the direct benefits of an activity and which may flow from the internal goods associated with that activity. Where satisfactions are derivative solely from the external goods associated with an activity, it is said to have extrinsic or instrumental value. As was discussed in section 4, however, this requires that the means to achieving those external goods is neutral. Both intrinsic and extrinsic value are subject-referring in the sense that they represent the reasons for engaging in an activity.

A subject, however, may or may not value both sets of reasons. So for instance, if someone does not value strategic skill or competitive intensity then the game of chess is unlikely to be valued intrinsically by that person. Whether or not something is valued intrinsically is a factual matter. It is tantamount to saying 'as a matter of fact I do (not) value this'. In deciding whether the game is potentially valuable or not one must take into account the features of the activity, and of persons, taken as a whole to see if they have the capacity to be productive of benefit(s). The capacity for being valued was called inherent value and was identified by the relatively stable and partially definitive internal goods of a practice. If, however, one values it for the former reasons such as strategic skill, then one's intrinsic value relates to the internal goods, which are inherent in the activity. Conversely, if one values chess exclusively for the reasons such as its capacity to earn money, where other options are equally available and efficient, then one may be said to value the game extrinsically. If these were the only type of goods procured by the activity it would be said to be instrumentally valuable. Again, it is a matter of fact whether one values a game extrinsically. If, however, the activity is valued relationally, then it is valued precisely for the relations of its internal and external features and the relations that hold between them and the participant. Of course one hopes that the reasons one gives for the value of an educational activity will be compelling to all. But this may not be the case. A demonstration of the internal goods is a necessary, though not sufficient, reason for an activity to be genuinely valuable. Whether an activity is valued intrinsically or extrinsically is a matter for empirical enquiry but articulating the capacity to be productive of value, and whether it flows from features internal or external to the game, is a conceptual one. Criteria must be given for the value of the activity which flow from a sensitivity to the nature of the activity, the culture in which it resides, the dispositions and abilities required of the participant and so forth.

It has been argued, then, that the process of reason-giving is necessary in order to conceive of the value of an activity but not sufficient to secure its being valued either intrinsically or extrinsically. A culture in which people never sat but only stood or kneeled is hardly likely to value furniture such as chairs. It is clear, however, that their capacity to be valued in cultures such as ours will relate to social factors such as being convenient objects on which to relax while conversing or watching television and physiological factors relating to the relative energy costs of various body positions.

The accounts of intrinsic and extrinsic valuing bear the hallmark of this relationality. In the first instance it has been argued that intrinsic value cannot be characterised independently of public criteria. Here the subject must value the activity for certain reasons which appertain to the activity. This does not require that each individual give a sophisticated linguistic account of the motivating features of the activity but that (a) this is possible and (b) the person has some insight into these features lest he or she does not know what it is that is valued. The relationality is bi-directional. It not only flows from subject to object but also from object to subject.

That is to say, if no-one ever valued an activity for its internal features it would be difficult, though not logically impossible, to see how that activity could be thought valuable.

The final problem to be addressed is whether there are any generalised criteria which may guide our choosing of activities to contribute to the living of full and valuable lives. These will be related to our interpretations of inherent, instrumental and relational value, and extrinsic, intrinsic and relational valuing. It has been argued that extrinsic valuing is best understood to refer to the instrumental relationship where X is seen as of value in so far as it secures good(s) external to the activity. The means are here seen as neutral to those ends. It follows from this that one's valuing of X is conditional or hypothetical to the extent that it does secure the derivatively valued ends. Further, it ought to be valued precisely to the extent that it does secure those ends. If some other means produces the same benefit more effectively then it will be of greater instrumental value. Moreover, if it achieves a greater amount of benefit (variously conceived) with the same amount of time, effort and so forth it will be of greater instrumental value. Similarly, if another activity secures a greater range of goods, where this range of goods is the source of its instrumental value, then that activity will be of greater extrinsic value. It will be clear that when seeking guidance for the selection of an activity for its extrinsic value, our criteria will be utilitarian. Means, in this instance, are of value in terms of their utility, which may be in terms of certainty, duration, extent, fecundity, intensity, propinquity and purity.[40]

As was argued in section 4 above, it would be a mistake to adopt this criterion for the complex activities. Simple utilitarian calculus is inappropriate here since one is not valuing solely the utility produced by our engagement in the activity but for the satisfactions of desiderata sought in the activity. Here one must look for criteria that distinguish some activities rather than others. It was seen in section 4 above, that the simple pursuit of pleasure was ipso facto inadequate to demarcate activities and that pleasures were not all of a kind. Furthermore, it was noted that some valuable activities require great effort, discipline and sometimes hardship before their ends are achieved. To talk of pleasure *simpliciter* as the basis was seen as problematic and therefore, in contrast, the notion of satisfaction has been used throughout. Intrinsic valuing is located in those psychological conditions that attach to the satisfaction derived from our direct engagement in that activity.

The notion that this type of valuing flows from a relationship between the valuing subject and the valued activity is important here. This helps us to recognise that some activities may be appropriate for some persons but not others. It is not a mere accident that the young are educated. The life plans of these persons are relatively unformed and uninformed. Their ability for evaluation may not be well-developed and their capacity to make qualitative contrasts between activities and therefore forms of life is embryonic. This is the motivation behind many educators' reserving the honorific title 'education' to intrinsically valuable activities (what has been called 'inherent value' here) whilst referring to those extrinsically (instrumentally) valuable activities by the less laudatory epithet 'schooling'. It is because these achievements are often the highest achievements of the culture in which they grow. They are often extremely complex, requiring enormous amounts of dedication to get on the inside of them. These goods can only be secured by entering into practices which require (though not in a logically necessary way) initiation from others more familiar with their features.

Some practices will have great appeal for some while not for others. So, for instance, one may see a strong capacity for inherent value in classical music owing to its internal goods. But this capacity may not be realised, that is to say may not be valued intrinsically, if an individual is, for instance, completely deaf or if the internal goods are not recognised in this or that subculture. It will not surprise us if an especially overweight woman does not value jogging, nor if a particularly frail man hates hockey. Contextual variations enormously affect what one values intrinsically. However, one may still say that the capacity for intrinsic value flows from its internal features which may be identified within a way of life even though it is recognised that they may not have compelling force for all.

Finally, there is the notion of relational valuing. An activity is relationally valued (or valuable), if it possesses internal goods (or offers the possibility thereof) and is a particular means of securing external goods. The goods it confers may be distributed over time (as is most likely the case with the intrinsic value of a practice's internal features) or may be immediate. It has been argued that this type of value and valuing is of greater significance since the activity or practice is conceived of in its entirety and not merely for its own sake irrespective of consequences or, conversely, for its consequences irrespective of the manner of their achievement. The mixed goods out of which these activities are valued relationally will similarly be open to contrast. Some activities may be of similar inherent value (i.e. may have similar internal goods) but one may be productive of fewer external goods. It would seem reasonable to value, *ceteris paribus*, the activity which was internally complex, which required greater discrimination, subtlety and so forth, but which also yielded external goods such as power, prestige and wealth.[41]

Notes

1 I am most grateful to Warren Fraleigh who gave me a copy of his paper on 'A Classification of the Values of Sport, Dance and Exercise' at the Philosophic Society for the Study of Sport at the University of Tennessee in 1991. While I was working on a chapter of my PhD thesis Fraleigh's paper gave me a chance to recognise more fully the contours of the problem, although I do not share his

general position as will become clear. My thanks are also due to Mark Hamilton for his response to Peter Arnold's paper on 'Sport as a Valued Human Practice' at the same conference. Considerable thanks are also due especially to Jim Parry, and to Paul Smeyers, Victor Quinn and Scott Kretchmar for some helpful criticism.

2 It should be noted as a caveat that no attempt is made here to articulate what distinguishes a leisure practice from any other sort of practice. The point, which will become clear, is that by introducing the term practice an attempt is made to consider seriously the idea that the value of certain activities must be articulated within a broader framework than is often assumed, for example, in games where the analyst often focuses on the consitutive rules of the activity. On the definition of 'leisure', see J. Parry and J. Long (1998) 'Immaculate Concepts', *Conference Proceedings*, 29 June–3 July 1988, Leisure Studies Association, University of Sussex.

3 Given present purposes discussion of value will refer solely to activities. The word 'object' will be used only in contrast to the subject who values things and/ or persons.

4 R. S. Peters (1966) *Ethics and Education*, London; George, Allen and Unwin, see chapter 5.

5 See N. Rescher (1969) *Introduction to Value Theory*, New Jersey: Prentice-Hall, chapter 1.

6 H. L. A. Hart (1961) *The Concept of Law*, Oxford; Oxford University Press.

7 I have argued elsewhere, following Charles Taylor, for a formal account of persons as beings for whom things have significance; who can form and reformulate life plans based on qualitative or contrastive evaluation. See M. J. McNamee (1992) *The Educational Justification of Physical Education*, University of Leeds Doctoral Thesis, unpublished. See also 'Physical Education and the Development of Personhood', *P. E. Review*, 15, 1, pp. 13–28.

8 K. Thompson (1983) 'The Justification of Physical Education', *Momentum*, 2, 2, pp. 19–23.

9 Ibid., p. 20. It should be noted that in the specific illustration of his point Thompson is referring to the activities of physical education. Notwithstanding this specificity the argument holds irrespective of the referent, as the quotation makes clear.

10 One is reminded of the preface to the chapter on 'Equality as a moral ideal' by Frankfurt where he reports an alleged conversation; first man: 'How are your children?', second man: 'Compared to what?'. H. G. Frankfurt (1988) *The Importance of What We Care About*, Cambridge; Cambridge Universtiy Press.

11 See L. Wittgenstein (1958) *Philosophical Investigations*, trans. G. E. M. Anscombe, 2nd edition, Oxford, Blackwell, §196ff. It is in no way suggested, however, that a Wittgensteinian position on value would necessarily be wholly unsympathetic to parts of the subjectivist thesis. Indeed one might expect them at least to be at home with the idea of agreement in practice and not merely in judgements.

12 Somatotype is the term which refers to one's body type. There are three axes according to which one is classified; endomorph (short and fat), ectomorph (tall and thin) and mesomorph (lean and muscular). Each individual may be classified with a rating from each category. The *locus classicus* of sports and somatotypical differentiation is W. Sheldon, S. S. Stevens and W. B. Tucker (1940) *Varieties of Human Physique*, New York: Harper.

13 For an account of the nature and philosophical sources of which, see C. Taylor (1990) *Sources of the Self*, Cambridge: Cambridge University Press.

14 R. Nozick (1974) *Anarchy, State, and Utopia*, Oxford: Blackwell, pp. 42–45
15 In a later book Nozick develops this theme a little. In addition to our considering how persons experience things from the inside he argues that account must
be taken of fact that both are (presumably this means both ought to be) desired:

(a) to be the best kind of person, and
(b) to have the best kind of life.

Furthermore, these two aspects are are to be considered as part of a whole. One
could imagine (a) without (b) and (b) without (a) but the most valuable life for
a person is one where the parts cannot be isolated thus. The kind of relation
where (a) and (b) are entailed he calls *leading* or *living* the most valuable life. R.
Nozick (1981) *Philosophical Explanations*, Oxford: Clarendon, pp. 409–413.

16 I am thinking in particular here of the purported association of video-watching
and subsequent criminal (notably violent) activity.
17 Aristotle, *Ethics*, Book Ten, trans. J. A. K. Thomson (1953) London: Penguin,
p. 317. The indiscriminate eating referred to by Aristotle is thought to refer to
cannibalism.
18 This is not meant to imply that any or all means are equally efficient at bringing
about X.
19 See P. W. Taylor (1961) *Normative Discourse*, Englewood Cliffs, NJ: Prentice-
Hall, chapter 1.
20 See for instance P. S. Wilson (1975) 'The Use of Value Terms in Discussions of
Education', *Journal of Value Inquiry*, 9, 3, pp. 186–200.
21 This problem is explored in T. S. Champlin (1987) 'Doing Something for Its
Own Sake', *Philosophy*, 62, 232, pp. 31–47.
22 Ibid., p. 36. An example of this isolationism can be found in Paton's commen-
tary of Kant's Categorical Imperative:

> The phrase the highest good is ambiguous. It may mean merely the good
> which is itself unconditioned and is the condition of all other good. In this
> sense 'highest good' and 'absolute good' mean precisely the same thing. But
> Kant is also making a judgment of value; for such a good is to be *esteemed*
> as 'beyond comparison higher' than any other good. *Its usefulness or fruit-
> lessness can neither add to, nor subtract from, this unique and incompar-
> able worth.*
>
> H. J. Paton (1967) *The Categorical Imperative: A Study in Kant's
> Moral Philosophy*, London: Hutcheson, p. 41, emphasis added

23 These values can be listed and classified. For such an account see W. P. Fraleigh
(1991) 'A Classification of the Values of Sport, Dance and Exercise', unpublished paper presented to the Philosophic Society for the Study of Sport,
Knoxville, University of Tennessee, 8–10 October 1991.
24 A. C. MacIntyre (1985) *After Virtue*, London: Duckworth.
25 Ibid., p. 187.
26 The issue of whether cheaters are actually playing the game or not is a perplex-
ing one, but outside present concerns. It is clear according to MacIntyre that
they are not. For an interesting discussion on which see C. Lehman (1982) 'Can
Cheaters Play the Game?', *Journal of Philosophy of Sport*, 8, pp. 41–46 and W.
P. Morgan (1987) 'Formalism and the Logical Incompatibility Thesis', *Journal
of Philosophy of Sport*, 14, pp. 1–20.
27 With the game of chess MacIntyre says that the internal goods cannot be had
except by playing chess or 'some other game of that specific kind' but it is not
clear just what this latitude opens up.

28 MacIntyre, *After Virtue*, pp. 189–191.
29 Ibid., p. 190.
30 Ibid., p. 193.
31 Ibid., p. 194.
32 Ibid., p. 191.
33 T. K. Seung (1991) 'Virtues and Values: A Platonic Account', *Social Theory and Practice*, 17, 2, pp. 207–247.
34 Ibid., pp. 207–208.
35 For a critical analysis of the concept of human potential and three interpretations of it, see I. Scheffler (1985) *Of Human Potential*, London; Routledge.
36 The chess example is borrowed from A. Kolnai (1966) 'Games and Aims', *Proceedings of the Aristotelian Society*, 66, pp. 103–127. The idea, however, is not exclusively his. Kekes operates with a similar idea in his discussion of internal and external goods which borrows from MacIntyre but differs significantly from it. He argues that external goods such as power, prestige and wealth may be intrinsically valued (1) because they are public recognition of our achievements and (2) as specific content that forms of appreciation have. J. Kekes (1989) *Moral Tradition and Individuality*, Princeton: Princeton University Press, pp. 185–200.
37 Ibid., p. 188.
38 See, for example, Peters, *Ethics and Education*.
39 Plato (1974) *The Republic*, 357–358, trans. D. Lee, 2nd edition, revised, London: Penguin, pp. 102–104.
40 For the *locus classicus* of the quality and quantity of pleasure see J. Bentham (1789) 'An Introduction to the Principles of Morals and Legislation', especially Chapter IV 'Value of a Lot of Pleasure or Pain, How to be Measured', reprinted in M. Warnock (1962) *Utilitarianism*, Glasgow: Collins.
41 The *ceteris paribus* clause here is an interesting one. Given our focus on the value of the specific ways of achieving certain goods an interesting problem is raised as to how one would know whether the intrinsic value of one activity was greater than another. The question, however, is beyond the direct scope of our present concerns.

Index

Page numbers in *italics* denote tables, those in **bold** denote figures.

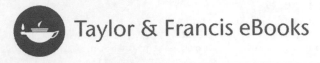

Taylor & Francis eBooks

Helping you to choose the right eBooks for your Library

Add Routledge titles to your library's digital collection today. Taylor and Francis ebooks contains over 50,000 titles in the Humanities, Social Sciences, Behavioural Sciences, Built Environment and Law.

Choose from a range of subject packages or create your own!

Benefits for you

» Free MARC records
» COUNTER-compliant usage statistics
» Flexible purchase and pricing options
» All titles DRM-free.

 Free Trials Available
We offer free trials to qualifying academic, corporate and government customers.

Benefits for your user

» Off-site, anytime access via Athens or referring URL
» Print or copy pages or chapters
» Full content search
» Bookmark, highlight and annotate text
» Access to thousands of pages of quality research at the click of a button.

eCollections – Choose from over 30 subject eCollections, including:

Archaeology	Language Learning
Architecture	Law
Asian Studies	Literature
Business & Management	Media & Communication
Classical Studies	Middle East Studies
Construction	Music
Creative & Media Arts	Philosophy
Criminology & Criminal Justice	Planning
Economics	Politics
Education	Psychology & Mental Health
Energy	Religion
Engineering	Security
English Language & Linguistics	Social Work
Environment & Sustainability	Sociology
Geography	Sport
Health Studies	Theatre & Performance
History	Tourism, Hospitality & Events

For more information, pricing enquiries or to order a free trial, please contact your local sales team:
www.tandfebooks.com/page/sales